Undeniably
Indiana

AN IMPRINT OF
INDIANA UNIVERSITY PRESS

Bloomington & Indianapolis

Undeniably Indiana

Hoosiers Tell the Story of Their Wacky *and* Wonderful State

Edited by
INDIANA UNIVERSITY PRESS
Introduction by Nelson Price

This book is a publication of

Quarry Books
an imprint of

INDIANA UNIVERSITY PRESS
Office of Scholarly Publishing
Herman B Wells Library 350
1320 East 10th Street
Bloomington, Indiana 47405 USA

Manufactured in the United States of America

Library of Congress Cataloging-in-Publication Data

Names: Indiana University Press, editor.
Title: Undeniably Indiana : Hoosiers tell the story of their wacky and wonderful state / edited by Indiana University Press ; introduction by Nelson Price.
Other titles: Hoosiers tell the story of their wacky and wonderful state
Description: Bloomington : Quarry Books, an imprint of Indiana University Press, [2016]
Identifiers: LCCN 2016009608 | ISBN 9780253022264 (pbk. : alk. paper) | ISBN 9780253022349 (e-book)
Subjects: LCSH: Indiana—History—Anecdotes. | Indiana—Social life and customs—Anecdotes. | Indiana—Biography.
Classification: LCC F526.6 .U55 2016 | DDC 977.2—dc23 LC record available at http://lccn.loc.gov/2016009608

1 2 3 4 5 21 20 19 18 17 16

Table of Contents

Preface

Well, fellow Hoosiers, you've gone and done it. In honor of Indiana's upcoming bicentennial, we at Indiana University Press asked for you to share what's meaningful to you about our state. The word went out through social media, and you responded—many times over. Boy, did you share. So much poured into our office—reminiscences of growing up on farms, in small towns, and cities; legendary tales of the past; reflections on the ever-changing Hoosier weather; events both wonderful and calamitous; unforgettable and infamous people. And, of course, basketball. Although praising the state, a number of you also recognized its challenges. Together you built the first crowdsourced book at the press, and one of the first ever by a university press.

Using your words, your stories, we wove together a tapestry of the wonderful and sometime wacky goings-on that are undeniably Indiana. Some caveats are warranted, here. Unfortunately, because of the sheer volume of responses received, we were not able to include everyone. It should be noted that if your submission was already available in a publication, then we tended not to include it as your marvelous stories were already available to readers. A handful of tales we needed to edit, for brevity and clarity. Finally, it should be readily acknowledged that this book does not purport to be comprehensive in its geographical, cultural, or historical coverage of the state. You wrote in 2015 of what interested you the most about Indiana, and we put the book together accordingly.

So, sit back, pick a section, and dive into some charming, moving, and sometimes downright funny tales. We bet you'll learn a new tidbit or two, and come away with a smile, appreciating once again why it will always matter to be a Hoosier.

Indiana University Press

Introduction

First off, I'm mighty proud to be a Hoosier—and a fifth-generation one to boot. Like many of us locals, I get revved up about sugar cream pie; the movies *Hoosiers*, *Rudy*, and *Breaking Away*; young Abe Lincoln; and roadside motels as well as the lavish West Baden Springs Hotel.

Also like many of us, I don't give a hoot about the derivation of "Hoosier." That intrigues newbies and out-of-staters far more than those of us who have lived with the designation all of our lives. Long ago, we moved on to revel in the rest of our colorful folklore, of which Indiana undeniably has a mountain.

Speaking of which, although Indiana doesn't literally have mountains, we do have hills, including some mighty steep ones—despite the myth that the state is as flat as a pork tenderloin, one of our favorite entrees. When Indiana became the nineteenth state in 1816—the same year that seven-year-old Abe Lincoln moved here with his family—most of the terrain was a deep, dense forest consisting of towering trees. According to folklore, a squirrel could have jumped from the Ohio state line clear across to our Illinois border without ever touching ground, accomplishing the aerial odyssey entirely by leaping from towering tree to tree.

So much for another misconception, that Indiana was a Plains state like Kansas or Nebraska. To the contrary, the Native Americans here were Woodland Indians, tribes such as the Shawnee, Miami, Potawatomi, and Lenape (Delaware) who flourished in the forests, not like their Plains counterparts. The forced evacuation of Native Americans to faraway places—that's where the link to Kansas comes in—was not the proudest chapter in our Hoosier story.

Even after two hundred years, though, the Native American heritage endures in many of our place names. Consider the Potawatomi, who controlled nearly all the region north of the Wabash River (that's almost one-fourth of Indiana) during the early 1800s. They lent their names everywhere from Lake Maxinkuckee (our second largest natural lake) to the town of Wakarusa (some natives translate that word as a Potawatomi term for "stuck in mud") and Pokagon State Park. The park in our far-northeastern corner has been renowned since the 1930s for its spectacular toboggan run that was created on the slope of, ahem, a steep hill.

In regard to place names, this state is, admittedly, as illogical as Garfield the cat. (The strip drawn in Delaware County by PAWS Inc. founder Jim Davis became, shortly after the turn of the twenty-first century, the most widely distributed newspaper comic in the entire world. The antics of lasagna-loving Garfield are enjoyed by readers from Tokyo and Madrid to Salt Lake City and Muncie.)

A sampling of our inconsistency: South Bend is located in the far north, while North Vernon can be found in the southeast. At least a dozen of our towns are not in the identically named counties. The town of Decatur is far from Decatur County; instead, Greensburg—the town with the tree growing out of its historic courthouse—is that county's seat. The town of Franklin isn't in Franklin County. Marion County consists of my hometown of Indianapolis, not the city of Marion. Alas, you won't even find our towns of Berne and Geneva in Switzerland County.

With all of that inconsistency, who would have predicted that more Carnegie Libraries would be built here than in any

Garfield. **PHOTO COURTESY OF GRANT COUNTY VISITORS BUREAU**

other state? Our trove of libraries constructed in the early 1900s is just one of Indiana's claims to fame.

Crown Hill Cemetery in Indianapolis is the burial site of more US vice presidents (three) than any other graveyard. Nine of the ten largest high school gyms are located in the Hoosier state. The exception in the top ten can be found, naturally, in Texas, where bragging almost is a cultural imperative.

In contrast, Hoosiers historically have been modest and self-effacing, traits that are endearing but that often cause our contributions to be overlooked. Consider just 2 of the 160 notable

Americans from all walks of life who are profiled in my book *Indiana Legends: Famous Hoosiers from Johnny Appleseed to David Letterman*. A pair of the twentieth century's literary greats were sons of prominent Hoosier families: Kurt Vonnegut ("Even my adenoids are Indianapolis," he once said, referring to the state capital's influence on him) and Booth Tarkington, one of only two novelists to have won the Pulitzer Prize twice. (The other was William Faulkner of Mississippi.)

True, we have our eccentricities. Since the 1940s, some excitable residents in the town of Churubusco claimed to have glimpsed a giant turtle looming in a murky lake. Known as "Indiana's version of the Loch Ness monster," the massive turtle's presence never has been verified even though Fulk Lake has been partially drained and scuba divers have searched. In the face of such persistent folklore, though, Churubusco residents made the shrewdest possible move: They toss a town festival to celebrate the "Beast of 'Busco," real or delusional. It's called Turtle Days.

Hoosiers love our town festivals, just like we adore our Indiana cuisine. There is such a thing as the latter, and it starts with the aforementioned breaded tenderloin sandwich, which a restaurant in Huntington, Nick's Kitchen, claims to have invented. Sugar cream pie—marketed as "Indiana's official state pie"—evolved out of farm kitchens in the 1800s because, unlike fruit pies, its ingredients (flour, sugar and cream) are staples available year-round, including during our harsh winters, as food historians note. Even today, Wick's Pies in the far-eastern Indiana town of Winchester remains the world's largest maker of sugar cream pie. Take that, Texans.

Winchester also drew national attention in 2006 when some civic-minded women in their seventies, eighties, and even nineties posed in the buff. The ladies, members of a bridge club, were appalled that the majestic Randolph County Courthouse was scheduled for the wrecking ball.

Inspired by a British movie titled *Calendar Girls*, the women shed their clothes to pose for a fund-raising calendar. This was done with decorum, as is the Hoosier way. The white-haired women shielded their most private parts by standing behind strategically placed small porcelain replicas of their beloved courthouse. The girls emerged triumphant; the courthouse, built in 1877, still stands.

Modest we may be, but we aren't pushovers. Nor are we rubes, stereotypes aside. And we have become a much more diverse state than many non-Hoosiers realize.

Fort Wayne, our second-largest city, has a larger community of Burmese immigrants than any other city in the country. In the Indy metro area, there are five Sikh temples. In cornfields near Bloomington during the late 1980s, a Tibetan Cultural Center was created; visitors have included the Dalai Lama and celebrity Buddhists such as Richard Gere.

Some other aspects of our Indiana tapestry: the Hoosier state now has the third largest Amish population in the country, behind only Ohio and Pennsylvania. And the Islamic Society of North America has been headquartered since the 1970s in Plainfield.

Let's stay in Plainfield, but time travel to the 1830s and '40s. The new frontier town was reliant on the National Road (now US 40), the federal government's first highway project. The dirt road had been built across the Indiana wilderness through the dense forests thanks to the arduous efforts of laborers who removed trees, stumps, and thick foliage. Bumpy and muddy, the National Road was in need of an upgrade, but President Martin Van Buren vetoed a bill that would have funded improvements.

Infuriated, Plainfield residents extracted revenge in 1843 when Van Buren, by then a former president, announced he would travel along the National Road. The locals paid his stagecoach driver to give his distinguished passenger a rollicking ride to remember. The driver revved his horses into a frenzy; the former president was unceremoniously dumped into the mucky National Road at its intersection with Avon Avenue in Plainfield.

A plaque commemorates the offbeat presidential site where Van Buren endured a "hands-on" experience with miserable road conditions. Hendricks County residents have been telling stories about the episode (with occasional embellishments) ever since.

That, of course, is a perennial Hoosier pastime: colorful storytelling. Enjoy those that follow.

Nelson Price

Undeniably
Indiana

Who We Are

A Hoosier Abroad

"Where are you from?"

"From the states, Indiana."

"What's in Indiana?"

Here I am, in the middle of Athens being driven back to my apartment by a Greek man who isn't too familiar with the United States. He's asking me what my home is like, and this may be the only person from Indiana he ever interacts with, so I have to make sure I answer well.

But what is in Indiana? How do I sum up my home state, a place where I grew up? I could tell him about learning to ride my two-wheeled Barbie bike in a local business's parking lot. How furious I had been when I turned around and realized that my dad wasn't holding on to the back of the seat. I could tell him about playing flashlight tag in my backyard and having bonfires with my friends on hot summer nights. Or maybe I could tell him about how much fun I had in high school with my friends—getting to school early to goof around and film short stories for our own entertainment.

Then there's my amazing college experience at Indiana University. From the Little 500 bike race to the huge fundraiser IU Dance Marathon (which raises over $1 million!), I could paint a picture of how exciting the state can be. But it's not all fun and games—there's the great scenery of Indiana as well, which IU showcases perfectly. The amazing trees and scenic rivers that dot our landscape show the true beauty of the state. And let's not forget our furry little friends—Indiana can boast some amazing wildlife, from wild deer to chipmunks.

But maybe I shouldn't think of my own experience—maybe I should talk about what Indiana has to offer tourists. There's the Indy 500, which is pretty popular and might be known more for the drinking rather than the actual racing. There's basketball—a sport so ingrained in our history that Larry Bird is a known name in most households.

Or maybe I could speak to pop culture references. Indiana is the home of Leslie Knope (Go Hoosiers!), a vivacious woman in public government who is hardworking and fun to be around. Then there's *The Fault in Our Stars*, which boasts local hot spots such as Holliday Park where you can see replicas of ancient ruins.

I could tell him all of this, but even without knowing my way around Athens, I can recognize that we are getting close to the apartment. Even so, there is no way to really explain how amazing and unique Indiana is, despite the fact that most think the state dull and ordinary. This is the place where I grew up, the place I miss as I'm halfway across the world. So what do I say to make this man understand everything Indiana has to offer and what it means to me?

"Cornfields," I answer.

Stephanie Simpson

What Does It Mean to Be a Hoosier?

When I lived in St. Louis, I was aghast to discover that the word "Hoosier" is used synonymously with the label of "redneck." I could only gape in open-mouthed horror when native St. Louisans informed me that my beloved title was tantamount to a stereotype I had prejudicially associated with the South. This information was especially paralyzing because I had and have always referred to myself as a "double" Hoosier: that is, I'm Indiana born and bred, and I attended Indiana University Bloomington for both my undergraduate and graduate education.

But if being a double Hoosier makes me a double "redneck" in the eyes of a state whose name could be a synonym for misery, then a double Hoosier I shall be and will remain, because of the pride that comes with the label, in the Indiana sense of the word.

Based on this misinterpretation I uncovered (in our very own Midwest, no less!), I set out to discover exactly what the word "Hoosier" means to its rightful possessors: the people who identify with and live in Indiana.

On Facebook, I asked my Hoosier friends to describe what being a Hoosier really meant to them. I received a wide variety of distinct, yet seemingly linked, answers:

- Hoosiers are very family-oriented and linked to their communities.

- Hoosiers are very traditional, but with a hint of adaptability. Although Hoosiers remain immersed in the familiar, they can also adapt readily and extremely effectively to different situations. Take Indiana weather, for example! Hoosiers also have the greatest pride, whether it's in our sports teams, attractions, or local celebrities and personalities. Quirky is the norm for Hoosiers, and we wouldn't have it any other way!

- Being a Hoosier means being the best a person can be! Hoosiers have a way of challenging each other to the greatest possible extent, but also providing support to help each other surmount any kind of challenge.

- Hoosiers are very engaged in any type of college rivalry: teams to support include Indiana University, Purdue, and Notre Dame. (Oh, and Hoosiers intuitively have an intense dislike for University of Kentucky!)

- Historically, Hoosiers were frontierspeople who crossed the Cumberland Gap with Daniel Boone and ended up in a place populated by Native Americans, or the Northwest Territory. The governor of this locale was William Henry Harrison (who was president for only thirty-two days before he died of pneumonia).

- Although Indiana is technically "flyover" country, we still possess some of the prettiest landscape in the continental United States. (There's a reason Brown County is called "God's Country.") We're also down home and uptown, all at the same time!

- Hoosiers create the breadbasket that feeds the world.

- Hoosier hospitality is generosity at its best!

- Although Hoosiers are always depicted as kind of quirky on television and in the media (Woody on *Cheers* or the characters from *Parks and Recreation*), we're so much more than just corn and basketball!

- No matter where you live, once a Hoosier, always a Hoosier!

After reading these varied yet apropos answers, I couldn't help thinking that Indiana itself is like our weather: what we have to offer, and the characteristics that define us all commonly as Hoosiers, is actually as varied as our weather, which can go from 75 degrees and sunny to 15 degrees and snowing in a short span of fifteen hours!

After all, Hoosiers do have to be incredibly adaptable, not only to get used to such extreme weather changes, but also to actually enjoy them. In a sense, you never know what's going to happen next in Indiana. Perhaps that's why we Hoosiers are frequently depicted as being so quirky and unusual in media representations.

Although we remain grounded by and in our strong traditions, it is the very stability that such traditions provide that allows us to perpetuate the strong sense of community and pride that defines Indiana, and simultaneously, what it means to be a Hoosier.

By using these traditions as our core foundation, we can be open to new and unusual things. This is one core characteristic that truly defines our famous "Hoosier Hospitality." It also allows us to simultaneously challenge and support each other. It lets us maintain and sustain our strong loyalty to and pride in all things Indiana: our communities, our sports teams, our landmarks, and our attractions.

Grace Waitman-Reed

Indiana Is . . .

Billy Joel has his New York state of mind. The dudes from Led Zeppelin are going to California with an aching in their hearts. They can keep all of it—the *Daily News*, the footsteps of dawn, the ache. I'd take Indiana over the Big Apple and the Golden State any day.

This declaration would probably come as a shock to my friends from the coasts who think of Indiana, rather predictably, as flyover country. They can never remember where it falls geographically in relation to what they call "the 'I' states."

"So, you're from Illinois," they'll say, venturing casually into unfamiliar territory, their voices at once hesitant and unconcerned.

"Indiana."

"That's what I meant. Indiana. Which is next to Iowa."

"Not exactly."

To them, Indiana is a sock-shaped stereotype. It's corn, basketball, and casseroles. It's lakes in the north, hills in the south, and farm country in the middle. It's people in poorly fitting sweatpants, well-intentioned but closed-minded, sweet as box cake but white bread as Wonder. Right?

I don't live in Indiana anymore. I live in Washington State, and before that I called Oregon home, and before that, Iowa, but I dream about Indiana. Almost exclusively, and I have for years. The dreams are bright, vivid, practically Technicolor. In my dreams I'm ten again, playing Wildcat Baseball at the diamond across the street. I'm three, running in and out of the north Fort Wayne house where I grew up. Sometimes I'm seventeen, falling in and out of love with the same boys I did before I knew any better. More often than not, I'm ageless, huddling under the stairs with my family, waiting out a tornado.

I miss thunderstorms in my new life in the Pacific Northwest, but my dreams give them back to me, night after night after night. The green skies, the lightning flashes like synapses firing, the crack and the boom. The dreams often end the same way—with a thick black funnel cloud, train sounds, and a near miss, followed by a dazed walk up the stairs and outside to assess the damage.

It's homesickness, I suspect. A kind of stormy pining.

So I guess it's true when I say I don't live in Indiana anymore. Not physically. But my brain does. My heart does, too, and my pen. When I write about Indiana what appears on the page depends on my mood, the dream I had the night before, the last story my mom told me about what my hometown was like when she was a girl. I don't get in an Indiana state of mind. Indiana is my state of mind.

To me, Indiana is

> My dad in the driveway whistling me home for dinner.

> My mom standing at the stove, smoking and telling me to set the table.

> My brother throwing a Frisbee into our neighbor's garden.

> Our neighbor handing the Frisbee back and inviting us to help ourselves to the fattest grapes on his vines.

> Our other neighbor carrying her pet raccoon around on her back while she dusts.

> My Grandma Zurbrugg running out of vegetable oil for a cake and using beer instead.

> My Aunt Cindy squinting up at the green sky over an above-ground pool, saying, "Don't worry, Deb. It'll blow over."

> Picnics, birthday parties, entire weekends ruined by storms that didn't blow over.

> My Uncle Rick teaching me how to sail.

> The smell of summer, which is the smell of lake water and flooded boat engines.

> The smell of winter, which is wet wool hats drying off on heating grates.

> Piles of leaves to jump in and burn.

Piles of sticks to pick up so Dad can mow.

Tiger lilies by the roadside, drooping over gravel, petals falling into potholes.

Peonies in the backyard covered in fat black ants.

Strip malls. Miles and miles of strip malls. My mom telling me, "No, you can't buy that."

Chain restaurants. Fast food. My dad telling me, "No, you can't eat that."

But also Lexy's pizza, Hall's Big Buster platters, Hilger's strawberries.

All-night skates at Roller Dome North.

Early morning fishing trips at Clear Lake.

Whole days spent lying under the Norway maple doing nothing.

Our elm tree before it died. Our ash tree before it died, too.

Mosquitoes buzzing my ears when I'm trying to sleep.

Mosquitoes eating my ankles when I'm trying to star gaze.

Mosquitoes. Mosquitoes. More mosquitoes.

The Auburn fair—doughnuts, darts, hard-won stuffed animals whose ears fall off in the car on the way home.

The Custer boys hitting a deer on our way home from the Auburn fair.

The Custer boys dragging the deer back to their house to make venison.

The Custer boys killing my pet turtle with a BB gun the very next day.

The taste of the Custer boys' venison on a cracker with cheddar cheese.

Hiking up the belly of a bear.

Looking out over a field of green corn, knee high.

Visiting the graves of my great-aunts and -uncles, my grandparents, my father, an older brother I never met.

Home.

Deborah Kennedy

Da Region

Only in Indiana do you not belong in Indiana. At least that's how it felt sometimes, growing up in Da Region.

Northwest Indiana is a true oddity. Comprised of just five counties (Lake, Porter, LaPorte, Newton, and Jasper), it's a blip on a map of ninety-two Indiana counties. And we don't do things like the rest of the state. For one, we follow Central Time—a shift that proves each spring we are not like the folks around us.

But things really get strange when you consider Lake and Porter counties, two pieces of Northwest Indiana nestled right up to Chicago. That positioning has earned the area a Bearsworthy nickname: "Da Region." (Too bad few people from Da Region actually call it that.)

That's where I grew up, in a town of 3,000 people called Hebron. We followed Chicago time; listened to Chicago radio; watched Chicago news; learned all the Chicago commercials ("588–2300 EMPIIIIIIIIRE"); played in Lake Michigan, where we could get a glimpse of the Chicago skyline on a clear day; and hopped on the South Shore train that took us into the city.

At the same time, we were in farm territory. My dad worked the fields in the summers when he wasn't teaching history. My babysitter owned a farm where I learned to shear sheep and pull up carrots. My mother, a music teacher, played the organ at the local Methodist church. And my older sister and I visited many a pioneer reenactment village with our parents.

It was a great way to grow up, with access to silos and sky-scrapers, tractors and taxis, potluck dinners and professional sports teams. It's probably the reason I still can't decide whether I'm city or country at heart. And the rest of Indiana and Illinois . . . they're not sure what to make of the paradox either. Having lived on both sides of the fence—and on the fence—I can attest to that.

During my time at Indiana University, people from outside our area would constantly point out the way I said things. "Pop" instead of "soda." Or my nasal tone on all vowels ("Hi, my name is Jeeeeeeyackie").

After college, I moved to central Illinois. People knew only a few things about Indiana—how to get to Turkey Run State Park and Indianapolis, and that somewhere in Indiana was a town called Fort Wayne, so surely I grew up near there, right?

And then I moved to Chicago. My Chicago friends thought Turkey Run was a Thanksgiving 5K and laughed at the idea of Northwest Indiana being a collection of Chicago suburbs (even though I repeat often that we grew up closer to the city than kids who grew up in Naperville).

So there you have it. An oddity. A unique culture. An area all its own, that only those who reside there truly understand and claim. But there's so much to love and to know about Northwest Indiana and the Region in particular. Here are a few:

- You've never seen a county fair better than the Porter County Fair in Valparaiso. The fair brings in top musical acts from the Beach Boys to Luke Bryan, and its vast layout allows fairgoers to experience everything from deep-fried Oreos and magic shows to petting zoos and amusement rides.

- In the '90s, we called Gary the Murder Capital of the United States, which technically it was for a few years when its murders per capita outranked Washington, D.C. The city continues to work on shedding that image, with a fun and cozy minor league ballpark and a respected airport. But what people really love to talk about when it comes to Gary is the fact that Michael Jackson grew up there—and not just Michael but also Tito and Janet and the whole family.

- MJ isn't the only celebrated Hoosier in the Region. Though he was born in Clay County, Valparaiso holds a Popcorn Fest (complete with running events and the nation's second-oldest Popcorn Parade) in honor of Orville Redenbacher each summer.

- In the era of Al Capone, gangsters were said to have dumped the bodies of their victims in the Region, and Capone himself is believed to have had a hideout there. In 1934, notorious bank robber John Dillinger escaped from the Lake County Jail in Crown Point. When Johnny Depp starred as Dillinger in *Public Enemies* in 2009, fans were thrilled to see the actor up close during filming in Crown Point.

- The Indiana Dunes offer visitors untouched beauty and serenity. Easily accessible from towns such as Chesterton and Michigan City, the protected Indiana Dunes National Lakeshore is 25 miles long. The dunes themselves, formed through glacial movements, are massive hills of sand that sweep down into Lake Michigan. It's the perfect spot for a weekend of sunbathing, hiking, camping, and bird-watching.

- Speaking of the paradox, the steel mills are visible from the dunes. Region steel mills provided materials for both world wars and sold not just locally to Chicago but globally. Beginning in the 1980s, the steel mills went through mass layoffs, with more than one mill closing completely, an upheaval that residents are still dealing with today.

- Things are a little more lighthearted at Region high schools. I spent nearly every Friday night of my childhood at a Porter County Conference basketball game or boys' volleyball match (because we were too small a school to have football). Sometimes the whole town would turn out to watch a bunch of high school kids in a dimly lit gym compete for an oaken bucket. In nearby towns like Lowell or Merrillville or Schererville, Friday nights were and still are all about football. We could give Texas a run for their money.

I landed in Illinois, but the truth is my heart will always be in Northwest Indiana. I still have my 219 phone number, and I left the city to find a house with a garden because I feel the urge to pull up carrots again. I'm not at all ashamed of my city friends finding out that I secretly want to live on a farm.

That's how all of us Region folk are—proud of our Indiana roots. We spent our weekends visiting Indianapolis or Indiana Beach, we attended Purdue and IU and Ball State, we learned all the words to "Back Home Again in Indiana." We're Region Rats, but ultimately, we're Hoosiers. And even if we're an odd bunch, we do belong.

Jackie Walker Gibson

What's in a Name?

In the spring of 1884 my second great-grandfather, Benjamin F. Branam, was fined thirty dollars in a Monroe County court for malicious mayhem. It appears that during an altercation with Marion Robinson, my second great-grandfather bit off part of Mr. Robinson's ear. The article did not state whether left or right ear, but the fight occurred on the levee, Bloomington's historic bar district west of the courthouse square. The original headline was "Hunk of Ear Costs Him $30" in the *Bloomington Saturday Courier* on May 3, 1884.

Both men were residents of the farming village of Dolan, along the banks of Beanblossom Creek in northern Monroe County. The term "Hoosier" has multiple origin stories, including references to hill people and country bumpkins or regarding the toughness of the men when asking "whose ear" was lying on floor after a fight. Benjamin F. Branam (1843–1902) is a true Hoosier on both counts.

Tony Branam

Indiana is the only state named for a Methodist circuit rider, "Black Harry" Hoosier.

John Robert McFarland

I have heard it came about because back in pioneer days when someone knocked on a cabin door, the occupants would say "Who's there?" but in their lower midland accents, it sounded like "Whoozherr?"

Laura Pinhey

I love that we have no idea, but aren't upset by that.

Jennifer Pfeifer

"Hoose" is an old English word for hill, and "ire" I believe is French for dweller . . . so, hillbilly!

Janey Taylor

I thought it was because people migrated from other states. Often asked newcomers "Hoosier state?"

Marcy Tanski

Having grown up in southern Indiana during a time when no one locked his or her doors and neighbors dropped in whenever, I have to go along with the theory of "whose here?"

Karen Walker

Hoosier: A kid who left Kentucky and found his first love at a basketball game.

John C. Updike

It means happy people.

Judy Young

Just Plain Peculiar

The Thorntown Gorilla

GORILLA TERRORIZES THORNTOWN. That's what newspaper headlines around the country exclaimed in 1949! Folks were convinced that there was a gorilla on the loose in Thorntown, Indiana—and with good reason. Three good friends, Homer Birge, George Coffman, and Asher Cones, were tired of hearing about Gobby Jones's fishing successes. All he ever did was fish! After one too many fish stories, they hatched a plan: they would make an animal to scare him away from Sugar Creek!

What animal would be better than a bear? So they set out to make a bear. Homer and his wife made the suit out of an old horsehair coat (some sources declare that it was a buffalo coat), which had once belonged to a family member, sewed over some old overalls. The effect wasn't quite enough, so Asher Cones tracked down another coat that he remembered another town resident once wore. He offered ten dollars to the guy for his coat (again, some sources say twenty dollars).

They used a wire frame to fashion a head, inserting tiger eyes to shine in car lights. They cut eyeholes just below the tiger eyes and added in a set of tin teeth, painted white. To wear it, you had to hold it on with one hand.

These three guys decided it was time to teach this guy a lesson. Homer suited up, George led Gobby to the spot—and they scared him so bad he lost his wallet in the water and scaled a bank he could never have climbed under normal circumstances! Gobby, however, didn't believe he saw a bear. He thought he saw a gorilla! So, that's how it became the Thorntown Gorilla and not the Thorntown Bear.

You know how small towns are: word gets around. So when these pranksters would hear that someone didn't believe that there was a gorilla on the loose, they were quick to make a believer out of the doubter. Homer, George, and Asher worked out a way to get people to where they needed them and developed a signal (flashing car lights) to let whoever was dressed as the ape know that the car they needed was right behind them, right where they wanted them! After the gorilla had been spotted the car driver (often Asher) would turn around, pick up whomever (usually Homer), and they would hit the road. They had that down to such a science it took them thirty seconds to clear out!

Not stopping there, they even cut out wooden feet that matched a gorilla footprint. Attaching the feet to old shoes, they would make clear, unmistakable footprints around the riverbank and in farmer's cornfields.

Now remember, this was 1949. There's a good chance that some of the townspeople had never even seen a live gorilla before. So when word began to really spread about this, when naysayers suddenly became believers, well, the story was bound to get around. And get around it did. Newspapers from around the country, from New York to California, reported on the Thorntown Gorilla, speculating on how it got there and what to do next. Men grabbed their guns and, in great groups, scoured the woods and cornfields for the gorilla.

The fishing spots were empty, kids were afraid to visit the old swimming holes, and one man missed work because his wife was too afraid to be alone! But what would you expect when the gorilla could appear anywhere, like the time it popped up in the window of an elderly couple's house, scaring the poor woman so badly she went over backward in her rocking chair?

The three pranksters say that they had usually planned who was going to see the gorilla. Asher admits that he told his wife because when the phone rang, he would head out. Don't you just wonder what she thought about it?

Although George had called it quits long before the gorilla drives and the airplanes flying over the area looking for the gorilla, that's what it took for Asher to end it. Homer kept it going until Asher gave him a talking to. Together, they placed the "gorilla" into a box, nailed it shut, and stored it in Homer's attic. Of course, no one else knew about it—but the sightings continued off and on. They did find a "demented" woman (as Asher Cones's statement said) at the area where they had been a couple of times, wearing a fur coat.

They didn't let anyone know it was them until YEARS, if not decades, had passed. Some people were really mad about the whole thing. They definitely didn't want to get into trouble! If anyone had gotten close enough, they would have seen through the disguise for what it was: a shabby coat and mask.

Funny enough, the former owner of the coat, the one who sold it to them for ten or twenty bucks, never made the connection between the sale of an old, heavy, decidedly furry coat at a strange time of year and the sudden appearance of a gorilla. That could have ended this story right there. But then again—if he had figured out the true story of the Boone County gorilla, would anyone have believed him?

Asher Cones was the last survivor of the gorilla group. He passed away at the age of 101 on Christmas Eve 2014. Oh, the stories I bet he could tell! The town held a wonderful event at the Thorntown Heritage Museum, which is supported by the Thorntown Public Library, to commemorate his life.

Interestingly, a website includes the Thorntown Gorilla in its listing of Bigfoot sightings from 1818–1980, and it also appears in a book written in 1982 by the couple behind the website. Gorilla to Bigfoot, that's one practical joke that certainly stands head and shoulders above the rest!

Jessica Nunemaker

The Tipton Mummy

Almost nothing has stirred up more intrigue in the Central Indiana city of Tipton than its revered 4-foot-tall "Indian princess" mummy that occupied a place of honor for almost three decades at the Tipton County Courthouse.

The preserved princess—with her mud-colored body; her lusterless black, shoulder-length hair; her long, spindly fingers and toes; two knoblike knees; and an oddly fetching, sardonic smile—was a curiously captivating thing to behold.

The mysterious mummy first graced the front page of the *Tipton Tribune* on September 3, 1954, after her petrified remains were discovered in an old barn. According to local legend, the mummified princess had migrated from the American Southwest to Tipton County some seventy-five years before and was promptly claimed by a family that capitalized on their acquisition by carting her from carnival to carnival, charging ten cents a look. Shortly after World War I, however, they handed down their moneymaking curio to the next generation, who opted to stash it in a barn, where it remained unattended and forgotten until early September 1954.

Once resurrected, the mummy snagged the attention of a Tipton High School teacher, who persuaded one of the local organizations to provide a custom-made glass display case. Shortly after, the mummified remains took center stage at the local history museum on the ground floor of the Tipton County Courthouse, where it soon overshadowed scores of turn-of-the-century artifacts and a variety of stuffed birds and small game.

And so it was, time and again over the next twenty-nine years, hundreds of thrill-seeking children dashed to the courthouse's lower level, pressed their tiny noses against the glass that separated them from the museum's star attraction, and gaped wide-eyed down at her. Their little voices were heard echoing throughout the concrete passageways, squealing, "Ewww, she's green! . . . She's so skinny! . . . I can smell her!" During that same time span, participants of field trips, club outings, holiday events, and festivals—accounting for thousands of visitors—came to the courthouse history museum to see Tipton's amazing "Indian princess" mummy for themselves. It was almost as if her career as a carnival sideshow attraction had been reprised.

But, alas, all things must come to end, even things that are mummified. Sadly, that was the case for Tipton's celebrated, mummified "Indian princess."

For her, the end came in the spring of 1983, when the Tipton County Historical Society undertook a reorganization, restoration, and renovation of the courthouse-based museum. During that process, the museum committee chairman thought to ask if anyone had ever validated the mummy's authenticity. Surprisingly, the answer was "No," prompting the Tipton County coroner to have it X-rayed.

Yet even before the historical society knew the result, the members held a special vote that sealed the fate of the popular Tipton relic: if the mummy were deemed real, they would either respectfully return it to storage or give it a proper burial. On the other hand, if it turned out that the mummy was a dummy, it would be dealt with swiftly and harshly. The public would learn the coroner's verdict and the mummy's fate at the society's meeting, scheduled for the evening of May 26, 1983.

Earlier, that day's edition of the *Tipton Tribune* asked the historical society's president about the famed museum relic, but the president remained mum, saying only, "We aren't releasing any information on the findings of the X-rays."

However, in the same news report, a source, who asked to remain unnamed, broke the silence, revealing that the mummy was a "fake," that the "body is wood, and the face and appendages are made of paper mache." Indeed, when the historical society meeting convened, the coroner disclosed that the "Indian princess" was constructed of "paper, wood, tacks, and nails." The announcement sparked an outburst of laughter, but the discussion quickly turned serious with the reading of a letter from a descendant of the family that had originally owned the mummy. They wanted it back.

In response, the society's president stated firmly that returning the artifact was impossible.

"The mummy has already been taken care of," she said, adding that the mummy fell under the museum's loan provision, which dictates that any article given to the society can be kept indefinitely or destroyed. With that, the society looked to the coroner to explain what had been done.

"We X-rayed it, proved it was a fake, and destroyed it," he said.

And that was that. The next day, the *Tribune* reported that a motion to close the subject silenced further discussion . . . permanently.

Although the subject was officially closed, a generation of Tiptonians refused to stop talking about their beloved mummified "Indian princess." Perhaps she had been counterfeit, but the love for her was as genuine as it was enduring. And that is why even today her story lives on, vividly preserved in the hearts and minds of all her admirers, who long ago as youngsters pressed their little noses against a glass case in the Tipton Courthouse museum and squealed, "Ewww."

Janis Thornton

Professor Edward M. Worth's Museum of Oddities and Curiosities

Long before Robert Ripley's museums of oddities, Professor Edward M. Worth had amassed an enormous collection of historical artifacts and curiosities. Worth was born around 1838, and his first museum was said to have been in Detroit, Michigan. There in the 1870s farmers started finding strange and ancient artifacts that could not be explained as belonging to a specific group of people. Some thought the markings on the objects to be Egyptian, offering pictures from their encyclopedias as evidence, while others who claimed them to be Hebrew countered with samples from their Bibles. If the writings were Hebrew could this then be the remains of the biblical "Lost Tribes"? Many thought so, and imaginations soared!

Within the course of the next few months, additional unexplainable pieces were unearthed in the area of Michigan northwest of Detroit: a copper stiletto, a small clay box, and a large slate tablet, each bearing undecipherable markings and strange cryptic characters.

Many of these artifacts fell into the hands of Worth, who displayed them in his Detroit museum. Later Worth moved his museum to New York, where he displayed the items for nearly forty years. In 1906, he decided to relocate to Indiana to be near his only living relative, his sister Anna, who as a child had been sent here on one of the Orphan Trains of the late nineteenth century.

Worth purchased some land near Springport, Indiana, and moved himself and his artifacts to Henry County, where he built a large museum in the shape of a cross (some say a starfish). The museum's reputation grew so that on some Sundays in summer as many as 600 people streamed through the museum to view the fantastic collection of over 5,000 artifacts.

Worth had started collecting as a small boy in 1848, and in addition to inscribed stones, he had a vast collection of coins, an outstanding collection of fine oriental pearls, and George Washington's sword. Other strange pieces in the collection were a Monster Devil Fish and a transparent baby.

But the most fascinating display for most museumgoers was the head of Charles Guiteau, the assassin of President James A. Garfield. The head, excepting the skull and brains, was enclosed in a square glass case set in a round glass case filled with water and standing on a pedestal. This pedestal was sized so that the top of the head stood just at the same height as the living Guiteau. Accompanying the exhibition were several portraits of Guiteau.

In 1916 Professors Worth's museum burned. From the ashes of that fire, some twenty pieces of the Michigan artifacts were recovered by Thad Wilson. Five of those pieces sold to Philip Schupp of Chicago in 1924.

After the fire that destroyed nearly all of the Springport Museum and its artifacts, Professor Worth's health began to decline. He planned to rebuild the museum, but was not as satisfied with the idea of displaying his artifacts as he had once been. On August 18, 1917, Edward Worth died at his home in Springport, Indiana, at the age of seventy-nine years. His body is buried at Springport's Woodlawn Cemetery.

Mark Sean Orr

Hell on Wheels

I was going to my daughter's house, driving west on I-80/94, getting near the Indiana-Illinois state line. It's like driving in a video game: overpasses, merges, perpetual roadwork, trucks, motorcycles, and fast cars. But if you want to get to a Chicago South or Westside suburb, you end up on this ribbon of death traps, like it or not.

To steady my nerves, I had the radio tuned to NPR, to play along with *Wait, Wait, Don't Tell Me*. I'm the white-knuckle kind of driver. You've seen me, older lady hunched over the wheel. I had just slipped through a truck sandwich of a chemical tanker and an auto carrier, and suddenly, right in the middle of the news quiz, which I'm winning by the way, music pours out of my radio.

So what? Public radio has music breaks, you say.

This was not, however, NPR-type of music. This was praise music, the kind heard at contemporary church services where songs are projected up front on slides with a dove motif.

So I listened for a few minutes, thinking maybe NPR was experiencing technical difficulties, and a panicky intern at the studio slapped in a CD from her church.

But the music went on for quite a while.

You're thinking—Why didn't you check your radio dial?

Well, I did my best. I turned a knob, blindly because trifocals have no range for far-to-your-right. One click of the knob and the praise music stayed on. Another click and it was still syrupy praise music oddly on several stations.

Then it hit me: Today is Saturday, May 21, 2011. Could this moment really be the RAPTURE?

Yes, that day had been predicted by Harold Camping, evangelist of international Family Radio, to be the Rapture—the day the chosen would rise to heaven. Those left behind would face earthquake and fire.

I wildly twirled the knob click, click—the praise music just stayed there, rising and falling like buzzing bees in a wall.

I pawed the dashboard for the Sirius radio tab.

Nothing. Silence. Are the satellites dead?

Maybe angels, proficient as Katniss Everdeen with bows and arrows, had knocked that technology out the spheres, a *Hunger Games* sort of thing. I hit the AM/FM tab again. Back to praise music. Apparently taking over the radio stations was the first angelic mission.

Is the music outside too? I actually opened the window.

I'm not a subscriber to end-time scenarios, but I was alone and captive as an astronaut in that galaxy of traffic. Belief was beginning to look very good.

A fast car zigzagged across several lanes. God damn that speeder—what's the rush!

Then—Is there a rush? I checked the rearview mirror for the Horses of the Apocalypse, equine Stealth bombers coming down on Northwest Indiana and this highway with its billboards for strip clubs, casinos, divorce lawyers, and fireworks.

Suddenly, the traffic tightened like beads drawn on a string. I was crawling next to other drivers, apparently people left behind like me. I was tempted to open the window and ask about the radio stations, but—well.

Caught up in the soaring music, I tried to make an assessment. Do I deserve to be saved? Oh, where does one begin to look for the answer?

Just then, the traffic holdup became clear: natural order had indeed dissolved!

Cows stood, and sadly some lay, on an overpass and along the embankment where their overturned carrier had spilled them out. Black, white, and red.

So, apparently, today was not The End.

The praise music? In gripping the steering wheel, I must have squeezed the radio button onto an AM Christian station, and the dashboard knob I twirled again and again was the temperature control. The missing satellite transmission? There are some very wide underpasses along 80/94.

Joyce Hicks

More of the Peculiar

Willard Aldrich was born around 1840. He made his home with his mother in Mishawaka. Willard's mother was thought to be a witch, and people kept their distance from her. Willard was an eccentric young man, who many thought was a horse thief because he would disappear from Mishawaka for weeks, and upon his eventual return he would have several fine horses for sale.

Unfortunately, Willard contracted consumption (tuberculosis) and knew he did not have long to live, so he had a local undertaker create a coffin in which he could sit upright.

Upon his death in 1882, his body was placed in the specialized coffin and put on the back of a wagon for its final trip to Mishawaka's City Cemetery. People lined both sides of Main Street just to catch a glimpse of Mr. Aldrich's odd-looking casket. The casket was lowered into a 5×7-foot vault that contained a card table on which there was placed a deck of cards, a pipe, tobacco, and a shotgun—in case the devil showed up.

There is no marker erected at Willard Aldrich's final resting place, just a large slab of concrete that was used to cover his specialized gravesite.

Travis Childs

Barbee Hotel.

* * *

The Barbee Hotel and Restaurant, located in Warsaw, Indiana, was a safe haven to many Chicago gangsters, including legendary American gangster Al Capone, in the 1920s before it started catering for parties and banquets. Each time, Capone stayed in room 301 and would clear the hotel of the rest of the guests so he could be alone. Hotel and cleaning staff members said they could frequently smell cigar smoke coming from his room. Since his death, hotel staff members have said they have seen a "ghostly" man sitting in a booth in the hotel bar after closing. The figure does not respond when staff members try to engage with it. Additionally, many also reported to have seen footsteps on the stairs and throughout the hallways.

Legend also says that the Barbee Hotel was a popular place for gangsters to bring their girlfriends. However, one time, a gangster brought the girlfriend of another rival gangster to the hotel. Upon finding out about her unfaithfulness, her boyfriend murdered her at the hotel. Since then, people have reportedly heard wailing at night, and they feel cold spots throughout the hotel.

Actress Rita Hayworth was also a frequent guest of the Barbee Hotel. Some people say her spirit manifests as a faint light that can be seen from outside the building.

The hotel is also a popular site to see orbs and apparitions, reportedly.

Tori Lawhorn

* * *

The old Whitley County Sheriff's House and Jail, located in Columbia City, Indiana, was built in 1875. The combination of a sheriff's house and a jail allowed Sheriff Franklin Allwein to easily oversee the inmates at any time. One of the inmates, Charles Butler, is assumed to haunt the jail.

Butler was an alcoholic who abused his wife, Abbie, and their son. During a drunken rage in 1883, he shot his wife in her back. Though he was put in Whitley Jail, he later escaped with four other prisoners through a door used for the second-floor cells. However, Butler was caught shortly after his escape when the sheriff found him passed out in a bar in Ohio. He was tried and sentenced to hang. Unfortunately, Butler didn't fall hard enough to break his neck immediately; he strangled for approximately ten minutes before he died.

His ghost is said to cause cameras to malfunction and batteries to drain. Visitors to the jail have also reportedly seen display costumes move on their own and heard footsteps, laughter, and voices coming from different rooms. Others have said they believe Allwein also haunts the jail. His spirit is said to have been seen coming down the stairs from the jail to the sheriff's part of the building. People also claim to have heard his spirit walk down the hallway beside the cells. Additionally, a door at the top of the stairs that leads to the top of the jail is said to open by itself.

An unknown female is also said to haunt the jail. A woman's ashy footprints have been seen on a wall on the third floor and attic areas.

Additional paranormal manifestations include footsteps and scraping along the walls, moving curtains, and a blurry apparition that has been known to touch the hands and shoulders of living visitors.

Tori Lawhorn

* * *

In 1894, an Indiana physician named Dr. Edward J. Goodwin attempted to square the circle. This meant finding a round number for the ratio of a circle's circumference to its diameter, rather than the long number we know as pi, i.e., ~3.14159. Goodwin tried to assert that pi was equal to 3.2.

Not only did he make this bold claim, but he then proceeded to write a bill for the state representatives that incorporated his ideas. In 1897, it became House Bill 246, or the Indiana Pi Bill, and was quickly brought up for debate. It is believed that it passed the Indiana House of Representatives only because the members were confused by all the mathematical language.

As the bill gained more media attention, a professor from Purdue University, C. A. Waldo, learned of it and immediately sought to end it. He happened to be at the Statehouse already, lobbying for Purdue's budget, but felt he had to step in when he heard of the attempted mathematical legislation. Professor Waldo knew that Goodwin's claims were ridiculous and recognized that squaring pi is impossible.

By the time the bill reached the Indiana Senate, Waldo had already talked to the senators and "coached" them on the realities of Goodwin's claims. When the senators reviewed the bill, they ridiculed it for half an hour by making puns and other jokes. The bill was then postponed indefinitely, as the senators were scared that the bill was opening up Indiana to ridicule by others for even considering it.

Alison Roth

* * *

In the summer of 1877 John Oscar Henderson, editor of the *Kokomo Dispatch* newspaper, received a letter seeking a "curious favor" from him. The letter, written by an assistant editor at the *Anderson Democrat* stung at having his poetry rejected by eastern publishers, proposed that the two men combine forces to spring on an unsuspecting public a ruse designed to "stir things from the comatose condition."

The young Anderson editor James Whitcomb Riley proposed that he would prepare a verse in the style of a popular deceased American poet (Edgar Allan Poe was selected), and Henderson would print this new discovery in the columns of his newspaper. After having made his point that having a famous name attached to a work—and not its quality—assured its success, the young poet, with Henderson's assistance, would announce his authorship to the public and "bu'st our literary balloon before a bewildered and enlightened world!!!"

Henderson, who just a month before had praised Riley as beyond a doubt the finest poet in the Hoosier State, eagerly agreed to carry out the plan, which he called "a capital one and . . . cunningly conceived." He printed the poem, titled "Leonainie," in his newspaper's August 2, 1877, edition.

At first the hoax seemed to be succeeding, with newspapers from New York to California announcing the discovery of a heretofore unknown Poe poem. Henderson wrote his accomplice that people in his community believed the poem was a "true bill" and that he had even been able to bamboozle his rivals at the *Kokomo Tribune*.

In spite of the scheme's early success, however, newspapers caught on to the ruse and raised doubts as to the poem's authenticity. On August 25 the *Tribune*, eager to obtain revenge on its rival, exposed the hoax to the public. The *Boston Evening Telegraph* spoke for many when it wrote of the incident that if Poe had actually written the poem "it is a consolation to think that he is dead."

Although he publicly apologized for the deception, Riley lost his job at the *Democrat* and endured scathing comments about his character in other newspapers in Indiana and around the country. "It was the most dismal period of my life," Riley, a former sign, house, and ornamental painter, admitted years later. "My tinsel throne was crumbling. Friends stood aside—went round the other way." Fortunately for Indiana literature, Riley successfully recovered from this temporary setback to his promising career.

Ray E. Boomhower

Zoar, Indiana—an unincorporated community straddling the Dubois and Pike County line—is undeniably Hoosier. You see, Zoar's population is 100 on one day a week: Sunday while church is in session. Zoar consists of one United Methodist Church (established in 1844 as a German Methodist congregation), a one-room schoolhouse (which served the children of the community from 1897 to 1933), a picnic grove (home to annual picnics and fests), a cemetery (with as many stones engraved in German as English), and five homes (surrounding the church-topped hill at the community's center).

The church, schoolhouse, and a handful of houses are in Dubois County—while the picnic grove and a few more houses stand in Pike County. The cemetery, well, it straddles the county line. In Zoar, Indiana, it is possible to have family members buried in the same cemetery, but in two different counties.

During the 1970s, when Dubois County observed Eastern Time and Pike County followed Central Time, the New Year would arrive in the church an hour earlier than the houses standing at the bottom of the hill.

And if one wonders how the community received the name Zoar—it comes from the Bible in the book of Genesis: fleeing Sodom and Gomorrah, Lot finds safety in the town of Zoar. What does Zoar mean in Hebrew? Small. Zoar, Indiana: the name fits.

Lee Bilderback

It was in the mid to late '60s, '65 to '67, that this story begins. On our farm in Washington County, Indiana, we raised swine. This episode was the first time that I had ever seen the birth of baby pigs, so I did not know what to expect. I was with my older brother at the barn and we noticed a sow beginning to deliver. What came next was odd; I could not make out really what it was, but after it came perfect shaped little piglets, one after another after another, about thirteen in all. We went to the house and let our dad know that one of the sows had a bunch of babies and that one had what looked to be two heads. Our dad, being a man who had raised pigs most of his life, did not think of it as anything special. Even though the little pig with the big head tried to stand, walk, and crawl, it just could not. My dad reached over into the pen, picked up the pig, put it in a five-gallon metal bucket, and placed it by the gate to the barn lot.

This could have been the end of the story; however, my dad enjoyed a cold beer from time to time. When he went to the local tavern, the Bluebird in Vallonia, Indiana, he told the story of having a two-headed pig, but no one seemed to believe him. They thought he must be drunk. However, the bar owner, Dan Wheeler, did believe my dad, and they drove to the farm to get this strange animal. My dad traded the pig for a case of beer. Dan Wheeler took the pig to the local funeral home and had it embalmed and put in a clear gallon jar filled with embalming fluid for all the customers to see.

I never saw that strange pig again until I turned twenty-one and went to the Bluebird, where the pig was still on display. I related the story to the people there. Time took its toll, and eventually the pig was buried. I often wondered whether if we had taken the pig to the vet instead of the bar it would have lived.

Ron Doyle

The Gooood Life

Gravel Lanes

There is nothing more undeniably Indiana than the gravel lanes that thread their way across the state. Winding randomly between cornfields, along creek bottoms, dead-ending in surprising spots: the best way to see Indiana is from the vantage point of an old farm road.

For those not native to Indiana, the curlicuing country roads present a puzzle. "Why don't these county roads run in a straight line?" This from a transplant from the West Coast, who was considering living outside the city limits.

"These farms are old," I responded. "Some go back over a hundred years in the same family. The fields came first, so they ran the roads around—not through."

My acquaintance snorted his disgust. "It's the twenty-first century, for heaven's sake!"

I sighed. There's no point in explaining to someone from Southern California the importance of every square inch of tillable soil in a farmer's field. Black gold, that. And if my acquaintance didn't see the romance in spending an evening driving around in the country with the windows rolled down, lights glowing on the dash, the scent of freshly cut hay in the air, well, he just wasn't going to be educated, was he?

If you grew up here, you know. Getting lost in a maze of cornfields in high summer is a rite of passage for every Indiana kid once they receive their driver's license. It's a requirement, almost a state law, no less than having a basketball hoop in every driveway. Crawling around in the dark with the headlights on low, mist rising from the fields, is tradition.

If, like my California friend, you want to use the country roads to get somewhere—not just ramble—there's an art to it, a methodology of travel, rules of the road, if you will. Those rules don't necessarily correspond with the driver's manual that the BMV hands out for driver's tests.

The first rule is the speed limit must be no less than 50 miles per hour, as you drive down the middle of the road until oncoming traffic appears. At that time, pulling to the right and decreasing speed slightly is recommended.

Second, one must always be aware of farm vehicles, grain trucks, combines, and the like moving at a much slower speed. These vehicles are particularly prevalent in the spring and fall. During those seasons it is a good idea to consider adding extra time for your trip. Since they take up the entire roadway, it will be an exercise in self-control to follow at 10 miles per hour until the farmer can find a spot wide enough to move over and let you pass. They always do, but it can take a few miles, so it is best not to get too impatient about the situation.

The third basic tenet of country driving is that all roads lead to somewhere. They may not lead to where you were planning to go, but you will end up somewhere. That place might be a farmer's barnyard, the crossroads where a one-room schoolhouse still sits, or even a small town. There is always a place at the end of the lane. Remember that.

If you recognize that most county roads are constructed on a grid, moving outward from the courthouse at the county seat, understanding where the road goes isn't too difficult. For instance, I once lived at 430 North 500 West. What that means is I lived 4.3 miles north of the courthouse and 5 miles west. As long as you don't have directional dyslexia or can follow the sun, you will never get lost in Indiana.

You can see amazing things on an aimless summer excursion. Wild turkey, fox, or deer slip in and out of shadows. Rounding a curve, you might experience the breathtaking moment when deep woods alongside the road give way to an unexpected pond, waterfowl quacking and honking in the late afternoon sun. A field of soybeans suddenly turns to open pasture, filled with prairie flowers; a redwing blackbird's unmistakable call lets you know you aren't alone. It is still possible to find stands of blackberry canes tumbling through an old barbed wire fence, the plump purple berries ready to be picked for tonight's cobbler or pie.

Old cemeteries crop up along the roads, the surrounding ancient iron fences overgrown in wild morning glory vines, gates propped ajar, layered in time and weeds. The headstones date back to the early nineteenth century. Reading the weathered slate tilted drunkenly on one side, you realize the luck it took to survive to adulthood in the early days of our state. A faint echo, a touch of mist, lets you know someone was here.

Even older whispers float along creek beds and hollows where the road dips low. Arrowheads can still be found; some of these lanes must have followed trails Native Americans made, paths worn into the land over time.

People get creative with their mailboxes; roadside art flourishes, constructed of old gears, posts, and tractor parts. As you head northwest, the land opens into long-grass prairie and windmills sprout from the earth, great blades turning languidly in a dance with the breeze.

These days I have to drive deep into the country to experience the thrill of gravel crunching under my tires. Some years ago an overzealous county commissioner saw to it that all our

county roads were paved. I suppose it's a kind of progress. Paved or not, the lanes still exist. They allow Hoosiers to experience Indiana at its roots, along a quiet, narrow road, cornstalks rustling, the rasping buzz of cicadas in your ears. You can't say you know Indiana until you do.

Casey Shipley

First Paycheck

I grew up on a farm in Huntington. From the ages of fourteen to seventeen in the late '60s to early '70s, I worked as a hay baler for six to eight weeks during July and August. A neighboring farmer would come by in an old pickup truck and I would hop in the back. We had a few others to pick up—the nearest neighbors were a quarter mile away, but the nearest boy was probably a mile and a half away.

Once we got to the farm, the strongest and senior-most boy got to ride on the wagon as it bounced around the field behind the hay baler. This was the prize job—you were in the open air and the breeze. The wagon was connected to the hay baler, which raked and compressed the hay and pushed it out in square bales weighing 80 to 100 pounds. You used a hay hook to get the hay bale and drag it onto the wagon. Stacking from the back and piling toward the front of the wagon, you made stacks about seven bales high—meaning the last two had to be thrown above your head. And sometimes you got a bale with a bumblebee nest in it that you had to get out with the bale hook!

The other boys would be at the barn. There was an elevator to move the hay bales from the wagon up to the top of the barn window. You'd wait for a bale at the window and start stacking, bottom to top. The hard job was in the barn—no breeze, hay dust flying around terribly thick and all over your body. Dirty, hot, and sweaty. But we'd be laughing and showing off our strength. It was a challenge to see how fast we could unload the wagon and stuff the barn! If you went fast, you'd have a few more minutes of rest until the next wagon came. At one farm, a lady brought us a drink we called "Granny's juice" in a one-gallon glass jug to cool us down.

We made fifty cents an hour, working eight-hour days about five days per week. I stuffed many a barn around my house, and to this day it still shows up on my social security as my first income.

Marvin Burns

Boilermaker with the
Heart of a Hoosier

My dad was born in a farmhouse in Elkhart County, November 17, 1939. His dad was a dairy farmer, and all my dad wanted was to be a farmer. But my grandfather, Homer Horace Virgil, decided his eldest son, Victor, needed a college education and sent him off to Purdue, where he joined the Farmhouse Fraternity. Dad was so used to milking cows at four o'clock every morning and again in the afternoon that he never traveled far from home, and never, ever slept in past sunrise. He became a county extension agent, raising hogs and melons and three children on the side.

Back then the way you got a promotion in the extension office was to move to another county. Dad started out in DeKalb County, where my brother and I were born in 1962 and 1963, respectively. From there he moved to Kosciusko County, then down to Switzerland County, where my sister was born in 1967. By the time I was in kindergarten, we'd moved to Miami County. Dad's background was in agriculture and livestock, but the Miami County position included being the area horticulture specialist for eight counties. Even as he worked full time, he drove his old Ranchero pickup back and forth from Peru to West Lafayette in the evenings to earn his master's degree in horticulture from Purdue. As he studied, he developed a real love for trees, shrubs, and landscaping, too.

Finally, Dad settled in as county extension agent of Kosciusko County from 1974 to 1994. He helped organize the Kosciusko County Area Plan Commission, and in 1990, he began the Master Gardner program, where his goal was to bring newcomers to the Midwest together with county natives in a process he called "Hoosierizing." He also served as a board of zoning appeals member, a 4-H adviser, and a livestock auctioneer. After all of us kids graduated from high school, Mom went to work at the Farm Service Agency, and between them, they knew just about every farmer in Kosciusko County.

So I grew up in "the boonies," which means we lived about 10 miles from the nearest stoplight. We always had a huge garden for canning and freezing, not counting the "truck patch" where we grew melons and vegetables to sell at the farmer's market. We heated our house with firewood that we chopped ourselves. Dad taught me to drive the old Ford pickup (a three-speed on the column) when I was fourteen years old so I could haul the John Deere garden tractor all over the boonies mowing lawns. If there was any money changing hands for my labor, I never saw a penny of it. I recall objecting on the grounds that it wasn't even legal for me to be driving. Dad raised his eyebrows and gave me one firm nod. "Then you'd better be careful and not get caught." Somewhere in my law-abiding father's brain was a "farm-kid" exception to the driving-without-a-license law. There was no "traffic" in boonies, only people doing an honest day's work the best they knew how.

Long before Nike coined the phrase "Just Do It!" my father impressed the concept upon me. Although he did this through-out my life in many small ways, all of those combined pale compared to the task he set me to during the summer of my six-teenth year. I was filled with the anticipation of freedom—my first summer vacation with a valid driver's license! I could actu-ally drive where I wanted to go. Out of the boonies and into the bright lights and big cities like Warsaw and Plymouth, maybe even South Bend or Fort Wayne! But Dad had other plans. He was going to chain me to our old red barn.

Dad unveiled my fate on the first Sunday after school let out. While driving the family home from church, Dad eyed me in the rearview mirror. "Laurie," he said, "I've got a project for you this summer." I closed my eyes and held my breath, dreading the impending doom. "You're going to tear down the barn," he said. Not a barn. THE barn. The enormous, weathered barn that stood next to our house. Mom said nothing. My siblings snickered quietly at my summer sentence.

Slowly and steadily I exhaled, trying to wrap my mind around the mission I would be forced to accept. "Do you expect me to start at the top and fall through," I asked in disbelief, "or do you want me to start at the bottom and let the whole barn fall on me?"

Dad didn't laugh. He wasn't kidding. The next morning, Dad took me out to the barn with our four-wheel-drive truck, a heavy tow chain, and a monster maul. "You just wrap one end of the chain around a supporting beam of the barn." I wrapped the chain around an old wooden beam in the very center.

"Now hook the other end to the back of the truck." I dragged the other end of the chain to the truck parked just outside the barn and wrapped it around the ball and hitch.

"Pull forward real slow until the chain stretches tight; then floor it." I put the truck in first gear and gradually let up on the clutch, inching forward until I could feel the chain holding me back. I sent up a silent prayer, ready to sacrifice the truck for the barn. Then I popped the clutch and floored it. The truck lurched forward, gravel flew from the tires and behind me I heard a sound like lightning striking a tree.

"Stop!" Dad shouted. I stopped the truck. "Now back up a foot or so to give yourself some slack in the chain." I threw the truck into reverse and inched back.

"Whoa!" Dad called. I got out of the truck and surveyed the damage. There was one wooden beam about the size of an electrical pole attached to the back of the truck. Dad helped me unhook the chain. He picked up the monster maul. "Now you just chop up the wood, throw it in the back of the truck and haul it around back to the burning site." He took a couple of swings, and then handed me the long, heavy ax.

So I was out there every day, all day, all summer, except Sundays. Thank God for a day of rest. At first, I would wake up in the middle of the night thinking about that big barn. The task was insurmountable. How could one kid tear down a whole barn by herself? No one but Dad believed I could do it. He was unrelenting.

Every morning I went back to work tearing down the barn. Eventually, I stopped focusing on the great big barn. I stopped thinking about an entire day's work. Sometimes even the thought of another hour was too much to bear. Instead, I focused on pulling down each beam, chopping it up into pieces I could move, and cleaning up the debris. And little by little, piece by piece, I tore down that big old barn.

My husband attributes our marriage to my tearing-down-the-barn story, which I told for the first time when he interviewed me for an associate attorney position and asked me about my work ethic. I definitely got my work ethic from Dad. He was proud that I went to law school, but more than a little miffed that I went to IU. "But Dad," I pointed out, "Purdue doesn't have a law school." And so he forgave me.

Dad loved Purdue and he loved farming, but even more than that he had a heart for people. When he retired from the extension office, he became a pastor of visitation at Pleasant View Bible Church, a Warsaw congregation with approximately 600 members at that time. When Dad passed away in 2014, crowds gathered to remember him as a friend, farmer, master gardener, county agent, and pastor. But most of all, they remembered him as a Boilermaker with the heart of a Hoosier.

Laurie Gray

Encounters with Town and City Folks

Some years ago, I was part of a church group of college-age people that included quite a few who had come from out of state to attend Indiana University. We had a party planned at the family farm of one of the local members of the group. During the hayride, the activities chairperson who had planned the party—who happened to be from a different part of the country—decided to play the tour guide, and intoned with mock seriousness, "And to our right, you will see a field of corn." All of us who were native Hoosiers burst out laughing as she gestured toward a field of soybeans.

Elizabeth Venstra

* * *

Our family has been Hoosiers since some time after the Civil War when my great-grandfather, Marvin—always called Frank —Kester (born September 25, 1862), moved to Wabash from Miami County, Ohio, to take a wife, Mary Ann Singer (born October 24, 1864), in Wabash, Indiana. They married January 18, 1883, and raised seven children. My grandfather Homer Wiley Kester, being the next to youngest, was born a Hoosier on January 9, 1898, and grew up following along with his father as he worked various jobs, including lumbering throughout northern Indiana. The lumbering he had learned from his father, my great-great-grandfather C. W. Kester. Pictured is great-grandfather's *Scribner's Lumber and Log Book* published in 1874 and purchased in 1876.

So when an enterprising young man found my grandfather's woods many years later, he was sure he could make some extra money for himself from this probably naive older gentleman

who never had a lot to say. The young man inspected the trees, chose those he thought he would do well with, and said to my grandfather, "I can give you a certain price for each board foot, but since you seem a gentleman I would be willing just to give you a price for each tree." My grandfather recalls, "I knew at the time, from my experience, that the price per tree was a losing proposition for the young man, not the bonus he was hoping to receive, but agreed to take his offer per tree."

Later the young man came around with payment and a sheepish look, saying, "I thought I had made a good deal, but there was not the board feet I thought. I really lost my shirt on this deal!" My grandfather's response was, "I knew you were in for it when you made the offer, now give me the board-foot price, that's fair. I hope you've learned to just be fair and not try to take advantage." I recalled this account some years later as a part of his eulogy, but learned it many times over as I followed him in my youth, much as he had followed his father.

Edward E. Kester

* * *

In the mid '80s, my father worked as an engineer at a large fertilizer plant that supplied ammonium nitrate to regional farmers. Local famers would often stop by the office to discuss yields, talk production, or show off corn.

One afternoon my dad was sitting in his corner office on a business call when a local corn farmer who farmed the land next to the plant popped his head inside my dad's office. The farmer didn't want to interrupt; just had a quick question to show some Hoosier hospitality to my dad. Noticing my dad was on the phone, the farmer quietly asked if my dad wanted a few "rows" of corn planted to take home to the family. My dad—half engaged in the phone call and half attentive to the hard-working farmer standing in his doorway—mouthed, "Sure, I'll take two rows" and returned to his phone call. The disclaimer: my family was a recent transplant from northern Pennsylvania and my father, a very wise man, had overlooked the fact that "two rows" of corn in Indiana could seemingly go on and on FOREVER.

That summer, every evening, our family was greeted with at least one large black trash bag, sometimes two bags, of Silver Queen corn in the bed of my dad's white pickup. After sharing with our neighbors, my dad, sister, and I would sit in our backyard and shuck ears of corn while my mom searched her cookbooks for new and exciting corn recipes. Creamed corn, corn fritters, grilled corn, corn on the cob every way possible, roasted corn in the husk, and the list goes on. After that summer, I didn't enjoy eating corn again until my mid-thirties!

Erik R. Anderson

* * *

Every August, I drive about four hours from Valparaiso to Knox County to buy watermelons. Why? Because Knox County watermelons don't need a good reason. They just are . . . THE BEST. My latest trip there was perfect.

Melon Acres in Oaktown and Sandy Ridge, exactly on the Knox-Sullivan line, are both on US 41. You just never saw so many watermelons—and the "cashier" at Melon Acres uses the honor system, another undeniably Hoosier trait. The woman at the office said, "We trust you," when I called to inquire about paying. One would assume that wholesalers buying melons might work under different rules than farm-stand shoppers.

So why drive four hours to buy a watermelon? I got a trunk-load of them because they make great Christmas gifts!

John C. Updike

* * *

For many years, my father, Roy Blunk, worked at Price Implement Company, a John Deere implement and repair shop in Portland in Jay County, Indiana. Daddy had been born in southern Indiana and raised all over southern and east central Indiana, but after my parents married, they resided in Portland their entire married lives. Mother never lived more than 5 miles from her birthplace in southern Jay County.

In the 1950s, Daddy was working at the parts counter when a farmer came in with his seven-year-old son. Farmers often brought their sons with them, and this boy had seen his dad deal with the implement store many times. This gentleman farmer was what my dad called a "big" farmer, with large acreage, and was successful, upgrading his mostly John Deere equipment frequently. The boy had seen his father trade tractors regularly, and on this particular day, they approached the parts desk and the man said his son had some business. The boy then proceeded to place a very worn toy John Deere tractor on the counter. It was an older model with the little cast metal farmer man forever sitting in the seat, driving the tractor.

The boy said, "I want to trade tractors!"

Daddy said, "Well, what do you want to trade for?" and the boy replied that he wanted a newer model.

Even in the 1950s those older model John Deere toy tractors were becoming collectable and hard to find. Daddy agreed to the boy's request, went and bought a brand new toy tractor himself, and then traded with the boy.

The farmer and his happy son left the store and Daddy worked on the tractor at home, fixed it, and repainted it with genuine John Deere green paint, of course, and that tractor was one of his favorite items for the rest of his life.

Becky Blunk Schneider

Toy tractor.

I recently learned that the outhouse I hated so much as a child in southern Indiana in the 1950s was actually the Cadillac of outhouses. It had been built during the Great Depression as a Works Progress Administration (WPA) project with the purpose of improving sanitation in rural America.

I was a city girl, having spent my formative years mostly in Fort Wayne. But in the summers our family went to stay at our farm in Washington County, in southern Indiana, near Campbellsburg. This was where my mother had grown up.

My parents, now deceased, were teachers, who taught in Fort Wayne. They had taken over the family farm after my grandparents died. As teachers they had the summers off work, allowing us to spend much of our summers at the farm.

Because we were not at the farm year-round, my parents rented the farmhouse to another family. That left us with no

The Shack.

place to stay when we were at the farm. So, my dad fixed up an old summer kitchen on the property for us. We called it the "Shack," which aptly described it.

As best my brother and I can remember now, the Shack was a small two-room affair. The outer room contained a kitchen and eating area, and the back room had two double beds on each side, one for my brother and me and one for my parents.

We had a propane tank on the outside of the Shack for the gas stove. Occasionally, we would go to the farm during spring break or Thanksgiving break, and it could get pretty chilly outside.

I remember Mom would try to the heat the place when it was cold by lighting the gas stove oven and leaving the door open. I think the Shack must have had electricity and must have had some sort of refrigerator, but I was a kid, so I really don't remember.

Trixie waits for the author's brother outside the WPA outhouse.

Most importantly, the Shack had no running water. There was a pump in the yard of the farmhouse, and we carried water in buckets to the Shack. I don't remember a thing about how we bathed. I do remember Mom heating water on the stove. So, we must have used that for "sponge baths."

Of course, with no running water, we had no indoor bathroom. That left the outhouse, which was several feet from the door of the Shack. Since I was a city girl and used to a regular flush toilet, I hated that outhouse.

Summers can get quite hot in southern Indiana, and I remember that outhouse being stifling during the summer. The June bugs and other insects buzzed all around the outhouse, scaring me, the city girl, almost to death. And the smell of the outhouse in the summer—there is really no way to describe it.

It was only recently when my brother was at the farm that he took our photo of the old outhouse out of its frame and discovered notes my dad had made about the outhouse. Dad's notes said the outhouse had been built by the WPA during the Great Depression.

I had no idea that the WPA built outhouses, so I had some doubt about my father's notes. I should have trusted him. It didn't take me long to research and learn that, indeed, the WPA had built outhouses in rural areas. In fact, WPA workers had built thousands of outhouses.

As outhouses go, the WPA ones were pretty nice. The WPA outhouses had concrete floors and a concrete foundation for the toilet area. Having concrete floors greatly improved sanitation over the dirt-floor ones by reducing the incidence of hookworm and other waterborne diseases.

The way the WPA project worked was that the farmer was responsible for providing the materials to build the outhouse, and the WPA paid the wages for the workers to build it. The WPA outhouses all were built using the same design, and our photograph of the old outhouse fits perfectly with the design description of the WPA outhouses. My brother remembers that our outhouse was much nicer than the one the neighbors at the next farm had.

I don't remember that our outhouse had a concrete floor, but my brother remembers that it did. Maybe I don't remember because I shoved the memory of the outhouse out of my mind since I hated it so much. Or maybe it was because my brother spent the most time in there while our dog, Trixie, waited for him outside.

The outhouse and Shack are long gone, having been torn down at some point by my father after he and my mother left Fort Wayne and retired to the farm. Sometime prior to my college years, my parents built a nice house at the farm for themselves, of course with indoor plumbing.

That house is now mine. I inherited it after the death of my parents. The two bathrooms in the house are small by today's standards. But before I complain too much to my husband about the small bathrooms in our house at the farm, I should remember that stinky WPA outhouse that I hated so much.

Karen Walker

* * *

One workday back in the '80s, I was driving to my job in Indianapolis from my home in Kokomo, when in those darkened hours of early morn, I thought I detected something massive in the road just ahead of me. I slowed down in anticipation, but I did not expect to see a huge cow standing in the middle of US 31, taking up both lanes.

Not having cell phones back then to call for highway help, I didn't know what to do except to pull over to the side of the road and see if I could get this poor baby to a safe place. I couldn't just leave it there to get hurt or killed by other drivers traveling before dawn or to put other commuters in danger as well. I had not one clue as to what I was going to do.

As I exited my car and started running toward Sad Eyes (I felt I had to give her a name), I wondered what in the world I was thinking. I must have imagined myself ripping open my blouse, with buttons popping, exposing the Wonder Woman insignia across my chest.

While approaching my newfound friend, appropriately attired with cowbell and ear tag, I realized that this was going to be no easy task. Just how does one city gal transport one country cow from busy highway back to grazing pasture?

I went ahead and swallowed what pride and dignity I had and attempted to moooooove Sad Eyes back up north to the only farm I could see, across both south and north lanes, not to mention through the sloped median. Picture my hands on her rear, trying with all my might to get her back into her familiar surroundings to be reunited with her significant others. But the stubborn bovine chose to remain motionless.

Imagine, if you will, this femme fatale wannabe (looking more like a cross between Brooke Shields and Olive Oyl), professionally dressed in the finest faux designer power suit, accessorized with dangling earrings and multiple clanging bangle bracelets, towering over the cornfields in intimidatingly high Aigner heels, trying to push some oppressive cow down the highway. All I needed was a sudden downpour or passers-by with cell phone cameras like folks have these days, slowing down to take a shot of me to share with the masses.

Upon closer inspection of the property from which she escaped, I realized I had to get her back over a 4-foot-high barbed-wire fence, for there was no obvious visible gate or space that she could have slipped through. I started to get that sinking feeling that one of my "spikes" had attached itself to one of the many fresh pies (and not of the apple or lemon meringue variety) scattered across the ground around my feet. Alas, it was definitely time for me to let go of any Wonder Woman aspirations and acknowledge defeat. I had really stepped into it this time, so now I was on a quest to find me a farmer!

Leaving Sad Eyes behind, I slipped off my shoes and ran bare foot down the highway, banging on doors and windows of this big old unkempt farmhouse until some curmudgeonly farmer in bib overalls took pity on me and hesitantly agreed to come to my rescue.

Running ahead of slowpoke Farmer Brown (I felt I had to give him a name, too, especially since it was obvious he wasn't one for introductions), I found Sad Eyes in the same spot. To my amazement, I had not seen any traffic on that normally busy road during the whole time this *I Love Lucy* episode was unfolding.

Upon hearing the farmer's keys jingling from a distance, Sad Eyes took one look at me and then made a mad dash across the highway, through the ditch, and over that fence in fine Olympian form, landing on a dime as a gymnast would after a performance on the parallel bars. It was all over in just the blink of an eye.

When Farmer Brown finally showed up, everything appeared normal as if nothing had happened. It was quite obvious the farmer doubted my credibility, and I started to wonder what excuse I could give my boss for being late, for I was sure he probably wouldn't believe my story, either. But then again, I thought, why wouldn't he? After all, just one whiff of me and the proof was in the pudding!

Nowadays, whenever I hear the phrase "till the cows come home," I automatically think of ol' Sad Eyes. Then a smile washes over me as I remember her and her fifteen minutes of fame and freedom as she took that unforgettable trip "over the moon."

Cheryl Soden Moreland

Ever since my husband and I sold our house in Chicago, I commute an hour between my office in that city and my home in rural Indiana. The landscape of my trip home changes dramatically in the 50 miles of this daily voyage. It starts with the strange duality of inner-city Stony Island Avenue, where Chicago has planted lovely displays of flowers on the median strips, but whose wide boulevard is flanked by rows of used car dealerships, auto repair garages, and the charred ruins of a spectacularly burned muffler repair shop. The skyway of I-90 takes me out of the city at 79th Street, past the oil tanks of Hammond and the largely defunct steel mills of Gary. Even before Gary, there are hints of the rural landscape to come—Wolf Lake, where once wind surfers competed in the shadow of power lines, and later the Calumet River threading its way through the industrial wasteland.

Nineteen miles from the city limits, where I-90 branches off to I-94 toward Detroit, the scenery shifts to become agricultural. Horizontal acres of corn and wheat spread out from the highway, alternating with rolling hills covered in woods and dimpled with ponds. Because it is Indiana, I also pass the world's largest firecracker outlet and several huge emporiums of cheap cigarettes. My last mile, past Trail Creek, the Cool Spring branch of the La Porte Library, and a number of modest homes set on large tracts of land, is as peaceful as a Ray Bradbury story.

Even more marked than the altered landscape, however, is the change in personality I encounter a scant 50 miles outside Chicago. For a lifetime city dweller, it is like entering the *Truman Show*. Somewhere in those 50 miles, people's basic attitudes toward each other seem to undergo a profound change.

People extend themselves to help each other, even if it makes them late. They treat everyday encounters with pleasure, not as a series of nuisances that retard their ability to work efficiently. People are generally honest. Really.

Let me serve up some examples. My grocery store has a greeter. This person stands at the entrance to the store and says hello to each person who comes in. For eight hours. Oh sure, he or she asks if you need a cart, but basically this person is there to make sure that someone has smiled at you when you enter and leave.

Then there's the story of my snowplow service. As a typical city slicker, I didn't think about snow until that first Thanksgiving, when 18 inches fell, burying my La Porte house and the entrance to the garage. With a 300-foot driveway and no city snowplow crews, my husband and I were afraid we would be there until spring. So what did I do? I walked down to the edge of the driveway and stood in the middle of the road. All these teenage boys with big trucks drove by and I hailed one down at random.

"Wouldn't you like to plow my driveway?" I asked.

"Well, ma'am," he said, "that's my father's business. If you like, he'll be at your house at 6 PM tonight."

And he was. We wrote up a contract, stating that he'd plow the drive every time it snowed more than 3 inches, and he'd send me a bill once a month. He's never missed a snowfall.

People here take being helpful to heights that make me positively dizzy. I ran into a woman's car several months ago and she offered to help me pay for the damage.

It happened this past spring when, having just left the cleaners and thinking about my next errand, I backed my car into the front left tire of a woman who was, herself, backing out to leave. The impact made an awful "thwack," and the lady's tire began hissing like a cat facing an angry dog. You'll note that I have NOT mentioned the victim screaming at me for my imbecility.

"Oh dear," I said, or something equally inadequate. "I'm so sorry."

"I'm on my way to a wedding," the lady in the other car replied.

I stared down at her tire, which was now as flat as three-day-old roadkill, and finally looked back at her.

"Come with me," I said. "We'll find a place to fix your tire or I'll buy you a new one."

Did this woman know me? No. Could I have been a crazy dangerous person? Definitely. In fact, by my driving you might well assume that my incompetence had already been established. But she got in the car with me as we sped off to a nearby tire store, telling me she was sure I hadn't meant to do it, and that my car had the bigger dent, which was true.

We arrived at Tire Barn and waited in line behind a young man who was buying tires for his mammoth truck. He took about twenty minutes and spent $1,200 on tires large enough to carry King Kong. Clearly delighted with the world, he moved aside to wait, while I explained to the man at the desk that I had inadvertently ruined this woman's tire and I needed someone to go get her car, bring it in, and fix it.

"We'd love to help you," the attendant said, "but we just sell tires here. We don't have a towing service."

"That's okay," spoke up the young man waiting for his humongous tires. "My cousin has a towing outfit. Shall I call him for you and get him to pick up your car?"

"Why thank you," my new victim/friend and I said together, having exchanged a number of confidences on the way to the tire store. "That would be lovely."

So the young man's cousin drove out and, on inspecting the damage, told us that I had just clipped off the air valve. The tire was fine. He put the spare tire on her car so we could drive her vehicle to the tire store and get them to replace the valve on her damaged tire.

"How much do I owe you?" I asked.

"Twenty-five dollars," he said. I only had twenty, so my victim offered to pay him the other five.

"Forget it," he told us. "Twenty is fine. You take care."

Back at the tire store, we were rushed to the front of the line. When the attendant heard that it was just the valve, he repaired the damage in ten minutes.

"What do I owe you?" I asked.

"Oh nothing," the man at Tire Barn said. "It was my pleasure."

Is this real? I asked myself at the time, while I embraced my new friend before she sped off to her family's nuptials. Have I fallen into a Disney cartoon? Do I care?

Obviously, the rule of civility is sometimes broken in Indiana. The county where I live has its share of wife beaters, thieves, drug addicts, and even the occasional murderer. So crime does creep in. But my interactions with people in Indiana retain a sweetness that makes me jump into my car to get back home.

I am certainly a city junkie for all the glorious cultural benefits a city provides. I love Chicago's music, art, and theater, and the attention paid to creating ever more parks.

In the end, though, the kindness of my neighbors looms large as the most important aspect of a quality life. Oddly enough, it's in rural Indiana that you can count on finding it.

Stephanie Wilson Medlock

Home

Upon graduation from Indiana University, I knew one thing for certain: I no longer wanted to be a Hoosier. Other states seemed so much more exotic—warmer, too. I was young, single, and without a tether binding me to the state of my birth.

Weeks after I donned the cap and gown, much to my parents' dismay, I loaded up my meager possessions and headed out West. I landed in Texas and spent the next two years listening to "ya'll" and "bless your heart."

The weather was warmer. The people were friendly. The landscape was expansive and diverse. But it wasn't home.

I ached for Indiana. The days when my heart hurt the most I was dreaming about a little Hoosier farm that generations of my family have called home.

The farm sits in Danville, Indiana, 40 miles west of Indianapolis. Visitors traveling from Indianapolis pass by dozens of retail stores and fast food restaurants before the landscape changes. The busy highway transforms from commercial overload to small town charm.

The farm is located a few miles past Danville's quaint downtown. It's perched amid the cornfields and commands the attention of passersby. The house is stately, handsome even. One may call the home elderly; it has stood on that same patch of farmland since the Civil War. I prefer to call it mature. Red bricks cover the sides; ornate historical touches add character.

At one point, a dilapidated log cabin shared a piece of the land. The history of the log cabin? No one quite knew. But for a while it was interesting to gaze at the cabin's sagging sides and wonder about the families that once called it home.

The farm did not lack in acreage. The landscape was expansive and unobstructed. An endless supply of cornstalks took the posture of guards protecting a fortress.

My great-grandparents were the first ones in our family to occupy the farm. My grandparents followed. My father, my mother, and my siblings lived in suburban Indianapolis. I was used to manicured lawns and abbreviated play areas. Traveling to the farm was like walking onto the set of *Little House on the Prairie*. Instantly, I transformed into Laura Ingalls.

Our favorite part of visiting the farm was Grandpa's tractor rides. He would jump into the driver's seat, and the grandkids leaped into the wagon trailing the tractor. Grandpa snaked the tractor around the property. We traveled along a dusty trail that sliced through the cornfields, and then encircled the murky pond dressed in cattails.

My grandmother preferred to walk us about the property. She'd stop and point to wild flowers and plants. I vividly remember her motioning to a dainty white cluster and calling it Queen Anne's Lace. It was beautiful. The white buds fanned out in a lovely, intricate design. I deemed it my favorite. Still today, the sight of Queen Anne's Lace brings back memories of those hikes and my grandmother's careful explanations.

The pond provided endless fascination. In summer, Grandpa fastened squiggly worms to the ends of hooks. He cast the line under the water, and we plopped down on the grass and waited. Our goal was not to land a fish (even though we swore it was); the fish were just tossed back into the water. I was there to hear my grandpa's fish tales, ones he told with a twinkle in his eye and a laugh in his voice.

In the winter, we laced up ice skates and timidly stepped upon the frozen pond. Skating on a pond made the artificial rinks seem lame and unimaginative. We would glide upon the pond with snowflakes drenching our faces and covering our smiles.

A tire swing hung on a tree branch by the pond. Upon arriving at the farm, it was my first destination. I spent hours swinging back and forth. With each rotation of the swing, I would inhale childhood, and exhale happiness. When my grandmother passed away, my father cut down the tire swing. Safety reasons, he explained as he chiseled at the rope. As the tire thumped to the ground and the fractured rope landed on the grass, I felt like a little piece of my childhood had detached with the tire.

What I remember the most is the holidays, birthday parties, and even the funeral dinners held at the farm. Relatives from all over "tarnation" descended upon the property. The farmhouse seemed to swell to accommodate all the family. Everyone had a signature dish, the item they were expected to bring to all family functions.

But Grandma's dishes were always the stars of the show. She treated butter and lard like food groups. She lathered up naked vegetables, stripping them of the title of health food. Her cinnamon rolls earned her family fame. More than one relative begged for the recipe, but Grandma seemed a bit like a baking savant. She created masterpieces without the constraint of instructions listed on a 3 × 5 card.

I loved when my grandmother whipped up persimmon pudding. She plucked the persimmons from the trees next to the house. The pudding was best served with a fistful serving of whipped cream. Somehow Grandma infused love and family into every spoonful.

Every family dinner began with a prayer. All the relatives formed a circle and clutched hands with aunts, uncles, and siblings. The senior-most family member did the honors. Little children found it comical. They squeezed the hand of their neighbor so hard that the relative would wince in pain or let out a giggle.

I remember little of what was ever said during a prayer, but I do recall the feeling I had while standing amid the group. It was a feeling of being loved and accepted. It was a feeling of being at home.

When I lived in Texas, I never felt this feeling. The farm sat in Indiana, states away. Relatives lived nowhere close. Within two years, I packed my bags and rented a U-Haul. Once I crossed the state lines, I breathed a sigh of relief.

I was home.

Rebecca Wood

Those Magical
Younger Years

A Miraculous Catch of Fish in Sullivan County

Anyone who has spent much time in Sullivan County, Indiana, knows of its abundance of "stripper pits"—small lakes that are left over from a coal mine having "stripped" the land to dig after a vein of coal. Thousands of acres of wetlands, containing hundreds of these pits, provide the people of Sullivan County ample opportunity for fishing and other forms of outdoor recreation. I grew up on a property adjacent to one neck of the Greene-Sullivan State Forest, near Dugger, that contains roughly a half-dozen of these stripper pits, and as a boy I would frequent many of them for fishing, exploring, or mischief of various sorts.

A favorite spot for me and my buddies to go was a little waterfall at the end of a creek that ran into one of the larger pits in the forest (it was given the official title of "West Lake" by the DNR, I believe). We had numerous adventures in and around that creek and its small waterfall. One spring day, for just one example, we witnessed carp trying to jump up the waterfall, just as salmon do as they travel up tributaries in the Northwest. It was amazing to see those fat fish flop against the sides of the rocks, one after the other. To my knowledge, none of them ever made it.

But perhaps the most memorable day at this spot occurred in the early summer when I was about twelve or so. My friend and I took our fishing poles back to the waterfall with a few worms. This particular day, the fish were biting well. In fact, in only a few minutes we'd used up the few worms we'd dug up and brought with us. Fortunately, the grasshoppers were thick that year, and a walk through the weeds on the bank landed us some hoppers to slide on our hooks. Every cast landed a fish, but we were tired of having to go back through the weeds to catch more grasshoppers. I think I was the one who had the idea of just throwing my hook in the water to see what would happen with no bait. And here is the miracle: cast after cast we continued to catch fish after fish with **nothing but** bare hooks! The stringers were so heavy with bass and bluegill we almost didn't want to carry them back the house.

It may not seem like much of a miracle to anybody else, but to my twelve-year-old mind it became an indelible part of a childhood full of the magic and mystery of nature. It's how I remember the special place where I was born and raised—such an abundance of natural beauty, a miraculous storehouse of God's riches given through nature.

N. S. Boone

A True Morel Mushroom Hunting Tale

We three brothers and our tagalong little sister loved the Hoosier woods of Vigo County near the small town of Blackhawk, especially in the springtime. Wildflowers were blooming, birds were singing, trees were leafing out, and morel mushrooms were peeking out from under the previous fall's blanket of leaves. On weekdays during mushroom season, we excitedly exited the school bus and stopped by our home for a quick snack from Mom, usually planning the mushroom hunt while we snacked. Then we hightailed it into the woods in back of our house.

One late afternoon's planning ended up with me in one section of the woods and my two brothers in another part of the woods. Their return trip would take them by a giant elm tree that had died from Dutch elm disease the previous year. We all knew that gray morels sometimes grew in abundance under an elm tree, especially if the elm had died the previous year. I somewhat reluctantly reminded them to check under the giant elm, because if there were mushrooms there, I really wanted to find them myself. After some mushrooming success in my assigned patch of woods, I slowly made my way back.

On the way I met up with my brothers. They were beaming, because they had found 117 morels under the giant dead elm! When they discovered the big patch of morels, they were in a bit of a dilemma. The morels were fresh, about 2 inches tall, and would undoubtedly grow more if left there for a few more days. (Yes, dear reader, gray morels will continue to grow for a while if the weather is cooperative. The old wives' tale that morels spring up full-grown is fiction.) But a patch this big could be discovered even by the neighbor, who we thought was generally clever but blind as a bat where morel mushrooms were concerned. So my brothers wisely picked them.

Later that evening after supper, there was a knock on the door. It was the neighbor. We instantly suspected he would be snooping about mushrooms. The conversation eventually got around to him inquiring about our mushroom-hunting luck. We were noncommittal about finding very many mushrooms. Then he mentioned finding a huge number of morel stems, pinched off just above the ground under a large tree. "Oh, is that so?" we said. He looked thoughtful, and then remarked that it looked like someone had mowed those mushrooms off with an ax. Oh my, that was sad indeed. Finally we shared some mushrooms with the neighbor, and he left with a smile on his face.

Now we had been trained to pinch the mushrooms off next to the ground, since pulling them out would disturb the mycelia and inhibit next year's mushroom growth. We resolved from then on to cover any large number of morel stumps with dead leaves. No sense in getting the neighbors riled. Oh, did I say that morels could be found under elm trees? Well, that was a mistake, as everyone knows they are found under pawpaw trees, and occasionally inside abandoned groundhog holes.

Paul Wassel

a Parke County Church Childhood

It has been said that the most magical place on earth is in Florida and involves a large-eared mouse. I have to respectfully disagree where my childhood is concerned. That place, in the '70s and '80s, was Parke County, Indiana.

My maternal grandparents, Albert and Rose Williams, answered the call of God and moved from their roomy house on North 9th Street in Terre Haute to a small parsonage on Highway 59 south of Bellmore. It was 1970 and my grandpa was the new pastor of THREE United Methodist churches at the same time: Otterbein (located across from the parsonage), Beech Grove (located just over the Parke/Putnam county line in Putnam County), and Sand Creek (located east of Rockville). The megachurches of today with their multiple services had nothing on my grandpa! He preached his first sermon at Otterbein in the morning, and then they would have Sunday school afterward. The other two churches would take turns having alternating Sunday morning and evening services.

My grandparents lived just a few doors down the street from us, and I was only four years old when they moved. The first trip we made to their house was very memorable for me because it was the first time I had seen a house with no furniture. I also remember thinking that my grandma and grandpa were moving a million miles away because it felt like it took almost the entire day to get there. (In reality it was about a forty-five-minute trip, but to a young child that was LONG.)

Going to visit Grandma and Grandpa was now an all-day excursion and a novelty instead of an everyday occurrence. As with many families of that time period, we had only one car. My mom would drop my dad off at work, then we would stop in North Terre Haute and pick up my recently widowed great-grandma, Bertha Johnson, and off to Parke County we would go!

While the parsonage was rather small, it did have a wonderful floor plan because small children could start out at the front door, run through the living room into the dining room, then run into the hall with a right turn into my Aunt Nancy's bedroom, and straight back to the front door again! And I must emphasize the word "run" because that is what my cousins and I did, and it drove my grandma nuts. The parsonage had a very large yard with an equally large evergreen tree of some sort between the house and the garage, which dropped tiny needles of the "sharp and stabbing to the bottom of tiny bare feet" variety. This was quite annoying because who wanted to bother with shoes in the summertime?

We had free run of the entire yard except for one VERY strict command: "Do not go down by the road." This was a highway and dangerous for small children. But that didn't faze my older cousin Jane. When we were about six or seven years old she thought it would be a great idea to hitchhike. I wasn't even sure what that meant, and I knew that we were not supposed to be by the road, but I wanted to do what she did, so down we went! When my grandma discovered us, she YELLED at us. I didn't know that grandmas ever yelled at their grandkids, and I started to wonder if they were allowed to spank, too. I'm positive that she was very scared when she finally found us and reacted as such. (As a parent now, I know I would have done the same thing.) I'm glad to report that the incident passed without physical punishment, but I can honestly say that I never went down by the road again alone, until I was at least ten years old or so, and that was at my grandma's request to get the mail.

Most people think of church buildings as purely utilitarian, but to a child whose grandpa is the pastor, they are DELIGHTFUL places to play! So many rooms, staircases, doors, aisles, and hallways to discover. Empty church sanctuaries were also the best way to play "wedding." The same before-mentioned cousin and I would get a blanket or old curtain and pin it to our head for our veil and down the aisle we would go, over and over again. Not possessing a groom didn't bother us; the fun was in the walking!

But the best part was that the Beech Grove church had an incredible novelty: a cemetery on a hill! Did you know that they make the perfect place to play hide and go seek? To this day I don't ever think of a cemetery as some place creepy or morbid. I did wonder about the people who were buried there, reading the names and dates with curiosity, but in a typical childlike fashion, the thoughts didn't stay long.

There was one thing that all three churches DIDN'T have that was rather bewildering and disgusting to my childish mind: indoor plumbing. Any time we were going to be at the one of the buildings for even five minutes, Grandma required each of us to go the bathroom before we left, whether we felt any physical need or not. But after a trip or two to one of those smelly, spider-filled outdoor facilities, we readily agreed to use the much cleaner indoor one, even if we felt it wasn't necessary at the time!

As my younger sister and I got older, we were allowed to spend longer periods of time with our grandparents, which meant that we would venture around with them. Parke County of the mid- to early '70s wasn't the tourist destination it is today. While Turkey Run was as popular as ever, the Covered Bridge Festival was just in its infancy, Raccoon Lake was a brand new park, and the Amish population hadn't moved there yet. Those things notwithstanding, there were still so many fun things to do! Sometimes we got to go to the laundromat! We got to go to not just one grocery store, but two, the smaller of which had wood floors and barely enough room in the aisles for two people to pass. Sometimes we got to go to Billie Creek Village. Once we got to dress up in our *Little House on the Prairie* dresses, and with all of those old buildings I felt like I really was Laura Ingalls Wilder. But the best place to go to was Murphy's 5&10! If they didn't have it, you didn't need it. Row after row of all sorts of things, and my grandparents didn't mind going into aisles to look at things they didn't need. This was the place where Grandma stocked up on a staple that every grandparent needs and every grandkid requires: CANDY! She even let us choose from the large bins at the Brach's Pick-a-Mix stand ourselves.

Being older, we could visit them during church functions, too. This included the occasional Sunday morning service, but it mostly involved church dinners. And could the Methodists of Parke County do themselves proud! I don't know if they had a lot of dinners, but between the three churches it seemed like there was always at least one every time we visited for an extended time. We would sometimes go along when our grandparents visited their friends, which in Parke County meant that there was a 99 percent chance they were farmers. To a city girl, this was terrific! We got to see the corn growing and all types of livestock up close and personal. I learned that it doesn't take more than a couple of houses and a store to make a town: Ferndale, Bellmore, Hollandsburg. Every area of Parke County had something different than my boring city life.

It was during these times seeing my grandparents interacting with their congregation that I got a glimpse into how other people viewed them. They were the first ones their congregation members called during their highest highs and their lowest lows. Grandpa conducted numerous weddings and many funerals. People came to him for advice about their lives and trusted him to lead them spiritually. When Grandpa passed away in 2005, there were too many people to count who said they wouldn't have the relationship with God today that they did if it wasn't for "Pastor Al." These people honored my grandparents and consequently me, because I was their family. It was fun to be considered special and treated as such. It made visiting them magical, and that's why Parke County, even though I didn't grow up there, will always be "home" to me.

Debby Harbour Cacovski

The Senior Cords Craze

A high school fad that was unique to Indiana and Hoosier Hysteria was the senior cords craze. Yellow corduroy ("cord") pants were all the rage at ball games. High school seniors had the sole distinction of wearing them proudly decorated with their personal artistic "graffiti" as a statement of their individuality. Students would embellish the trousers and skirts with colorful drawings depicting anything from cartoon characters and school mascots to friend's names, extracurricular activities, and year of graduation.

Worn in pep blocks of the late 1950s through the early 1970s, the cords, or "whistlers," as they were referred to by many

Senior cords.

because of the "swooshing" sound they made through the halls of the school, were either purchased or sewn from scratch using the original bolt of fabric. Lots of sweat equity went into the making and decorating of these garments, so the finished product became somewhat of a status symbol.

The Hoosier tradition actually started at Purdue University around 1904 when the college seniors began wearing, and later decorating, their "Boilermaker gold" cords, after seeing a bolt of the fabric in a tailor's shop window. As the craze picked up steam, the custom evolved into a senior tradition. Eventually sororities, fraternities, and other organizations jumped on the bandwagon. Little did they know the craze would soon be emulated by high school seniors in search of the coolest new trend to showcase their personality!

In Marshall County, senior cords were popular in the late 1950s, 1960s, and early 1970s. In 2015, some fifty years later, an exhibit at the Marshall County Museum highlighted those formative years by asking now "senior citizens" to dig through their trunks and storage bins and pull out those infamous icons of Indiana. The display brought back lots of memories and nostalgia for those crazy days that celebrated an era that was undeniably Indiana!

Mindy Langdon

The Day I Shot Down the Sun

In the late 1950s I was a student at Purdue University living in the Pi Kappa Alpha fraternity house at 149 Andrew Place. The year before I had been drafted into representing the fraternity in the intramural archery competition, and I grew to love the sport. Under some expert coaching I became quite proficient with the bow and arrow, and I won the intramural championship the next year.

The Kappa Sigma house sat just across North Street, and a friendly rivalry existed between the KΣs and the Pikes. Each year during "Hell Week," the KΣ pledges hoisted a papier-mâché sun into a large tree in front of the house at sunrise. Each evening, they took down the sun and hoisted up a papier-mâché moon. As part of our interhouse rivalry, the Pike pledges would steal their moon and hold it for some trivial ransom. One year the Pike pledges challenged the active brothers to steal the sun.

Our Pike pledge master, knowing it would be nearly impossible to pull off such a heist in broad daylight, bargained with the pledges by offering for the actives to destroy the sun. The pledges readily agreed, not realizing the pledge master had a plan for achieving that goal.

He surprised me one evening by asking if I could shoot a fire arrow into the sun from the balcony of our house. I mentally calculated the distance involved and decided I couldn't guarantee accuracy at that range. I told him I'd have to get closer.

The next day we surveyed the terrain for any location offering good cover and a reasonable shot. We found that the banking in front of the house offered enough cover if we could catch a moment when there were no witnesses. We decided lunchtime offered the best opportunity.

I prepared two fire arrows using old shafts I was going to discard anyway. These arrows bore no heraldry to identify the shooter. I practiced with the heavier point ends, and informed the pledge master I was ready.

The next day at lunchtime, we crept into range. I nocked an arrow, and he lit the lighter fluid–soaked gauze tied around the point. Taking careful aim, I loosed the first shot. The flaming point grazed the sun and flew onward, avoiding any of the bare tree's branches, to land, still blazing, on the roof of the Methodist church at the end of the block. We watched in horror, praying the arrow would not ignite the entire roof. Fortunately, the West Lafayette Fire Department had a station at the other end of the block, so help was not far away. To our relief, the arrow stopped burning with no apparent damage to the church.

I nocked the second arrow and sent the burning bolt straight into the KΣ sun. To our surprise, it burst into flame immediately. We didn't wait for a response from inside the KΣ house. We ran at top speed across the street to the Pike house and watched from a window as the KΣs ran out the front door in total shock and surprise. Of course, the sun was completely consumed by this time, and any attempt at saving it was useless. That evening the pledges saluted us during dinner.

Many years later I sat in a particularly boring meeting about some aspect of the soon to be defunct Manned Orbital Laboratory. A representative from one of the aerospace contractors present noticed my Purdue class ring and the gold ΠKA on the stone. He asked when I graduated, and I told him. He said he'd graduated the same year and was a KΣ. At the break I told him about shooting down their sun. He was thrilled to learn the actual cause of the fire. They had believed the sun was a victim of spontaneous combustion. He said he would make sure the story was included in the next issue of the chapter's newsletter. I never knew if the story was published.

Years after that incident, I found myself on the Home Association Board of the BΦ chapter of ΠKA at Purdue. A fellow member was a minister who served at the Methodist church I nearly burned down. I never told him about the incident, and until this story is published, only two other people know of it. That is, unless it was published in the KΣ chapter newsletter.

James M. Thompson

Wandering Indiana

We didn't have to leave Indiana to step back in time and enjoy the simple pleasures of camping with our children and grandchildren. Some days we picked berries along ancient Indian trails, and later watched juice ooze out of the berries, then bubble over the crust of the cobbler baking over a wood fire. Around every bend Mother Nature provided wonders and educational experiences enjoyed by the young and the young at heart.

At Turkey Run State Park we pitched our tent under the shelter of tall trees, hiked along trails where Miami Indians once walked, and crept around huge rock formations formed from glaciers. Drifting down Sugar Creek when the water level was low led to an incident I'd rather not experience again. After the canoe caught on a sand bar I jumped out and pushed it into deeper water. I was in about chest-high when I spied a water snake swimming straight for me. I shot out of the water and landed smack dab in the middle of the canoe just as the snake slithered past.

Another year, our kids couldn't wait to explore Spring Mill's pioneer village and soak up the rich history of growing up in the 1860s. The blacksmith's hammer rang as he heated metal over a hot forge and then pounded it into a horseshoe, while a woman dressed in a long pioneer dress spun sheep wool into thread as another skillfully wove it into cloth on a huge loom. All this before she hand-sewed it into a dress or shirt.

Over at the three-story gristmill, rushing water flowed over the huge wheel that turned the gears that ground corn into cornmeal. Later around the campfire, butter and honey dripped off cornbread fresh baked in our iron pot over a wood fire.

Later we enjoyed feeling the temperature drop in the Twin Caves as we searched for blind cavefish on our canoe tour. At the nature center, native snakes, curled up in glass cages, gave me the willies. I even spied one that gave me nightmares of the snake on Sugar Creek. The kids enjoyed the box turtle and the ranger talking about the history of southeastern Indiana.

The Gus Grissom Memorial, created for the Hoosier native who was the second man in space, tugged at my heartstrings. I was still in school when the *Liberty Bell* and later *Apollo 1* blasted into space. Now my kids were reliving his space history.

At Potato Creek, Grandpa taught the grandkids to fish. We rented a paddleboat and toured the lake, hiked the Miami Indian trails, and cooled off splashing at the beach. On Sunday, we sat on wooden benches and enjoyed worshiping with fellow campers in a log church.

The thrill of sledding down Pokagon's Toboggan Track at 35 to 40 miles per hour was worth the long wait in line. Once at the bottom of the run, we tramped through the snow to get back in line. During the summer, we enjoyed camping and the trails until our bones grew weary, and then we enjoyed the luxury of sleeping in a cozy room in the Potawatomi Inn and eating a delicious meal in their dining room.

Our kids didn't need to be entertained with modern electronics. We just rolled up our sleeping bags and explored Indiana's wonders for lasting memories.

Esther Thompson

Eatin' Out

Miller's Restaurant—Now in Onion Ring Heaven

A fire left Miller's Restaurant of Colfax, Indiana, in ruins. It was a cremation in the year 2000—a killing of our chance to ever again take a muggy summer night's drive from Lafayette down Highway 52 with a hungry stomach to a burg whose "courthouse" was a catfish canteen.

An arsonist fried the landmark crisper than the cornmeal-dusted catfish once served there on thick, white plates by waitresses in snow-white dresses.

Miller's was Colfax. When we had a craving for catfish on a Friday night, we said, "Let's go to Colfax," not "Let's go to Miller's." Over the years, the restaurant grew room by room to fill an entire block in the center of town—a town so small you could stroll its boundaries in about thirty minutes. My husband and I walked Colfax while waiting to hear our number called over the Miller's loudspeaker that blared through the streets and wafted amid nearby bungalows: "Number 96, party of two, your table is ready! Number 96, party of two, only!"

James Miller and his son, Mike, owned the business. James, known as Junior, was the man responsible for perfecting the catfish that brought clamoring people from as far away as Chicago and Indianapolis. Even during its prime—when Miller's served copious numbers of catfish per night—the fish were dressed in their delicate cornmeal coats only on demand. They were not prepared in advance. Breading-as-needed was part of Junior's secret to tender, flavorful "whiskered walleye."

We stood in line, packed like sardines on the linoleum floor. Busboys dressed in the staff uniform of all white parted the waiting crowd as they strong-armed heavy trays loaded with freshly prepared fish on their way to a swim in the fryer.

After more than an hour of suffering the agony of smelling the delicious aroma of the "catfish suppers," our number was called, and we sat down in plastic '50s chairs in a room decorated in red-flocked bordello-like wallpaper. The waitress approached, order pad in hand, and asked, "Are we having 'feesh' tonight?"

"Yes!"

"French fries?"

"Yes!"

"Onion rings?"

"OOOOOOOh, yeah!"

Miller's onion rings were the pinnacle, the scale by which today my husband and I still judge every restaurant ring. Halos of sweet, pearly-white loops were dipped in an ultrathin glaze of batter and fried feathery crisp. Miller's onion rings were gold upon the tongue. They were Colfax caviar.

And they were fried by Elvis.

Junior's son, Mike, stood at the fryer in the Miller's signature white shirt and pants. For brow-wiping, he hung a white towel around his neck—"Elvis-style." Plus, he had Elvis-like hair, so you can see how I made the connection between Mike and "The King." Mike would walk out of the kitchen, and I'd say, "Elvis has left the fryer."

Fish was served with a plate of white Wonder Bread. Theory was, if you choked on a bone, the bread pushed it down your craw. The tables were covered in brightly colored oilcloth.

"Suppers" were served with packages of moist towelettes. Two-foot-tall framed portraits of the Miller clan hung on the walls. It was a family place. It was kitschy before kitschy was cool.

And sadly, it's now smoke in the ozone layer.

Yet on sizzling June nights, I still smell catfish and hear a voice from a loudspeaker swirl up and out into the corn and soybean fields calling me to Colfax.

Oh, to taste one more Miller's onion ring.

Angie Klink

Gene's Root Beer

My grandmother always loved when my dad or uncle would pick her up a Spanish hot dog from Gene's Root Beer stand around the block from her Anderson home. Isn't that how nostalgia starts?

I can't ask her about it, but I can ask my dad. He's been a fan since the '60s. Along with a few other old-timers, he remembers what it used to be called before it changed its name to Gene's. I don't remember, but my dad is a tireless convincer, especially when it comes to the superiority of things from before 1980. Things Aren't As Good As They Used To Be, regardless of the subject. It took years, but by the time I went to college he passed the Gene's bug on to me.

Once taking it as my own, I'll admit I went a little nuts for it. Just about every weekend when the restaurant was open, I'd go with a friend or two and eat a ridiculous number of those Spanish dogs. Some friends who rode along got hooked. The others didn't think it was worth the effort. I have nothing to say to the latter.

A visit to Gene's was a commitment. We lived on the southeast side of Indianapolis, so the drive was usually an hour each

Gene's Root Beer.

way. Once you added the time spent there actually ordering, waiting, and eating, it was an evening's activity. Going there during the week typically meant that classes would be skipped. That was worth it if I could eat three times my GPA in Spanish dogs. The best group to hang out with on weekends was the group that didn't mind blowing a Saturday night with a trip to Gene's. Which we did. Repeatedly.

What is a Spanish hot dog that makes it worth the trip? It is a kind of Coney dog. Smaller than a grocery-bought hot dog, with a steamed bun, finely chopped onions, and meat sauce. Small enough that eating seven of them is a feat, not a marvel. The sauce is a bit spicier than what you might find elsewhere, but to a degree that wouldn't offend the sensibilities of those who like their salsa mild. Why Spanish? No idea. I have my doubts that the recipe originates near the Iberian Peninsula. The wiener dog in the logo wears a sombrero. Mexico, Spain, Coney Island, what the hell. Call it a Spanish dog. It simply is. Don't worry about it.

The root beer is served in cold mugs without ice. It tastes good, and is great with a Spanish dog. It is popular enough that you can buy a gallon to take home. I think they still make their own, but I'm afraid to ask. I like it and don't want to ruin the mystery. It's good. Don't worry about that, either.

Gene's is one of many secret handshakes for people who know Anderson. One of my first jobs was working with an Anderson University graduate, and her eyes lit up when I mentioned Spanish hot dogs. I also spent a few years living and working in Virginia. One of my coworkers grew up in Anderson in the '70s and '80s, and of course she knew Gene's. The Facebook page is full of people in different states longing for a taste of home.

Nationally, the focus continues to shift away from the smaller towns and toward the cities. There are the typical chain restaurants off the I-69 exit, but the town is still full of anachronistic businesses and restaurants that have served the locals for generations. Sometimes sixty minutes in a car serves as a just fine time machine.

Eric Denney

Kunkel's Drive-In

Kunkel's Drive-In might not be the last curb-service diner in Indiana, but it's a cinch it's one of the most enduring.

A Connersville landmark for sixty-plus years, Kunkel's has defied the ages. It isn't the sleek nationally smooth model of McDonald's or Arby's or Wendy's, but it just keeps hopping along.

It's home to the Kunkelburger, well known to practically everyone who has visited Connersville since 1954, before Ronald McDonald even thought about painting his face.

According to a history printed on its menu, the restaurant was founded on the family's farmland and was owned by brothers

Kunkel's Drive-In.

Albert and Josh Kunkel until 1990, when the Cartwright family bought the operation.

So just slither up to the speaker and tell 'em what you want.

The fries are big and fat. When you get a large iced tea, you get a LARGE iced tea.

Prices are comparatively similar to . . . well, modern times.

So continues the history: "Its iconic neon sign, 20 outdoor drive-up booths and timeless home-cooked diner food are a source of pride and nostalgia for the community."

As Connersville has changed over the years, particularly along the retail strip where Kunkel's is located, this unique restaurant has remained the same.

John C. Updike

The Scoop on Ivanhoe's

Ivan Slain, owner of Ivanhoe's Drive-In in Upland, was the king of ice cream in Grant County. Patrons of his restaurant have 100 shakes and 100 sundaes to choose from, not to mention the full menu of salads and sandwiches. Trying to decide what to order when visiting Ivanhoe's can create a real dilemma!

Slain, who worked in a factory for fifteen years, wanted to change careers, but had no idea what he would like to do. He had never given any thought to owning a restaurant until he saw the "For Sale" sign in the window of a local drive-in back in 1965. Within one week, Slain had purchased the restaurant, while admitting that he didn't even know how to cook! The restaurant offered hamburgers, French fries, and milkshakes, each priced at 15 cents.

The Slains decided on the present name for their restaurant after a high school student who worked for them called his employer Ivanhoe. It seems the student was studying knights in school, and upon learning that there was a knight named Sir Ivanhoe, he thought his boss deserved the title. The name stuck!

Slain and his wife closed down their restaurant each winter, to head to the warmth of Florida. During their drive, they would think about ways to improve their business. The first spring, they decided to add five new milkshake flavors to the existing vanilla, chocolate, and strawberry. The next year they added ten more, and each year thereafter they would add new flavors, until the menu reached 100 different flavors of milkshakes and sundaes.

The process for creating a new flavor went something like this:

1. Think of a new flavor

2. Think of a name

3. Make up a recipe

4. Try it!

Some ideas worked, and some didn't. To this day, new flavors are created, but the total number of shakes and sundaes listed on the menu remains at 100. The list changes as the staff notices popularity trends.

According to general manager Mark Souers, who has worked at Ivanhoe's for more than twenty-eight years, the restaurant sold 7,200 gallons of soft-serve ice cream in 2004. Souers says that customer favorites are the Mint Chocolate Chip milkshake and the Turtle sundae.

To become a member of the 100 Club at Ivanhoe's, which earns you a T-shirt bearing the Ivanhoe's logo and gets your name engraved upon a plaque in the restaurant, you must eat each of the 100 different sundaes or shakes. The first member of the club was a Taylor University student in 2001. Since then, sixteen names have been added to the plaque. Customers thinking of joining the 100 Club face a tough assignment. The toughest part may be deciding what flavor to choose first—with names like Chocolate Peanut Butter Pretzel, Grasshopper, Peach Melba, Cashew Crunch, and S'Mores, it can be nearly impossible to narrow down the list!

Grant County Visitors Bureau

Dutch Mill Restaurant

It was my first job interview and I was nervous. Soon after my sixteenth birthday, Dad took me to the Dutch Mill restaurant in our town of Bluffton to help me apply for a job. It was the mid-1970s and the Dutch Mill was the best full-sized restaurant in town. It seemed huge as it stretched across a strip of land overlooking the banks of the Wabash River in Wells County. I had been in only one part of it. Mom was a teacher and Dad worked odd hours on the railroad. The opportunity for our family of five to eat together once a week on Thursday nights with napkins on our laps was celebrated at the Dutch Mill in one of its regular dining rooms on the south end.

In the middle of the building was a section called The Cupboard. This area focused on take-out orders. While some people ate in the small dining area, most meals were phoned in and packaged for on-the-go. I had never entered this small area.

The last section on the north end of the building was the "cool" area—the drive-in. A couple of friends worked there, and I hoped to be with them.

Also nestled among the Dutch Mill's labyrinth that had been built in 1946, shortly after WWII, were banquet rooms of various sizes.

Someone said the cavernous building could seat up to 500 people and that 85 people may have worked there at one time. I don't know. I just know it seemed like a big deal to apply for a job there.

The thought that I had never worked in a restaurant and would not know what to do ran through my head when Dad asked to see one of the owners, Mr. Glen Moser. Mr. Moser owned the restaurant with another local man, Kenneth "Kenny" Steffen. Shifting from one foot to another while standing in the front lobby area, I wondered if the owner would expect me to cook something. Hopefully not! I had never cooked anything in my life.

When Mr. Moser entered the lobby, he stood quietly listening to Dad tell him my qualifications. He may have recognized us from our weekly dining visits. Finally Mr. Moser nodded and said I could start right then. Dad said he'd pick me up after work, and I followed Mr. Moser into the deep recesses of the famed Dutch Mill.

Maybe I would be assigned as a carhop, I thought. After watching some 1950s movies, I thought that looked like a glamorous job—only in good weather of course.

Instead, Mr. Moser led me to the one place I had never visited and knew little about—The Cupboard. That night I became the "runner" for The Cupboard. The Cupboard handled mostly phone-in orders. Most people called, wanting a sandwich, fries, and a drink. Those were easily assembled by a small staff of mostly high schoolers.

Sometimes people came into The Cupboard to eat a full meal at a table or ordered the daily specials. The specials included chicken-fried steak, broasted chicken, fish, and sides of mashed potatoes and gravy, macaroni salad, or vinegar slaw. The Cupboard had its own fryer so the chicken and fish could be packaged directly. Other specials had to be retrieved from the front of the restaurant in the main kitchen. All of it was packaged in disposable containers and handed to customers, who ate it elsewhere.

As the runner, I "ran" back and forth during my shifts between the kitchen and The Cupboard with meals and orders. It was tiring but good exercise. It left me plenty hungry for an occasional chicken leg or piece of pie that a cook might feel like sharing at the end of a shift.

When I became trusted enough to graduate from runner to order taker, I met people who shared that they had driven from Fort Wayne, even Ohio, just to eat there. I always wondered why they didn't eat somewhere closer to home. "Don't they have good restaurants where they live?" I asked myself.

Now as a travel writer and blogger, I appreciate all of the facets that go into a successful restaurant and recognize that the customers did too.

First, great service—the Dutch Mill had a plethora of experienced waitresses. Some employees worked there for decades!

Dining options—no matter the occasion, you could find a clean, comfortable place at the Dutch Mill. We held our wedding rehearsal there, served family-style with trays of broasted chicken, chicken-fried steak, vegetables, and dessert. Businessmen were served shrimp cocktails in private dining rooms. Civic clubs met regularly for lunch meetings. Teens walked there after ballgames for lemon or cherry Cokes, Dutch Boy or Dutch Girl sandwiches (I can't remember their exact ingredients, but they were precursors of our current put-everything-on-it sandwiches).

Prices—although it was probably the fanciest restaurant in the area (maybe in Northeast Indiana?), Dutch Mill prices were kept well within our community's standards.

Food—now we come to the crux of the Mill's success. Their food was absolutely the best! Some favorites besides those mentioned were fruit salad with sherbet, giant (plate-size) sugar cookies, pizza burgers, and pies.

Ah, the pies! Dutch Mill pies were renowned. Almost everyone who ate there ordered a piece of pie to finish off their meal. I felt privileged while working there to see them made in the large Dutch Mill kitchen—my first experience being "behind the scenes" in a restaurant.

The banana cream, pecan cream, and coconut cream all used the same base and were mixed together early in the mornings. Such huge mixing bowls! The mixture was cooked on a stove, cooled, and poured into pie shells—dozens!

Strawberry pie was another favorite pie flavor, but probably the most popular pie ordered by customers was sugar cream. My grandma made this often so it was not special to me. Now I'm aware this is considered Indiana's state pie. The Dutch Mill pie was sweet, velvety, and always cooked to perfection. Anyone who has made a sugar cream pie knows you have to bake it until it is firm in the middle. Inexperienced cooks take it out of the oven too soon and serve it slightly gooey. Ugh.

During the eighteen months I worked at the Dutch Mill during high school, I got along well with the staff and had no complaints. It was nice working at a place that was famous, even more so than I had ever imagined before working there. However, not everything went according to plan.

One day while serving with two other servers at a family meal with thirty or so people eating in a banquet room, I leaned over too far while trying to serve salad dressings (there were three) and accidentally spilled French dressing on a man's suit. I was mortified, nearly crying as I stuttered an apology. "That's the end of this job!" I told myself, believing it would be right to dismiss me for such carelessness. Thankfully, Mr. Moser and Mr. Steffen didn't fire me. I guess they believed accidents happen. I'm sure they offered the man a free meal (or two). I never knew but was so grateful to not be unduly scolded. That taught me much about patience and forgiveness.

When the Dutch Mill burned to the ground in 1997, it was devastating not only to our community, but to thousands of people around the country, many of whom had worked there or eaten there during its long history. The cause of the fire was not known, though it was determined not to be arson. By then, Mr. Moser had retired. Mr. Steffen decided not to rebuild and to retire. It was disappointing but understandable.

Today, those of us who were around at the time understand why this part of our small town is named Dutch Mill Plaza. A scattering of businesses have located there. A couple of other restaurants have come and gone. A farmer's market is held there each week during warm weather months.

No restaurant has ever replaced the Dutch Mill for high-quality food and service and good memories. Some people claim to have held on to the recipe cards used by the cooks of the pies. This recipe was shared with me as one of them. It may or may not be the actual recipe used by the Dutch Mill cooks, but making it and tasting its comforting sweetness will evoke a good feeling about living in Bluffton and its culinary mark on Indiana. Enjoy!

DUTCH MILL SUGAR CREAM PIE

1/2 cup brown sugar

1/2 cup white sugar

1/2 cup flour (a good 1/2 cup, not level)

1 cup milk

2 cups heavy whipping cream

1/2 teaspoon vanilla

1 pinch salt

1/4 teaspoon cinnamon

Directions:

Whisk sugars, flour, salt & milk until foamy. Fold in whip cream and vanilla. Pour into pie shell. Sprinkle with cinnamon. Bake at 400 degrees until firm on top.

Kayleen Reusser

Custard Lady's Last Stand

Elinor Stingley was known as the "Cone Lady" at the Original Frozen Custard in Lafayette, Indiana. She began working at the Frozen Custard at the corner of Main and Wallace in 1952 and worked there until the last five years of her life, which ended in 2009. For me, Elinor was the story that got away.

In the 1990s, I worked on an advertising campaign for Lafayette Printing Company called "Local Color." The campaign was a collection of newspaper inserts promoting the company's four-color press. Each insert highlighted a colorful person in Lafayette and connected their multihued life with the four-color process.

Elinor Stringley. COURTESY OF *LAFAYETTE JOURNAL & COURIER*

I wrote stories featuring Arni Cohen, owner of Arni's Restaurant, Joe Rumpza of Rumpza's Farm Market, Evelyn Ball of the Ball Mansion, James Riehle, former mayor of Lafayette, Tony Zamora, jazz musician, Jerry Smith, downtown street sweeper, and many more. I wanted Elinor to be a part of "Local Color."

For when it came to colorful, Elinor broke the mold.

I remember Elinor from my childhood summer visits to the Frozen Custard. When I was in high school, I was scared of her. I'd tentatively approached her cone counter with hope that I didn't take too long, or order wrong, or give her insufficient change. She looked stone-faced, leaned her ear toward the hole in the window, and waited for me to talk. She was gruff and in a hurry. No one was going to slow down Elinor's line. No one was going to slow down Elinor, for that matter. Elinor Stringley was so well known in Lafayette and worked until such a ripe old age that on days when she was not there, "the Custard" displayed a sign that read, "I'm not dead; I'm just at the doctor."

There were window rules at the Frozen Custard, and Elinor was the enforcer. Many a Lafayette citizen felt trepidation when approaching the slight, gray-haired woman in the blue-and-white paper ice cream hat and matching smock.

Handmade signs were posted on windows and walls instructing patrons of each ordering window's purpose. The windows were a mere 2 feet apart, and the Frozen Custard staff behind the windows stood just an arm's length away from one another. Yet Elinor's window was for cones only. A patron was not allowed to order a soda or sundae at the cone window. If an unsuspecting new customer failed to read the signs, waited in line, approached the cone window, and ordered a chocolate soda back when she was still the cone window warlord, Elinor would bark, "Window over is for drinks! NEXT!" Elinor kept her line moving, and she had no patience for those who couldn't read the notices and abide by the Frozen Custard Magna Carta.

Another sign read, "We do not mix flavors." In other words, one scoop of chocolate and one scoop of strawberry could not cohabitate, touching like a pink and brown intermarriage, on a singular cake cone. This was the rule set down by Elinor's employers, the Kirkhoffs.

Charles and Florence Kirkhoff founded the Frozen Custard Igloo (as it was originally named) in 1932. Charles had been the general manager and mixmaster of the Frankfort Ice Cream Company in Frankfort, Indiana. He obtained mixing machines and then developed his own formula for frozen custard—a time-proven recipe that has not changed. Still today, the Frozen Custard churns out ribbons of frozen velvet.

Since his original lease forbade him from selling carbonated beverages, Charles concocted his now famous "Fruit Drink," a golden blend of refreshing secret ingredients.

The Frozen Custard is open only during Indiana's warm weather months. So like the first robin sighted, when the winter protective boards are removed from the ordering windows and the switch is thrown to light the "Open" sign in March, spring has been pronounced in Lafayette; the Custard is "open for the season."

The stand is a blue-and-white confection with a massive striped awning that shelters picnic tables. The terrazzo tile patio, glass-block windows, and curved architecture speak Art Moderne. On humid summer evenings, three rooftop neon lights shaped like an ice cream cone, soda, and sundae beckon passersby as locusts drone in the surrounding trees and custard is devoured before the heat melts it into a puddle. From across the street at Columbian Park you hear a crack of a bat at Loeb Stadium or, in the distance, see kids swooshing down Tropicanoe Cove's Banana Peel slide, while from the zoo wafts the sound of a goat bleat.

Elinor was in her nineties when I approached her to be featured in "Local Color." She was a customer of the drug stores my husband, Steve, and I owned. Because Elinor knew Steve and appeared to like him, I thought this would be an "in" for me. I asked Steve to help me convince Elinor to be interviewed.

On a brisk spring morning, we arrived at the cone window and asked to see Elinor. The fellow at the counter pointed across the street and said, "She's on her way." We looked up and saw Elinor walking from her nearby home. As she approached, her blue smock billowed. Shoved under her arm was a brown vinyl pocketbook. On her feet she wore threadbare house slippers wrapped in duct tape.

Like grandchildren asking for a cookie, we mustered up our best behavior and Elinor-worthy courage and asked her if she would consent to having her photo taken and a short biography written about her days working at the Frozen Custard.

"No. I just don't want to do it," Elinor said bluntly. "I don't need people coming up to me and telling me they saw my picture. It would slow down the line."

Steve groped for an angle and said hopefully, "It would be something for your grandchildren."

"If I did it for anyone, I would do it for you," Elinor said, actually smiling up at Steve. (It was then I thought we had a chance, and I patted myself on the back for having the foresight to bring him along.) "But I just don't want my picture taken," she added. "Now I need to get to work." (So much for Steve's boyish charm.)

I thanked Elinor as she shuffled away, her tape-mended slippers swishing on the terrazzo tile.

Even though she declined our request, in the days to come we were "in." On future visits when Steve stepped up to Elinor's window, he would tease her, and she would smile and verbally spar. One day, I was standing in a very slow and long drink-window line when Elinor had no line at her cone window. She motioned for me to approach. "What do you need?" she asked.

"A small Coke," I uttered, cautiously. "Can I order that here?"

"Sure," Elinor said. Then she yelled my order in the direction of the drink window workers. I had slipped past the window rules because Elinor granted me a privilege.

Today, a faded photograph of Elinor Stingley wearing her paper ice cream hat is tucked in the corner of a window at the Frozen Custard drive-up. Elinor lived to be 101, having retired from the Frozen Custard when she was 96. She stood sentry over the cone line for fifty-one years.

As I end this essay, my apologies go to Elinor. For when it's all said and done, it's, well, all said and done. I have written a story about the Cone Lady.

But up there at the big cone window in the sky, I bet Elinor approves. After all, I'm not holding up the line.

Angie Klink

First and Only, Biggest and Best

A Baseball First

Looking west across the St. Marys River on Fort Wayne's Thieme Drive is Camp Allen Park, the little playground tucked into a quiet portion of the Nebraska neighborhood. It was here that a momentous event took place in the history of baseball. However, through the years the story, cloaked in confused reporting, has become difficult separating fact from fiction. With the aid of the Society for American Baseball Research (SABR) the story of "Kekionga Ball Grounds in Fort Wayne" prepared by Bill Griggs and Jim Nitz has shed new light on what actually took place here.

Generally, Camp Allen Park on the old grounds suggests that a space for playing baseball might not fit into the small triangular space. A larger area was turned over to the military during the early years of the Civil War. Named in honor of the War of 1812 hero John Allen, it earlier had been the site for the Northeastern Indiana Fair Grounds. "Camp Allen," expanded to include the area north of Fair Street, was suitable for both infield and outfield play.

Base ball—first expressed using two separate words—was enjoyed as a "pick-up game" sport in Fort Wayne since 1862, when the Summit City Base Ball Club played a gentleman's version of the game on the northwest part of the Allen Hamilton

Homestead on the southeast corner of Lewis and Calhoun Street. Later, that became the site of the Fort Wayne Community School's administration building. After the Civil War a new ball club called the Kekiongas—named after the original Indian town at the Three Rivers—was formed in 1866 and played in an area today formed by Williams, Barr, Wallace, and Calhoun streets. The team played in a rough-and-tumble early professional circuit that took them to Chicago and Troy, New York.

On March 17, 1871, several leading baseball team owners gathered at Collier's Café in New York City and organized the nation's first professional baseball league, the National Association of Professional Base Ball Players—the forerunner of the National League. Among the first teams in the league along with New York, Cleveland, Boston, Philadelphia, Troy, Rockford, and Washington was the Fort Wayne Kekiongas. The Boston Red Stockings and the Olympics of Washington were also scheduled to play their first game on May 4, 1871. An untimely rain washed out the possibility for a game, and it fell to Fort Wayne and Cleveland to play the first game.

So it was, on the old Camp Allen's Kekionga Ball Grounds, that the nation's first professional baseball league game was played. It happened on May 4, 1871, when the Fort Wayne Kekiongas hosted the Cleveland Forest Citys. When the day of the game arrived, Fort Wayne fielded the youngest and most inexperienced team in the new league.

The game day, a rainy one, attracted about 500 spectators to witness the event. The Kekiongas won 2–0, stunning the home crowd, which expected a thorough thrashing by the Cleveland club. The Fort Wayne journalists called it a miracle. A Cleveland reporter wrote, "The fielding of both nines must have been of a very high order, and the batting remarkably weak."

As it turned out, the Kekiongas went on to compile a lackluster record that same season, notwithstanding that first professional baseball league game victory. Later in the same year, the team folded after its game on August 29, 1871. Although it is no rumor that the Kekionga team played and won that first pro baseball league game, a persistent rumor crept into baseball lore that the Kekionga franchise was taken up by a Brooklyn team. However, it was another twelve years before the Brooklyn Dodgers club was formed, and the notion that they took the place of the Kekiongas is but a myth.

Tom Castaldi

Roundabout Capital of the United States

Carmel, Indiana, has the distinction of having more round-abouts than any other city in the United States, totaling more than sixty in the entire city. It has been Carmel mayor Jim Brainard's goal since 1999 to replace the majority of Carmel's stoplights and stop signs with roundabouts. He got the idea after traveling to England as an exchange student and observing some of Europe's many roundabouts. The United States still has only about 3,000 in the whole country.

Carmel was featured on Anderson Cooper's CNN show in 2011 because of the amount of attention the roundabouts were receiving. Mayor Brainard explained in his interview that roundabouts improve safety and traffic flow, save the city money, and reduce gas use by 30 percent.

Because of the confusion roundabouts cause for some drivers, the city's website has instructional videos on how to drive through a roundabout for people who have never been on one before. One video, titled "Roundabout Rookie," features a woman from Carmel explaining roundabouts to her friend from out of town. The video is a (semi)realistic representation of what Carmel residents go through when having to describe to relatives and long-distance friends how to get around the city.

In February of 2015, Mayor Brainard announced plans to build more roundabouts on the east side of the city. And if he gets his way, he'd like to take his roundabout plan up to the next level (literally) by building an elevated roundabout at 96th and Keystone.

Alison Roth

Home of the Hog

Marion, Indiana, hosted the 1919 and 1920 Marion International Motorcycle Race, dubbed the Cornfield Classic. Motorcycle rallies aren't usually considered a sign of a rich history, but in the case of East Central, Indiana, the Hog Daze Motorcycle Rally celebrates the time and place that a Harley was first called a "hog." In 1920, the "Hog Boys" team earned their nickname when they celebrated their victory lap in the 1920 Marion (Indiana) International Motorcycle Race by riding with a pig around the Cornfield Classic track. The hog moniker stuck, and the Hog Boys' victory lap is now recreated annually at the Home of the Hog Motorcycle Rally and Ride.

Grant County Visitors Bureau

This Town's a Circus

In the center ring, flying trapeze performers capture the wide eyes of the crowd. Soon, the spotlight shifts to the end ring, and the audience gasps in awe at the elegance of the Roman rings spectacle. Next, clowns hold their attention at the opposite end, honking red noses and drawing laughter.

Peru Circus. COURTESY OF BRIDGETTE HARMON-SMITH, PERU, INDIANA

It's circus week in Peru, Indiana, where all 200 performers in the Peru Amateur Circus are local kids, ages seven to twenty-one. They're backed by dozens of volunteers who set the riggings, sew the costumes, and make the popcorn for the spectacle, held for a week every July since 1960.

The kids spend long hours in training, mastering the unicycle, taking flying leaps, and learning to juggle. They gain confidence and encourage each other, all while celebrating Peru's more than 130 years of circus heritage.

Peru and circus fame first met when the Great Wallace Shows (which later became the Hagenbeck-Wallace Circus) chose Peru for its home base in 1884, launching a run that spanned more than fifty years. Easy rail access soon had other circuses wintering over in Peru. At one time, as many as 4,500 circus industry workers filled the town.

That earned Peru the nickname Circus Capital of the World, a moniker the kids have kept alive.

The circus focus continued to sparkle when collections from the International Circus Hall of Fame museum arrived in 1988 after the museum closed in Florida. The town now sports a working calliope, a Cinderella coach, and a 1903 gold-leaf bandwagon.

Next came professional circus performances during the same week as the children's circus, with the two groups joining in for the culminating event, the Circus City Festival Parade on Saturday.

With Peru's stature solidified, visitors now flock to the town each summer for a glimpse of yesteryear, a lot of marveling at the young talent, and the fun that can be found only at a three-ring circus.

Kathy Mayer

The Chimney Sweep Industry Gets a Makeover in Indiana

The stereotype of chimney sweeps as an industry of soot-faced, dancing-fool relics of the Mary Poppins era got a much-needed overhaul in Y2K. But this image makeover didn't occur on a rooftop in England nor the northeast United States, where fireplaces and wood stoves are a common in-home source of heat.

On December 1, 2000, ground was broken atop a 1.5-acre parcel of land in Plainfield, Indiana, for the shared Chimney Safety Institute of America (CSIA) and National Chimney Sweep Guild (NCSG) CSIA Technology Center. Chimney sweeps wanted to build a centrally located 10,000-square-foot hub where they could train, be educated and certified, then go out and professionally inspect fireplaces from Maine to California. This strip of land in an industrial park area just southwest of Indianapolis International Airport became the site. Besides the new facility,

Twisted chimney.

the headquarters of CSIA and NCSG relocated from Gaithersburg, Maryland.

The work that sweeps do is no laughing matter. The US Consumer Product Safety Commission reported an average of 22,700 fires related to the chimney, chimney connector, or fireplace from 2010 to 2012. In our state-of-the-art facility, we teach professionals so they can educate homeowners and reduce the risk of unintended fires, carbon monoxide, and other risks.

Over 1,600 sweeps now are credentialed in forty-nine states, and CSIA has over 325 professionals that carry the only credential related to clothes-dryer exhaust venting, the C-DET. Yes, all that is at 2155 Commercial Drive in Plainfield, Indiana. We're known for our twisted chimney atop the building's front entrance. You've probably already heard of us—in November 2005, Mike Rowe of Discovery Channel's *Dirty Jobs* featured us on his program, which we show students four times a year at our world-famous six-day National Chimney Sweep Training School! We still get students who decide on a career as a chimney sweep as they see the program in reruns.

Tom Spalding

City of Democracy

Greensburg, Indiana, is known for a tree growing out of the courthouse—sometimes called the eighth wonder of the world. But Greensburg is famous for another reason, too.

On February 15, 1949, the United States Chamber of Commerce named Greensburg the "City of Democracy." The award informed the world that Greensburg was selected as a typical American small city. The March 26, 1949, issue of *Businessweek* magazine had a story about the selection of Greensburg as "Democracy's Typical City." Other publications followed suit.

After the announcement, the Greensburg Jaycees took on quite an impressive job. The members decided that a scale model of the city should be shown at the International Congress of the Junior Chamber of Commerce at Brussels, Belgium.

This perfect scale model of the center of the city of Greensburg included fifty-four buildings, several automobiles, businesses, hotels, and homes, and cost slightly more than $12,000 to build.

When it was completed, the scale was put on display for the citizens of Decatur County on April 10, 1949. Residents stood in line for more than two hours at times in order to see this wonderful replica of their county seat.

The scale model was then taken to Europe by five members of the Junior Chamber of Commerce: John E. Gelvin, Ray Lindboe, Thomas E. Downey, and Dr. and Mrs. Boyd M. Mahuron.

Part of the scale model was shown in London and Paris, and the complete exhibit was on display for nine days in the ballroom of the Hotel Atlantic in Brussels. It was shown later in Antwerp, Luxembourg, and in free Germany.

When it was returned to the United States it was again put on display in Greensburg. It was then taken to several cities in the United States, including Fort Wayne, Chicago, and Washington, D.C.

After that it was again taken overseas as part of the US Department of State's traveling educational exhibit on American life. It was shown in England, Scotland, Luxembourg, and Berlin.

Finally it was brought home, and that is the last anyone saw of the scale model of Greensburg, Indiana. Residents of the "City of Democracy" have tried to locate it and have also called upon their representatives to help. But it still has not been found. Can you imagine how excited Decatur County would be if they could put it on display again?

Pat Smith

A Foxglove Named Deam

Much of Indiana's upper quarter is replete with dunes, natural lakes, and wetlands just like our Great Lakes neighbor to the north. To the south, where the great Ohio and Wabash Rivers meet, bald cypress swamps appear as if transported from Louisiana (minus the alligators of course!). Our western sector, especially the northwest, is a land of grand prairies. There big bluestem and Indian grass once tickled the bellies of bison and at times fed the flames of regenerating prairie fires. And then of course there is the forest. Most of our state was the domain of trees, positioned here at the western edge of the expansive eastern deciduous forest that stretched to the East Coast.

This mashup of life is quite interesting to the biologist, but is Indiana strictly a melting pot with nothing uniquely our own? Actually, there is a suite of small animals found only in the Hoosier state. Unfortunately, at least for the claustrophobic, many of these are cloistered away in caves and other subterranean interstices.

For us surface dwellers, in the forested hills of far southern Indiana grows a wildflower that occurs nowhere else in the world. It is the only vascular plant in Indiana that can claim such a distinction. Most people might recognize it as a type of foxglove, or beardtongue. The plant, a good 2 feet tall with a wand of white snapdragon-like flowers, was first discovered by Bluffton druggist turned botanist Charles Deam. Deam's discovery was later determined by a botanical expert to be a new species, and in 1935 he christened it Deam's foxglove (*Penstemon deamii*). Deam is known to many as Indiana's first state forester and is the person for whom the Hoosier National Forest's Charles C. Deam Wilderness is named.

Plants of Indiana. MICHAEL E. HOMOYA AND ERIN HIATT

Several botanists have looked in surrounding states for Deam's foxglove, but none were found. Why it keeps such a restricted range is unknown and will likely remain a mystery. Perhaps it's just meant to be a one-of-a-kind Indiana original.

Michael A. Homoya

When Hoosier Boys Ruled the River

The Rising Sun Regatta was named Hoosier Boy Regatta in honor of J. W. Whitlock's line of racing boats, invented and built in Rising Sun, that ruled the rivers from 1909 to 1927.

In 1907 Whitlock built his first boat and kept up an intensive experiment with hull design and power. This was the era when packet boats plied the river at speeds of 12 mph.

In 1909 he brought out the first Hoosier Boy. The boat was 40 feet long and powered with a Buffalo engine. The boat won every speed contest that year in Cincinnati, Peoria, Toledo, and Buffalo.

Whitlock built his boats for endurance as well as speed. For a race in Peoria he drove the boat down the Ohio to Cairo, up the Mississippi and Illinois Rivers to Peoria, covering the 1,000-mile journey in record-setting speed.

Whitlock's first hydroplane was built in 1910. It was 24 feet long and powered by a 40-horsepower, 12-cylinder Liberty airplane engine.

Through the years between 1911 and 1917 the Hoosier Boy set records. In 1924 Whitlock and his Hoosier Boy made a record that still stands. On a swollen Ohio River, full of debris, Whitlock tried the unheard of: breaking the mile-a-minute speed barrier on a round-trip endurance race between Cincinnati and Louisville, a distance of 267 miles. He made the trip in 267 min-

Oil painting of the Haan Mansion Museum in Lafayette, Indiana.

utes and 49 seconds, driving without relief, accompanied by his mechanic, Harvey Byram.

Two of the Whitlock boats are housed in Rising Sun at the Ohio County Historical Museum on Walnut Street.

Sherry Timms

Haan Mansion Museum of Indiana Art

Bob and Ellie Haan didn't intend to create a museum, but their love of art inspired them to turn their home into one.

In 1992, their business, Haan Crafts in Otterbein, Indiana, was doing well selling sewing kits to middle schools and high schools across the United States. That year, they decided to start collecting Indiana art to hang in their home, the beautiful

Classical Revival building that they saved and restored at 920 East State Street in Lafayette, Indiana. This building was the Connecticut Building at the St. Louis World's Fair in 1904. After the fair, it was auctioned off, disassembled, shipped by rail to Lafayette, and reassembled on this site. One little boy who visited said, "It looks like the White House."

The Haans began building quite a collection, and curators came to visit. They asked to borrow art for museum exhibitions and publications. One day Rachel Perry, Indiana State Museum curator and author, came to select art for an exhibit. She said that she didn't need to look any further; the Haans had all of the art that she needed. Perry said of the Haans' collection, "It is hands down the best historic Indiana art collection in the country."

The museum is now known for its unparalleled collection of paintings by Indiana's most prominent historic artists. There you can see the best works of T. C. Steele and other Hoosier Group painters, prime examples of work by Brown County artists, major paintings of the Potawatomi Indians by George Winter, works by important Richmond Group artists, a major collection of 1930s Regionalist paintings, and other exceptional works.

In 2007, the Haans started giving tours. They began calling their home a museum, the Haan Mansion Museum of Indiana Art.

In 2014, Christmas came early to forty Indiana ceramics artists when the Haans became smitten with ceramics. Bob and Ellie decided to have the best Indiana ceramics collection. Many people feel that they have succeeded. The Haans amassed over 1,000 ceramic works of art.

The museum's mission is, in part, to preserve, protect, and share the best of Indiana art and the historic Haan Mansion. There is no other Indiana art collection of this caliber and depth, and no other museum (that we know of) solely devoted to Indiana art. The Haans created this sanctuary for Indiana art independently, with their own funds. They are passionate about the art, the artists, and the history, and they want to preserve and share it.

On July 13, 2015, the Haans gave away the mansion that they love to the museum nonprofit organization. This generous gift enables the museum to move forward, becoming a home for Indiana art for generations. They have started the process of donating the art collection to the museum.

The property includes a mountain bike path and nature trail with over thirty native Indiana trees identified. Both trails are open to the public. For 2016, plans are underway to install a sculpture garden and repurpose the Carriage House to become a visitor's center.

Flo Caddell

Hoops

Fifty Greatest Nicknames in Hoosier Hardwood History

It all began with Crawfordsville in 1911, and for nearly the next nine decades, Hoosier hysteria enchantingly exemplified what is undeniably Indiana. Other states may boast equally of their own versions of the 500, Studebaker, Eli Lilly, Hoagy Carmichael, and James Whitcomb Riley. No one, however, from Nome to New York, can deny the preeminence of high school basketball in our great state. For example, at its peak in the '50s, the Wigwam in Anderson boasted 6,000 season ticket holders, and the athletic director found himself testifying in divorce cases over the rights to season tickets!

The consolidation craze, which began in the late '50s, along with other rising tides of modernity, has unfortunately robbed high school basketball of the cultural cohesion it once gave Indiana. As a consequence of consolidation, many wonderfully quaint, quirky, and colorful school nicknames have vanished. Additionally, the newer schools have largely played it safe by choosing mundane monikers. Currently, over one-third of schools are known by one of eleven common and largely uninspiring nicknames:

1. Panthers (19 schools)
2. Warriors (18 schools)
3. Eagles (17 schools)

1949 Anderson High School basketball team.
COURTESY OF THE *INDIANAPOLIS STAR*

    4. Tigers (17 schools)

    5. Bulldogs (14 schools)

    6. Cougars (12 schools)

    7. Trojans (12 schools)

    8. Knights (11 schools)

    9. Wildcats (10 schools)

    10. Braves (9 schools)

    11. Patriots (9 schools)

Consolidations have also made it difficult for fans and for-midable students of state geography to identify many schools. For example, where the heck is Tri-High, Tri-Central, Tri-West, or Tri-County?

To pay homage to these lost sobriquets, I recently met in Bloomington with my family and friends to determine the top fifty Indiana high school nicknames of all time. The vote was based on lists compiled of over 820 schools. It was an enchanting evening of laughter, reminiscence, and due diligence. Some voters emphasized onomatopoeia, alliteration, and puns. Others tended to value whimsy. The majority of voters placed significant import on the pertinence of a nickname to the cultural or industrial heritage of a community.

For the purpose of full disclosure, a few balloters acknowledged a slight sentimental bias toward communities of which they had more intimate knowledge. However, election overseers were in place to monitor for voter fraud or intimidation and to ensure that no community was unfairly disenfranchised. Eleven of the fifty schools (indicated with an asterisk) still exist, while no school opened after 1960 made the list.

Here are the results, along with some interesting historical footnotes, and ruminations:

1. Stinesville Quarry Lads

(Now part of this consolidation: Edgewood)

Stinesville was our decisive number one! It embodies everything Indiana, as the school and gym were built from limestone mined locally.

2. The Epsom Salts

(Now part of this consolidation: North Daviess)

The Salts lost a heartbreaker to Washington 33–32 in the sectional final in 1933 under legendary coach Leo Cavanaugh "Cabby" O'Neill. He later moved to Jasper, where he led the 'Cats to a state title in 1949. Called "Cavy" by his friends and family in Daviess County, he was all-SEC at Alabama. A newspaper article mistakenly called him "Cabby," and the name stuck. From the '30s through the early '60s, players from Indiana like O'Neill dominated SEC and ACC rosters. Many teams, such as Vanderbilt, Ole Miss, and NC State often composed half of their teams of Hoosiers.

3. The Banquo Ghosts

(Now part of this consolidation: Huntington North)

Banquo is one of the main characters in Shakespeare's *Macbeth*. The ghost of Banquo returns in the third act to haunt *Macbeth*.

4. The Edwardsport Power House Gang

(Now part of this consolidation: North Knox)

The team was named after the mammoth coal-fired power plant in this town on the Wabash. A fire destroyed the school in 1951, and the original plant was demolished in 2012.

5. The Speedway Sparkplugs*

The team's deepest drive (pun intended) in the tournament came in 1973 when they fell to Franklin in the opening game of the semi-state. Gordon Johncock won a rain-shortened 500 later that spring.

6. The Delphi Oracles*

The Greek god Apollo gave some of his most important oracles (revelations) in Delphi.

7. The Fort Branch Twigs

(Now part of this consolidation: Gibson Southern)

To borrow shamelessly from the University of Maryland: "Fear the Twig!"

8. The Wheatfield Shockers

(Now part of this consolidation: Kankakee Valley)

This town was established in the Indiana wheat belt in 1882. In the early days, wheat had to be "shocked" (stacked) in 30-pound bundles in order to dry for a number of weeks until "threshing time." Indiana has approximately 700,000 acres of wheat under cultivation, and it is our number-four cash crop behind corn, soybeans, and nursery/greenhouse. The 1967 Shocker team was the best, falling to powerful Lafayette Jeff in the finals of the regional.

9. The Ireland Spuds

(Now part of this consolidation: Jasper)

This team was named, of course, for the famous Ireland potato famine of the 1840s that brought many immigrants to the United States. During a surprisingly successful season in 1963 with the colorful Pete Gill as coach, the team won the regional championship.

10. The Frankfort Hot Dogs*

The Frankfurter originated in the beer gardens of Frankfurt, Germany, as a highly seasoned sausage and became wildly popular in the United States around the turn of the twentieth century as the "hot dog" or "wiener." Fortunately, Frankfort chose the former! In 1923, twenty-two-year-old Everett Case was hired from among eighteen applicants to teach and coach basketball and track (the only two sports offered by the school) for $1,800 a year. The rest is Naismith National Basketball Hall of Fame history! Case won four state titles at Frankfort (1925, 1929, 1936, 1939), and then became coach at North Carolina State from 1946 to 1964, winning nine consecutive conference championships with the pipeline of players he imported from Hoosier high schools.

11. The Mecca Arabs

(Now part of this consolidation: Riverton Parke)

In 2009, the group received a $212,000 grant from the state to salvage and refurbish a gem of a gym, which is now used for many community activities.

12. Rising Sun Shiners*

The sun first comes to Indiana in this town along the Ohio River. The Shiners went fifty-three years between their first and second sectional titles (1930–1983).

13. The DePauw Blue River Echos

(Now part of this consolidation: North Harrison)

The school closed in 1951 and never won a sectional. One can imagine it's a name inspired by the fiesta on the river—bellowing bats, baritone toads, trees twisting in the wind, and waves routing waves.

14. The Farmersburg Plowboys

(Now part of this consolidation: North Central)

Farmersburg won the sectional title in 1954. An anachronistically hip nickname—like, what if James Dean had actually played his high school ball at Farmersburg rather than Fairmont? Unfortunately, Farmersburg is actually west of Eden (Indiana).

15. Shoals Jug Rox*

Named after the unique sandstone formation just west of Shoals on Highway 50, the poor Jug Rox have never won a sectional—coming close in 1964 when they fell to the Washington Hatchets in the final.

16. The Hartford Township Gorillas

(Now part of this consolidation: South Adams)

The school existed from 1918 to 1963. Their best run in the tournament came in 1948 when they fell to Portland in the Huntington regional final.

17. The Marengo Cavemen

(Now part of this consolidation: Crawford County)

While Mishawaka is also known as the Cavemen and play in "The Cave"—a legendary gym built in 1926—Marengo actually features real caves!

18. The Pimento Peppers

(Now part of this consolidation: Terre Haute South)

Inspiration from the garden isn't likely to instill fear in the opposition!

19. The Idaville Green Streaks

(Now part of this consolidation: Twin Lakes)

Jug rock.

According to local historian and retired schoolteacher William Henshaw, the name may emanate from the Devonian-Mississippi black shale of White County, which is laced with streaks of green.

20. The Arlington Purple Breezes

(Now part of this consolidation: Rushville)

This team won the Rushville sectional in 1940 and 1947. The gym was built in 1939 as a WPA project and still stands in near-pristine condition. It was considered a finalist for the central filming of the 1986 movie *Hoosiers*, starring Gene Hackman and Dennis Hopper. The Knightstown gym was ultimately chosen.

21. The Converse Borderman

(Now part of this consolidation: Oak Hill)

Converse sits on the border of Grant, Miami, and Howard Counties.

22. Jackson Township Stonewalls

(Now part of this consolidation: Eastern)

Thomas Jonathan "Stonewall" Jackson is the best-known Confederate general after Robert E. Lee. A revered and gifted tactical commander, he earned his nickname at the first battle of Bull Run when a fellow officer exhorted his troops to re-form by bellowing: "There stands Jackson, like a stone wall!"

23. The Vincennes Alices*

This team name is based on the popular novel written in 1901 by Maurice Thompson entitled *Alice of Old Vincennes*. Alice Roussillon was a spunky orphan girl who fell in love with a soldier commanded by George Rogers Clark, during the days of the American Revolution.

24. Chili Polar Bears

(Now part of this consolidation: North Miami)

Chili, Mexico, and Peru are all towns in Miami County! The vote on this one was somewhat polarized (pun intended). A few balloters found this moniker perhaps not quite as clever when one knows that the town is pronounced: "CHAI-lai" (with two hard "i" sounds). Most voters however, found the nickname cool enough to land it solidly in the top fifty. Chili had some good teams under Bob Macy in the '50s but never managed a sectional ring. The school closed in 1961, and its tiny gym is now a private residence.

25. The Martinsville Artesians*

The area is known historically for its rich mineral spas, which come from the many artesian wells (underground wells) in the area. With all respect to the Big "O" and Larry Legend, Martinsville produced the greatest of all Hoosier hardwood titans—Johnny Wooden. The "Wizard of Westwood" led the Artesians to the state championship in 1927.

26. The Huntingburg Happy Hunters

(Now part of this consolidation: Southridge)

The legendary gym was dedicated in 1951 and seats over 6,000. For a long time, it was the toughest sectional ticket in the state. Bob Hammel, the great longtime Bloomington sports writer, wrote a wonderful book about the last single class sectional played at Southridge in 1997 entitled *Hoosiers-Classified: Indiana's Love Affair with One-Class Basketball.*

27. The Battle Ground Tomahawks

(Now part of this consolidation: Lafayette Harrison)

Battle Ground was named for the Battle of Tippecanoe, where William Henry Harrison won a decisive battle against Tecumseh's Shawnee brother Tenskwatawa (the Prophet) on November 7, 1811. This battle essentially ended all Indian wars east of the Mississippi. Twelve counties in Indiana are named after American soldiers who fought there: White, Daviess, Dubois, Pike, Boone, Floyd, Gibson, Parke, Harrison, Warrick, Tipton, and Spencer.

28. The Cory Apple Boys

(Now part of this consolidation: Clay City)

In the early '20s, Mr. E. A. Doud started the orchard in Cory and made this town famous. At its peak, the orchard produced over 100,000 bushels per year and the hardwood quintet became known as the Apple Boys. Mr. Doud died in 1965, and the school and the orchard both closed in 1967. The town celebrates its heritage the last weekend in September with its annual apple fest.

29. The Griffin Tornados

(Now part of this consolidation: North Posey)

This team was named for the famous "Tri-State tornado" of March 18, 1925, which destroyed 150 homes in Griffin and killed many.

30. Cambridge City Wampus Cats

(Now part of this consolidation: Cambridge City Lincoln)

The Wampus Cat was born of Cherokee mythology and migrated into mainstream American folklore. Variously described as a freakish, fearsome variation of a cougar: "A six-legged cat—four to run at the speed of light and, two to fight, with all its might." The team won the Richmond sectional in 1951.

31. The Smithville Skibos

(Now part of this consolidation: Bloomington South)

This is the biggest mystery in all of mascot-ology! The Skibo mascot was a cute little penguin that would have made Batman's Penguin guffaw, but could have easily landed a part in the movies *Penguins of Madagascar* or *Happy Feet*. An exhaustive Internet search reveals no other associations of the words "penguin" and "Skibo," other than to Smithville High School. There exists a beautiful castle in Scotland called Skibo Castle, built in the thirteenth century and once owned by Andrew Carnegie. Skibo is the Anglicization of the Scottish-Gaelic *sgiobal*, which in turn, comes from the old Norse name meaning firewood-steading. The penguin certainly isn't the most menacing creature on the prowl. However, according to local historian

Rosemary Wisley, students took great pride in their mascot. There is no record of the decision-making process for the name of the famed penguin mascot. Smithville became known as the Skibos in 1924, when the team was doing well and they decided they needed a mascot.

32. The Spencer Cops

(Now part of this consolidation: Owen Valley)

Cops is an acronym for Center of Population Spencer. According to the 1920 census, exactly half of the US population lived west of Spencer, and half east.

33. The Ladoga Canners

(Now part of this consolidation: Southmont)

This nickname was chosen by principal G. H. Jackson in honor of a large tomato canning facility in Ladoga from 1903 to 1950. At one time the plant employed 300 people and sent many of its products to soldiers during WWII. The company furnished the team uniforms during the Depression. One wonders whether Jackson had double entendre in mind when he choose this moniker—Ladoga canned tomatoes in the factory and hoops on the hardwood!

34. The Swayzee Speed Kings

(Now part of this consolidation: Oak Hill)

As the nickname implies, these guys preferred polishing off opponents posthaste. Sardonically counter to this M.O., Swayzee played in the longest game in state history: a nine-overtime victory (65–61) over Liberty Center in the opening game of the 1964 Marion regional. The Speed Kings fell to Huntington in the final.

35. Monroe City Blue Jeans

(Now part of this consolidation: South Knox)

This team was named in honor of Monroe City native and former Indiana Governor James "Blue Jeans" Williams. While in office from 1877 to 1880, he wore suits made of the material to remind him of his humble roots. Williams is buried in Monroe City.

36. The River Forest Ingots*

This team was named after the local industry that makes ingots, which are masses of steel shaped in convenient forms for refining.

37. The Newberry River Rats

(Now part of this consolidation: White River Valley)

This sobriquet serves as a reminder of the many charming and unusual nicknames, now bygone, given to small bend-in-the-road (and river) schools, such as Newberry, which is located on the banks of the Wabash.

38. The Kirkland Kangaroos

(Now part of this consolidation: Adams Central)

Four score years before ESPN helped to popularize "streetball speak," the Kirkland Kangaroos were fabled for their ability to "get to the rim with mad hops!"

39. The Wingate Gymless Wonders

(Now part of this consolidation: North Montgomery)

State champs in 1913 and 1914, the school had no gym until 1925, when they purchased a livery stable and converted it.

40. The Union Sharpshooters

(Now part of this consolidation: Huntington North)

An utterly apropos appellation for a Hoosier hardwood squad!

41. St. Paul Blasters

(Now part of this consolidation: North Decatur)

This team was named for the blasting caps frequently discharged from the nearby quarry.

42. The Summitville Goblins

(Now part of this consolidation: Madison-Grant)

Given the close proximity of Summitville and Banquo, the Ghosts and Goblins likely had many ghoulish games. One wonders how the all-time series stands?

43. The Warren Lightning Five

(Now part of this consolidation: Huntington North)

The team named was inspired by a sportswriter who wrote in the early 1900s after a victory over a Goliath Marion squad that "The Warren squad was fast as lightening [*sic*]."

44. The Hobart Brickies*

This nickname is a reference to the old brick-making industry in Hobart. "Brickies" has unfortunately been morphed by modern-day hoop vernacular into either something wonderfully self-effacing or dreadfully misfortunate, depending on your perspective. Fortunately, for Hobart's gridders, the name Brickie evokes an image of strength (Think Vince Lombardi and Fordham's Seven Blocks of Granite). Perhaps this explains why Hobart has always been thought of as a football school.

45. The Andrean Fighting '59ers*

This is the only school in the state named for its street address: 5959 Broadway.

46. Pinnell Purple Dragons

(Now part of this consolidation: Western Boone)

The Purple Dragon is the embodiment of everything necessary in a nickname. Purple is the chromatic cachet of the coronation of kings and Cleopatra. It is the color of heroism and valor, like the Purple Heart. The dragon captures the imagination of any discerning mythological mascot-ologist. They imbue power and may be victorious under any circumstance. WARNING: Breathing fire will likely result in cremating the opposition. Dragons are seen symbolically as guardians of sacred places like Pinnell, and in ode to the modern mantra of Under Armour—"Protect This House!!"

47. The Bedford Stonecutters

(Now part of this consolidation: Bedford-North Lawrence)

Not as retro-chic as "the Quarry Lads," but nevertheless, the name is quite cool and definitely deserving of a top-fifty accolade.

48. The Buck Creek Cobras

(Now part of this consolidation: Lafayette Harrison)

The cobra should engender awe—unless, of course, the opposition apprehends that these guys should be hibernating during hoops season. The Buck Creek "Cobra" knife (made in Germany), is highly sought after by American blade collectors.

49. Dubois Jeeps*

This team was named after Eugene the Jeep, a character in the popular Popeye comic strips of the 1930s. Eugene existed on a strict diet of orchids and had the "the ability to go anywhere"—including to the basket! Some mistakenly attribute the nickname to the popular Willys overland vehicle used extensively in the Second World War and admired by soldiers for its "ability to go anywhere." The workhorse wagon of WWII was also named in honor of Eugene the Jeep.

50. The Scircleville Ringers

(Now part of this consolidation: Clinton Central)

Is this orthographically challenged institution a pun? Perhaps it's a commendable confession to a time in the early years when Scircleville tended to use ineligible players? Either way, it's a completely cool nickname and a great way to "round out" the top fifty.

Michael E. Ruff, MD

Kitchel Had Its Moment

On your way to Anywhere Else, you probably need to visit Kitchel.

Take US 27 south from Richmond and at the sign just north of Liberty, the one that points to Clifton . . . um . . . turn left. County Road 400 North. Go a mile or so to County Road . . . um . . . the road sign is missing. Never mind, turn right till you get to . . . County Road 350 North, unless it's called something else.

Kitchel monument.

Turn left and drive like lightning.

When you reach the railroad tracks, you are in downtown Kitchel.

If you reached the tracks, you may have missed the reason you went there. It's what the man in Kitchel described as a "real nice" monument to the greatest moments in Kitchel history. It's a brick-and-mortar bulletin board, standing about 4 feet high, proclaiming

HARRISON TWP. SCHOOL

A couple of inscriptions are inlaid. One of them is a bunch of names. The one on the right says:

Kitchel Cowboys
1942 & 1943
Sectional Champs

A couple of pots full of plastic flowers adorn the monument, which stands alongside four large pine trees, planted in a square configuration. Yeah, it's "real nice," this monument. It's surrounded by corn.

Something is missing.

Kitchel's school is long gone, swept away by a nation that said rural education was better served if it went to town.

Oddly, for many years, its gymnasium endured, defying time, gravity, and weather. If this is your first trip to Kitchel, none of this will make sense. If it's your ten-thousandth visit to Kitchel, it will still make little sense.

So, it helps to thump the dust off of your history book to get in step with the past, which led you to Kitchel in the first place.

Actually you would probably never go to Kitchel because there's little tangible evidence it exists. The sign points to Clifton, not Kitchel. There is no sign pointing to Kitchel.

Never mind that.

Kitchel was actually only a farm owned by a man of that name when Harrison Township decided to build its school there, serving all the families far and wide. The railroad tracks probably had some impact on that. Kitchel's farm was generally in the center of the township.

Meanwhile in 1924, in true Indiana fashion, the school organized a basketball team.

The Cowboys.

And they played in the various conferences and tournaments alongside a dozen or so other township schools from surrounding counties, all culminating in the Sectional at season's end in Connersville.

Big old Connersville won the Sectional almost every year, leaving Kitchel and the others to wonder . . . What if? Can we dream? Could we ever?

What if two months after the Japanese bombed Pearl Harbor America would face a serious labor shortage? Thus went Connersville, where all the factories were located. February 1942, a very cold and frightening winter. Boys were leaving school early in the day to work those jobs. The practice was not only accepted, it was encouraged.

Connersville's basketball team would be running on fumes.

When the Sectional started, big old Connersville was still the favorite, but the "dope bucket" of the day said the Spartans would need to beat . . . Kitchel.

True to form, the two met in the title game. The Connersville *News-Examiner* headline explained what happened.

KITCHEL WINS IN
DOUBLE OVERTIME
TO COP SECTIONAL
Cowboys Defeat Spartans
42 to 40 in Finals
To Upset Dope

("Dope" was apparently jargon of the day that meant "the odds" of winning.)

"Standing tensely, the crowd watched Clinton Bostick as he had reached the outer foul circle and was poised in the air for a left-handed hook shot. All was extremely quiet as the ball left his hand and swished through the net. Tumult broke the silence as Kitchel had won 42–40 in [the] most exciting and thrill-packed double overtime sectional game the Spartans had encountered in a long time."

It was Clinton Bostick's only basket of the game.

Evidently the Cowboys were pretty good. Bostick's brother Darrell was the star of the team.

One presumes the usual fanfare followed, complete with a parade through downtown Kitchel and back. Ah, the imagery just isn't there, sorry.

Then came 1943.

KITCHEL CAPTURES
LOCAL SECTIONAL
FOR SECOND TIME

"Last Saturday night with a one-handed push shot, Harry Dils became the hero of Kitchel High School. Last year at this time it was Clint Bostick. This year Dils became the hero when his shot clinched the Sectional title for the defending Cowboys in a double-overtime game. The final score was 36–35."

The final score reflects the rule of the time. You needed the first TWO points in the second overtime to win. Connersville had led by one point when Dils sank his game winner.

In both years, Kitchel was good enough to advance to the finals of the Rushville Regional, defeating Arlington 33–29 in 1942 before losing 55–33 to Aurora, and gaining revenge 43–33 against Aurora in 1943 before losing to Batesville 37–25 in the final game. Keith Stroup was the coach.

The Kitchel school was closed in 1961, and the school building itself was demolished a few years later. The sturdy gym, meanwhile, was left standing, primarily because township residents believed they could convert it to a community center. With a population of a half-dozen or so in a place that didn't even merit a highway directional sign, the plan seemed doomed to failure.

The old gym stood there, crumbling. The school grounds had been sold by the township to a neighboring farmer who finally decided in 2014 to tear down the gym.

The "real nice" monument remains.

The Cowboys? Ghost riders in the sky.

John C. Updike

The 1954 Milan Basketball Team

It was tradition in our family when my brother and I were growing up in Kokomo, Indiana, that our family would watch the Indiana High School Basketball Tournament finals at home on our black-and-white TV.

One year, our dad surprised us by suggesting that Mom, Dad, my brother, and I each put a quarter in the pot and draw names of teams. Whoever won would get a dollar. This sounded like a lot of fun, and we had never seen Dad gamble before. Our favorite team, Kokomo High School, was already out of the tournament, but it was still exciting. I could hardly wait because I drew the name of Muncie Central, ranked number one in the state. A dollar could go a very long way in 1954. My brother and I were laughing because Dad had drawn a name I had never heard of before—Milan High School!

Bob Thrasher

Stories of great basketball players and games have always been a big part of Indiana history. You can hear many older folks talking in the barbershop or local bar about games they, or friends, played either on a dirt lot or in their school gymnasiums. The memories and stories play as if they happened yesterday.

A story about basketball that has reached way beyond the borders of Indiana involves the small town of Milan. The stars began aligning in 1953, and before, for what was to become the most famous Indiana basketball championship game of all.

It was a time when small towns flourished with small department stores, locally owned factories, gasoline stations with service bays, and old-time barbershops. It was a time before televisions and telephones engulfed the majority of people, and teens spent their time playing basketball wherever they could find a hoop. And EVERYONE attended local high school games.

Milan High School enrollment was 165. Its basketball team consisted of young men who had been playing basketball in back-

Milan basketball team on the sixtieth anniversary of their 1954 state championship. *Left to right:* Kenny Wendelman, Rollin Cutter, Roger Schroder, Bob Wichman, Patty Bohlke Marshall, Ray Craft, Jinky Craft, Gene White, Bobby Plump, Mary Lou Wood (Coach Wood's widow), Glen Butte.

yard lots most of their lives. Once Marvin Wood was appointed the new coach, the team began to work its way winning local basketball tourneys. The Milan team reached the state level, and on March 20, 1954, it was named Indiana State High School Basketball Champions in Hinkle Fieldhouse, after defeating a team from Muncie Central (with an enrollment of 1,662).

Thousands gathered, not only at the fieldhouse, but also through the streets from Indianapolis all the way to Milan to celebrate the mighty men of Milan's against-odds victory. Some would say it was just a game, but it was more than that: it was the empowerment of a small community to think—and be—big.

The win was followed by the basketball players and then other students attending college, a road not usually taken by kids

Memorabilia of the 1954 Milan, Indiana, state champion basketball team.

in small towns. Many of the players, always humble, went on to become coaches—all of them being assets to the communities where they settled.

That was the official beginning of the story, but it has lived on in the hearts and minds of the players and those who attended the game and celebration. The memorabilia at the Milan '54 Hoosiers Museum draws the players back regularly, as well as many who have heard the story and want to learn more about our basketball heritage.

Already known worldwide, the story became even more popular when Indiana natives Angelo Pizzo and David Anspaugh decided to make a movie focusing on the big game called *Hoosiers*. The 1954 game inspired the movie, but other than the last shot, the story lines are very different because the true story lacked conflict.

Today the Milan '54 Hoosiers Museum has many items from the game, the players, and the era. The museum also holds the largest collection of memorabilia from the movie *Hoosiers*, including uniforms, costumes, and other items from the set.

While small-town Indiana is not the same, visitors can still experience the feel of the 1950s in Milan.

Katherine Taul

Fictitious "Fod's" Weekly Forecast

1954: It was the year that a team from small-town Milan, Indiana, won the coveted Indiana high school basketball state championship. It was also the year that a fictitious sports writer by the made-up name of "Doc Fod" started dangerously predicting the outcome of area basketball games at the *Plymouth Pilot-News*. Fod anonymously mailed his weekly picks to the sports editor, so only one or two people at the newspaper ever knew his real identity. He was portrayed in the paper by a caricature that seemed to somehow evolve and age over the almost thirty years that he agitated the folks who lived in and around Marshall County. In fact, in some respects, he seemed to strangely resemble the well-concocted *Mad* magazine mascot, Alfred E. Neuman, of the same era. Maybe it was best that Fod remained incognito. Emotions ran high when it came to basketball in the state of Indiana.

At first Doc Fod was a cute little cartoon-like face that affectionately appeared on the sports page making fun-loving forecasts of the weekly pairings, but when they turned into outrageous predictions, the townspeople turned on Doc. It was hard to keep harmony in a community when Doc's basketball forecast picked a small county school to upset the known powerhouse.

Readers started writing to the newspaper, vehemently voicing their disagreements with his sports forecasts. Eventually, as newspapers got delivered, subscribers began removing the rubber band, overlooking the day's headlines for an immediate glance at the sports page to discover whether they were going to be pleased or provoked. At one point, when passions became particularly profuse, a disgruntled school constructed a prototype of Fod and he was hung in effigy!

Sports headlines in the *Pilot-News* soon fueled the fire by running banners that read, "Bremen Fan Questions Ability of 'Old Master,'" "Fod: Less Said the Better," "Please Don't Kick Fod When He's Down," and finally, "Fod Suffers a Nervous Breakdown," giving this comic book–like character even more human characteristics.

Contests were started by the newspaper to keep the craziness going. One contest titled, "I Beat Doc Fod in the *Pilot-News* Sports Page," gave readers an opportunity to challenge Fod's predictions. Entry forms came from all over and at one point averaged over 160 per week. Occasionally Fod would meet defeat, and the skilled challenger would win the highly coveted T-shirt that read, "I BEAT DOC FOD!" When Fod took a well-earned vacation or got sick, some of the Fod family would fill in for him. His French cousin, "Jacques Fod," sister "Farrah Fawcett-Fod," and "Mama Fod" would allow him to take a short hiatus.

It's hard to say who had more fun—the *Pilot-News* or the readers! It has been said thirty years later that the identity of the real Doc Fod is still unknown by those who remember that era. It is one of those things that probably should never be revealed. The mystique of Doc Fod and the agitation of an entire community make for great "fodder" and remain undeniably Indiana!

Mindy Langdon

Sneaking into Market Square Arena

1975: Horns were honking! People were cheering and yelling, hanging out car windows waving black and gold pom-poms, driving to downtown Indianapolis on Madison Avenue.

This was the procession my friend Judy, my three children—Autumn, 8, Jason, 7, baby Evie, 2—and I were witnessing.

I'm from a small southern Indiana town called Loogootee (say Luh-GO-tee). It is famous for its fabulous high school basketball teams. They have played schools three times their size, and the coach at the time was Jack Butcher.

That March day in 1975, every car we saw driving in Indianapolis had "51A" license plates (you knew the folks were from Martin County). I shrieked at Judy: "Oh my gosh! That's Loogootee! My hometown went to State!!! I hadn't heard. This is HUGE!!! We've got to get there!" She said, "What? Get where?"

"They'll play at Market Square Arena," I said. "I've GOT to get to that game! Come on!"

She said, "We don't have tickets," but I knew we could buy some cheap ones from the afternoon game people.

I asked a dozen people. No takers. This was just sad. I looked up at the upper levels of Market Square Arena, saw throngs of basketball fans pouring from every door, and in a split second, decided to gather my little group and walk in, at the same time everyone was coming out!

Judy said, "What are we DOING?"

I replied, "I've got to get in there. All of Loogootee will be there and I'll see everybody I know."

"I won't," Judy said. "You're crazy."

"I know! Come on!"

Once inside, I felt a little wave of triumph, but it began to fade as I realized I hadn't thought it through. It was now 3 PM, and the night game didn't start until 8. Five hours away.

I had to think fast. I led my company to the restroom to ponder the next step. We stayed in the bathroom for half an hour, and Jason kept going out and coming back in. It was boring. I could see that this wasn't going to work.

We cautiously emerged from our hideout, not knowing what to expect.

Judy said, "This is making me nervous. What if they throw us out?"

I answered, "They could." I peeked around and noticed men with official-looking badges. I thought, "How am I going to entertain the kids for five hours?"

There was trash everywhere from the afternoon game. So I hit upon the idea of putting Autumn and Jason to work as part of the cleanup crew. They did great. Evie and I watched and walked. No one said a word to us.

Finally the arena was cleaned and there was nothing left to do. It was now 6 PM, and two hours to go until game time. I looked at all the paper cups and food containers and thought, "Concession stand! I'll go apply for a job! That will kill some time." We all moved to that end of the building. I took a lot of time filling out the application, stalling as long as I could.

Back to the restroom—one hour to go. Finally they opened the doors and fans started coming in. We did not have paid seats, and of course I knew we would be ousted no matter where we sat. We filed in, sat down, and the paid ticketholders approached us immediately and frowned.

We moved up several rows, and again were run out.

The nosebleed section was a winner. We got to see the whole game. I saw my dear Uncle Connie Arvin and lots of Martin County people. Even though the Loogootee Lions lost, it was a blast.

Three weeks later, Market Square Arena called me to come to work at their concession stand.

P.S.—I always felt bad that we didn't pay for our tickets!

Francine Arvin McCoy Schmitt

Basketball Rioting at Its Best

2002: The year that Indiana University was named the number-one party school in the United States was also the same year that the latest basketball riots occurred. That information should come as no surprise to any native Hoosier, nor any IU basketball fan. In the wake of the (somewhat) shocking firing of the head coach, Bobby Knight, two years earlier, Hoosier fans took to the streets like a people robbed of their life's blood and bread. And considering that the sport of basketball is like a second religion to many residents of Indiana, it should come again as no surprise that Bloomington students and others made their discontent with the decision vastly and intensely known, far and wide across campus, through the streets of downtown, and by Assembly Hall.

When the decision was not reversed, the team itself was left to uphold the vestiges of the basketball tradition that Coach Knight had built over his nearly three decades as the Hurryin' Hoosiers' head coach. So when the 2001–2002 season turned out to be a winning one (nearly, at least), with replacement head coach Mike Davis spurring on the remaining team members to the championship game (with an impressive victory over Duke along the way), it again should come as no surprise that the rioters themselves were out in full force yet again come the spring—this time for joyful reasons instead of the frustration and anger that had inspired the disturbances in the fall of 2000.

The riots continued and the rioters only increased their intensity as the Hoosiers proceeded through each successive victory toward the final game. It got to the point that the IU administration began to remove the fish statues from the Venus fountain in front of the auditorium, as it was a notable tradition to remove and redistribute those fish (heavy and made of metal though they were) every time IU's basketball team achieved another monumental victory. (For example, by the time IU beat Duke, the fish had already been removed; the same was true when IU beat the University of Kentucky nearly a decade later.)

Although the Hurryin' Hoosiers didn't quite pull through in the final game, the basketball riots can be seen as both a testament to the popularity and lasting impact that Coach Knight had on IU and the entire Bloomington (and Indiana) community and the extreme pride and support that IU basketball fans bring to Assembly Hall. They can also be viewed, to a certain extent, as the manifestation of and enactment of the religious fervor that is the sport of basketball for Hoosiers everywhere.

Grace Waitman-Reed

Town and City Delights and Reflections

Bicknell

My brothers and I grew up in Bicknell, Indiana, a small town in Knox County where, on sultry summer evenings, front porches served as living rooms and neighbors named Socks, Basil, Ott, GiGi, and Reva would sit and visit while the kids chased lightning bugs with Mason jars. In Bicknell, an ice-cold bottle of Nehi grape pop was liquid ambrosia and the Schwinn Stingray was at the top of the bicycle-riding food chain.

Though I do not recall nail-biting ghost stories or legendary tales originating from my hometown, I can honestly say it was as uniquely Indiana as one might hope to find. Imagine a town turning its Main Street over to countless children of all ages dressed as ghosts and goblins, hobos, witches, and superheroes (store-bought and homemade) for the annual Halloween parade. Or that same Main Street decorated in red and green ribbons and adorned with oversized ornaments and twinkling white lights for Christmas (in fact, if you think of your hometown every time you hear Andy Williams sing "Silver Bells," then you might just be from Bicknell). To this day the aroma of burning leaves takes me back through the ages to crisp autumn afternoons when I had the pleasure of helping my grandpa rake and pile leaves along the curb, only to have our wayward dog, Pooch, come bounding around the corner of the house to plow through them like a fur-covered freight train.

Uniquely Indiana? That would be small towns, those that dot the back roads and county highways of a state that defines what a small town should be, and in that sense there is no town more uniquely Indiana than Bicknell.

Brad Butrum

Bloomington

My Hoosier identity extends back through three generations, and I am happy to claim it despite misconceptions about our state. I am especially glad that it was in Bloomington where I spent my formative years. Born here in the '50s, I remained through my high school graduation, after which I made my way to college out in Santa Barbara, California (UCSB), sight unseen. By the beginning of my junior year I was back in Bloomington and enrolled at IU. What I had missed more than anything were the seasonal changes.

Upon receiving his PhD from UC Berkeley, Father got his initial teaching position at IU, where he remained on the faculty through his retirement and was awarded a distinguished professorship. It's rather rare to stay put at a single campus for the duration of a lengthy academic career.

My personal memories of life in Bloomington include going to the concrete atop the reservoir, just off 17th Street, to watch the fireworks on the Fourth of July and applying the yellow sulfur powder to ward off chiggers. A more regularly occurring pleasure came from evening trips with my dad to the experimental fields where he conducted some of his research. I had relatively free rein in the fenced-in expanse adjacent to the Hilltop garden center. Though I ran with abandon, I felt insulted when my dad informed me that as a girl I should soon start keeping my blouse buttoned, even on the hot and humid summer evenings. Mind you, I was only seven or eight, so this was an early introduction to gender-based restrictions or my first real awareness thereof.

I participated in Hilltop's summer gardening program for kids. Each garden plot, where we grew a variety of vegetables and a few flowers, was usually shared by two youngsters. I was so pleased the morning I arrived to find our shared garden rewarded with a blue star. This lasted for several weeks, only to be replaced by a red circle, much to our dismay. These were large wooden constructions mounted on a pole for all to see, indicating a well-tended garden or a breach of expected conduct. Our red circle was for leaving a tool in the garden and not returning it to its proper location at the end of our morning of gardening.

Until I was six we rented an upstairs apartment in a house on South Fess Avenue across from what was recently the Elm Heights Bloomingfoods. In my youth it had been Ellis's Grocery, and the owner's home was the stone house that still stands next to the store. It was a full grocery with a refrigerated meat closet where the Ellis daughter of my same age took me one hot summer day to experience the immediate cooling effect. I was stunned by the big slabs of a quartered beef that hung next to us.

A few years later our immediate family enjoyed picnics in Cascades Park after our piano lessons. The park is a Bloomington treasure where you can enjoy nature barely 2 miles from the center of town. An old well that had likely been a public source of water in an earlier era remains preserved in this most peaceful of settings. Children, both chronologically and in spirit, still play in the cascading water.

No adolescence in southern Indiana would be complete without the somewhat forbidden swim in one of the quarries. Ivory soap was sometimes brought along if you wanted to come away clean, the benefit of that brand being that it would float so you would not lose it irretrievably.

Bryan Park ball diamonds were my first introduction to Little League baseball, but merely as a spectator. The outfield chatter carried a good distance, so the minute I stepped outside our house a short block away, I could always tell when the competition was getting serious. I frequented the concession stand and saved a few baseball cards that came in a pack of gum. If I got an especially good one, one of the boys more knowledgeable than myself about what constituted a prize card would offer me several cards in exchange for the one. It seemed at the time like a good enough deal. Needless to say, I was never a serious collector. Another sporting event that we started to attend at an early age was the Little 500 bike race. Back then it was held in a stadium located where the arboretum now stands. During a concert in that stadium years later, a rainbow broke through the rain as Richie Havens performed "Here Comes the Sun." Outdoor summer operas were performed there with spectacular sets designed by Cesare M. Cristini. I had the opportunity as a high schooler to assist the lighting crew for the production of *Carmen*.

During the winter months, the Juke Box on Washington and Smith was the spot for teens to congregate for music, dance, and socializing. Now known as the Allison-Jukebox Community Center, it offered recreational classes to the public when not scheduled for teen events or sock hops. Just down the block on Smith at Walnut, in what is now called the Chocolate Moose, was an ice cream and sandwich shop, which opened as the Penguin in 1950—a favorite both then and now for a wide selection of ice cream–based treats. In our high school years it was rivaled by the A&W once we had our drivers' licenses and access to cars to cruise through their drive-in at 10th and College.

More recently there are a plethora of activities in which I've participated from both sides of the aisle, as an artist or a spectator or staffing a table, such as at the Fourth Street Festival of the Arts and Fine Crafts. The more recent GarlicFEST provides a welcome complement in the art, craft, and entertainment arena. Lotus World Music and Arts Festival has been one of many activities in which so many folks, both town and gown, take an active role. Many former friends and acquaintances gravitate back to town during Lotus. Not only is it one of the best opportunities to reunite with friends, old and new, but the vast array of musical performances is sure to offer something pleasing to a wide variety of tastes. The recent Bloomington Boogies festival created by Craig Brenner is sure to take on a similar annual role, even if on a somewhat smaller scale. The B'Town Jazz Fest moved just this year from Grant Street to a more comfortable and inviting space on the courthouse lawn. The inner part of the Square, as it is referred to colloquially, is the site of many other uniquely Hoosier activities that include the tasty strawberry shortcake offered during the annual Boys & Girls Clubs of Bloomington fundraiser.

These are just a few of the attractions in Bloomington that I choose to highlight. I maintain a heartfelt fondness for our little "sea of blue" in south central Indiana.

Cynthia Roberts

The most Bloomington thing I ever did was to leave Bloomington. Bloomington, Indiana; Population: 80,405, about half of which are Indiana University students. There are three annual folk arts festivals, a Tibetan restaurant, and one gay club in a pear tree. It is the top destination in southern Indiana to run away to if you have artistic tendencies, experience the overwhelming desire to grow organic vegetables, or don't fit neatly into whatever box was picked out for you at birth. All of this marks B-town as an Official Den of Sin, which was shouted at me by an earnest preacher and his van of followers as I walked to my high school job at the public library. They weren't protesting anything in particular, just the town's existence. If Indiana is the crossroads of America, my hometown of Bloomington is the wayward roadhouse tavern.

My own parents were internal Hoosier immigrants: musicians looking for that sweet spot of cheap rent, an arts scene, and a place within an hour's drive of an airport for touring purposes. A lot of events led to the decision to relocate to Bloomington, but I think they can be summed up by that time a man with a megaphone called my mother the Whore of Babylon while she strummed her guitar at a peace rally.

When we arrived in Bloomington, my mother sighed audibly with relief. "There are so many musicians here," she said in a voice full of awe, not dissimilar to the way I like to imagine my great-grandparents stepping off the boat from Italy and saying, "There are so many jobs here. And so little grape-plague. Let's stay here forever and raise opinionated babies."

Like so many second-generation immigrants I spent my childhood and adolescence listening to an endless narrative of how lucky I was to grow up in such a land of opportunity. I wasn't going to struggle like my parents. I would have free-range eggs, Green Party mayoral candidates, and flute lessons, and no one would call me the Whore of Babylon unless it was a consensual relationship where I was into that sort of thing.

My friends, most of whom were similar second-generation and third-generation Bloomingtonians, grew up with the same story. There were Deborah and Mona: their parents met at Oberlin, their dad came to Bloomington for the arts scene and set up shop as a professional hammer dulcimer player, and their mother was a doctor at the only Planned Parenthood in south central Indiana. There was Helen, whose parents were humanities professors employed by the University (in Bloomington,

Indiana University is simply "the University"). And there was Isaac: his devout lefty Lutheran parents met as art students at Valparaiso University; his mother was now a weaver and yarn shop owner and his father was a ceramist and public school art teacher. Our folks signed us up for theater camp and music lessons while they recorded albums and got doctorates and lobbied against I-69 coming to Bloomington and against the military going anywhere.

"My parents love this town," Helen explained. She had been born in Philadelphia. "They think it's so small and safe compared to the big city. But it still has opera and stuff." She was known mostly as "Professor Wood's daughter," similar to way Mona and Deborah and Isaac and I were identified by our parents' occupations. Our parents' magnificent dreams buoyed us and washed over us in turn.

Helen and I spent long hours at her house, which was covered in Turkish rugs from her parents' ethnographic field studies, playing with her dollhouse and running lines from our summer theater camp play, making up elaborate inside jokes the way you do when you pass a whole summer together. Sleep-deprived folklore and art history students wandered through her living room, the way sleep-deprived musicians wandered through mine; it was perfectly normal to Helen and me, and we were perfectly aware that this was not normal to other people outside of our small, hilly town. Our mutual combination of weirdness and conventionality was such a shared understanding that we never spoke of it.

This new world was good to our parents; Helen's dad got tenure and my parents began to find regional notoriety, which is not as lucrative as fame, but it helps pay the bills. Our folks joined fundraising boards, and opened co-ops, and had huge potluck parties for the Fourth of July and the summer solstice and for no reason other than that they wanted to see their friends. Helen and Isaac and Mona and Deborah and I ate sweet corn and tomatoes from our parents' gardens and spat out watermelon seeds as our parents argued about politics and sang folk songs under the stars, accompanied by cicadas and frogs screaming for sex in the humid August nights.

Our parents grew a community the way they grew their organic gardens, planting pieces of it carefully, unsure of what the harvest would be in the end. It wasn't without effort, but the soil was fertile and there were enough people committed to the work that they wound up with a bumper crop of odd-looking friends.

But nestled in this garden, my dissatisfaction began to grow. Like squash-blossom rot, it appeared without warning on an otherwise glorious day and produced blank confusion, followed by blame and increasingly ridiculous attempts at a solution.

On the outside, I was a good Bloomington girl. I played flute in the school band, sang second soprano in the University's children's choir, worked at the public library as a circulation page, volunteered for the Bloomington Teen Council and our Quaker meeting, got almost straight As, acted in civic theatre, ran for thirty minutes up and down hills every other day, and worried about the Balkans and PCBs and Planned Parenthood's funding being cut. I was overcommitted, but everyone around me was overcommitted. You don't make it as a working artist or academic if you're not overcommitted. I was blossoming, people told me. I was blossoming in this beautiful town and wasn't I lucky to have so many opportunities to play and volunteer and study and work and worry.

So I tried to blossom; I tried to be the passionate uncaged genius everyone else was, but I felt like a failure all of the time and I didn't know why and it scared me because no one else had this problem. If I sang, it was off-key; if I wrote a paper, someone else wrote a better one; at the library everyone else shelved books faster and didn't get lost in anxious speculation. Everything I did felt wrong, and I didn't know how to make it right. There was a tightness growing in my chest, like a briar patch, crawling up my throat, digging its sharp thorns in my brain.

I turned sixteen and got my driver's license, and after work and volunteer shifts and rehearsals I took long drives through the twisty country roads around Bloomington and stopped by Lake Griffy and sat and cried in the parking lot and wondered why I was crying, why I felt so helpless and trapped in my own skin. I doubled down on activities; volunteered more, studied harder, gathered up commitments like warding charms—it mostly didn't work. Instead of producing fruit like I was supposed to, I was rotting on the vine.

I longed viscerally to leave my life in southern Indiana. If I could leave, maybe I could start over again. I always loved buying new notebooks at the beginning of the school year, seeing all those unspoiled pages and thinking this year would be different. I would write neatly in these notebooks. I wouldn't smear the ink or pick at the metal spiral binding like a hangnail like last year's. I could start my life again, I would write neat and tidy sentences and my life would be neat and tidy and my feelings would be neat and tidy instead of these disturbing scrawls.

I tried to leave, but I failed at that too. I went to a tiny Quaker college about two hours away, but I came back every summer, much to my dismay. After graduation, I moved to Colorado for a decent job and doomed relationship and scurried back quickly when it became clear that the college boyfriend and I weren't going to work out. Afterward, I took a teaching job at a college in Mexico, but once again I found myself back in my hometown after a year.

As much as I wanted to leave, I was afraid to stray too far from the community I grew up in, where everyone knew me, shortcomings and all. Wherever I went, the sadness followed me—like my midwestern inflections—and I wondered, "What if the sadness overwhelms me and I'm among strangers? What would happen then?" And even worse. . . "What if there isn't anything better?"

All of the Bloomington transplants talked about what a strong community Bloomington was, and I had no reason to doubt them; it was evidenced from my parents' tight-knit circle and the fact that community was in the name of absolutely everything: Bloomington Community Garden, Bloomington Community Band, Bloomington Community Farmers' Market—I even interned at the Department of Community and Family Resources of the City of Bloomington. It was unusual to find such neighborliness, the transplants said, and nothing in my travels so far led me to think I could find anything like it.

Everyone around me was so relentlessly enthusiastic about Bloomington that my deep-down unhappiness was more evidence of how utterly messed up I was and how little point there was in leaving. Surely that many people couldn't be wrong. If I couldn't be happy in Bloomington, if I couldn't blossom in a town that was named after goddamn flowers, then maybe I couldn't be happy anywhere.

What do you do when you want to run away, but you already live in the town everyone else runs away to?

If you live in the Midwest, you go to Chicago.

Officially, my new boyfriend and I moved to Chicago because the University of Chicago offered me money for grad school and he was done with his coursework and could write his dissertation anywhere.

Unofficially, Indiana University had also accepted me into a doctoral program, and when I got the letter, my stomach seized up and my heart sank, which was deeply ungrateful of me and not what is supposed to happen when you get into grad school.

Unofficially, I had decided that even if I was meant to be miserable, I could at least be miserable with a scenery change.

Unofficially, Chicago was still close enough to home that I could retreat back to Bloomington if I really was incapable of being happy and things got too bad. I didn't know exactly what "too bad" looked like, but I didn't want to find out.

So the boyfriend and I moved, just as the economy began to collapse with all the grace of an arthritic elephant. I learned how to use the public transit system and what to look for in a real winter coat and met more improv actors than I knew existed. I got my master's degree and bedbugs and bicycled up and down the Lakefront path, marveling at the Art Deco buildings and fighting off lakeside geese that came after my bike with murder in their eyes.

In Chicago, it didn't matter where in Indiana I was from; being a Hoosier was always a punchline.

"Where are you from?" the improv actors would ask me at parties.

"Indiana," I'd say.

They would laugh, knowingly. "Yeah, I'm from Kentucky, had to get out before I got pregnant, you know?"

Or "I got you, I grew up in Minnesota—the only theater was Lutheran Christmas pageants."

Or just a pained "Iowa."

"Well," I would respond, "Sort of. I'm from Bloomington." I say it with the same self-deprecating manner you say, "I'm from Paris."

"Where?"

I'd try to explain my where I'm from, to make vague noises about Dr. Kinsey and musicians and bicycle races and they would nod, humoring me, counting down the seconds until they could tell me about their upcoming show.

The more I tried to explain Bloomington, the more I saw it from the outside, the more I started to see all of its flaws for the first time: the hypocrisy of our union-busting co-op; the way adults turned a blind eye to the bullying of gay kids at my high school; the constant, smug comparisons to Martinsville—a town about half an hour north of us that was a Ku Klux Klan stronghold in the 1920s and sundown town long afterward—comparisons that came at the expense of honest conversations about racism in our own community. It wouldn't have been so bad if we were another small town in Indiana, but we were Bloomington. We were supposed to be better. I became disdainful of Bloomington in the way you can only be disdainful of your hometown because Bloomington's failings were indicative of my own.

I would like to say that taking a more objective look at my hometown is what helped me learn to better navigate the deep down hopelessness, but that's only half-true. It is true that losing my blind faith in Bloomington helped to regain some faith in myself. The problem, I realized reluctantly, wasn't that Bloomington was paradise and I was unfit for it, nor a hell that I narrowly escaped—the problem was that we were both imperfect and I needed to find a way to sit with that truth and not drown in it.

But it is also true that I wasn't happy right away. I couldn't start over in the way I dreamed of; I was still me in the end. There would be no new notebook, but I did feel like I had a room of my own to write in, like Virginia Woolf used to say. In the Windy City I had anonymity for the first time, and no one to distract me from myself or tell me who I was. No one told me to blossom in Chicago; most people just bundled up in heavy coats and tried not to kill themselves in February, and that was accomplishment enough. Long dark winters are not great for depression, and neither is underemployment, but they do force self-reckoning. And between the revelations, and the space, and the anonymity, and a sliding-scale therapist I did slowly begin to extricate myself from the deep pool I used to live in. I never quite swam to shore; nowadays I mostly paddle in a canoe on the pool, accompanied by a few friends that sit in the boat with me. But that's enough.

The first time I went back to Bloomington, I was amazed at how small it was. I could walk the length of the downtown in ten minutes. I could sit at the Laughing Planet Café and at least three people I knew would stop to talk to me, every single time. It used to feel so big, so all-surrounding and all-knowing, but it really was just a largish town in the end; just a pretty, flawed, college town in southern Indiana.

My mother once told me, "People always want to move to their vacation spot. But when they do, they're always disappointed."

"Why's that?" I asked.

"Because it's not the place they crave, it's the state of mind."

Bloomington is a place, but it is also a state of mind. The runaways who come there long for a break with what they've known. They long for a community, they long for freedom, they long for a life full of passion, or at least contentment. Whatever their dream is, the runaways want it so badly that when a hint of it appears, they hold it carefully, breathing on it like embers. And they teach their children, in the clumsy, indirect way that we all teach our children, to look for what they want and to believe that they can find it if they are willing break with everything they know and to go someplace new.

I never really left Bloomington—I just went looking for it.

Amelia Aldred

Brownsville

Several branches of my family tree extend from the tiny Union County town of Brownsville, which sits on the Whitewater River. My grandmother Jobe died in 1968, but I well remember various stories she told about area history, mostly handed down to her from her mother, Sally Ann.

Sally Ann told her that when she was a girl, "the Indians came around and stood there until we gave them cucumbers from our garden." Fearing I would be considered a fool for inquiring, I asked a college Indiana history professor if this could possibly be true. He thoughtfully asked me about the location—was it a river town? And what was the year? When I told him the town sat right on the river and the year was the 1840s or so, he said that indeed, it could be true.

Grandma told me other stories: about the town's covered bridge that serviced locals from the 1840s to 1974, about how Brownsville had more than one saloon and a hotel, and about the time much of the tiny village caught fire.

But the story I loved the most concerned Sally Ann once again. It was one line, but with that line, my imagination ran wild. The one line was this: Sally Ann got up in the night to watch the Lincoln Funeral Train pass through.

That was it. No other details. For years during my childhood, I thought about those tracks and imagined this great-grandmother long gone, a young woman in her twenties at the time, viewing the Lincoln Funeral Train as it passed east to west through our little village.

As a young woman in my early twenties, I was crushed to learn that the truth was that funeral train never passed through Brownsville. I tempered my disappointment over the legend with a consolation prize: She probably watched trains of that period draped in mourning cloth, and while it wasn't the funeral train itself, she probably saw some kind of memorable train pass through that very night. But it wasn't the Lincoln train.

Or was it?

Decades passed and a few years ago, in my job as a newspaper reporter in New Castle, I was asked to interview a man from

Knightstown who was writing a book about the Lincoln Funeral Train. He told me that the train passed east to west along the National Road, now called US 40, and people came from miles and miles in the night, carrying lanterns, on horseback, and in carriages, to watch that train pass carrying the slain president.

I wanted to scream with happiness! He unknowingly had just confirmed the truth of this century-and-a-half-old family legend.

Since the National Road is about 10 or so miles north of Brownsville, it is highly likely that Sally Ann DID see the Lincoln Funeral Train pass. She DID get up in the night and go there. She may well have even seen the casket, as I understand the train stopped along the route and people could look in and see it.

I have asked people if they have this legend handed down in their families and have yet to find anyone with a similar story. I am grateful for a grandmother who listened and reported her mother's stories to her only granddaughter. As a newspaper reporter, editor, and novelist myself, I collect stories like some people do cups and saucers or books.

I am delighted to feel at peace with this long-ago family legend and realize that the mistake, all along, was mine. I assumed that the train tracks were in Brownsville. I mistakenly filled in a detail that didn't belong.

I am amazed that I was in a position to learn the truth. And to find a new link with a slain president and a great-grandmother, a central-Indiana link that I will always cherish.

Donna Cronk

Coal City

Life was pretty calm and peaceful most of the time in Coal City, Indiana. Everyone knew everyone's business and was ready to help if help was needed. It was easy to keep up because there were only five streets and maybe 300 people.

Extended families were very important. Most Sundays after church were get-togethers at Grandma Selma Dayhuff and Grandpa William Henry Harrison Hauser's farm with my mother's seven brothers and sisters. The fifteen cousins loved playing baseball and hide-and-seek in the barn. The food was excellent, and there was a lot of it. Grandma cooked most of the food on a wood-burning stove in the summer kitchen. On the side was a holding tank for warm water, which was always available. Water came from a cistern well close to the back door between the summer kitchen and main house. When the cistern ran dry (it was fed from rainwater) water had to be carried from a spring up a long hill behind the house.

My other grandma, Maude Van Horn (my father's mother), and I were very close. She had six sons and no daughter; therefore, she had a soft spot for a little girl like me. We lived up the hill from Grandma Maude and Grandpa James Madison Inman's house. As soon as I was big enough I'd go down the hill by myself to spend time with Grandma. She knitted doll booties for my dolls, and I kept them until they fell apart.

On warm summer nights there were free shows downtown. We took blankets and watched movies with stars such as Roy Rogers, Abbot and Costello, Our Gang, Hopalong Cassidy, Gene Autry, and Tarzan. The movies were shown on a makeshift screen—a tarp stretched between Daddy's barbershop and Mr. Welsher's hardware store. Sometimes the Busy Bee Home Ec Club, of which my mother was a member, sold popcorn. During the show many men went to the barbershop to get a haircut or a shoe shine, to swap jokes, or just to catch up on the latest gossip. Some of the women did their weekly grocery shopping at this time. After the movie some of the kids went to the drug store for cherry Cokes and ice cream. There was a croquet court by the garage, and some of the men played during and after the movie.

Another summer activity was 4-H Club, and Mother was our club leader. Finishing projects and exhibiting at the fair in the county seat of Spencer was fun. Winning ribbons and sending exhibits to the state fair was the culmination of many hours of hard work.

During fall, winter, and spring, the Coal City School (grades 1 through 12) was the hub of community life. All the community was involved whether they had children in school or not. Basketball was the most important activity in the fall and winter, and the school gym was standing room only for all home games (reminding me of the movie *Hoosiers*). In spring it was softball, baseball, and track. We had junior and senior class plays, class night when all classes performed skits, music programs, sock hops, and box suppers.

The box suppers were fun. The girls and ladies fixed a box of food for two and decorated the boxes. Men and boys bid on the boxes in order to win an opportunity to share the boxed supper with the lady or girl who prepared it. We tried to let our guys know which was ours so we could eat with them. Sometimes it worked and sometimes it didn't! The money raised went to the PTA to buy things for the school.

We didn't have a cafeteria so we all took our lunches to school, except on special days when the Farm Bureau, PTA, Home Ec Club, or home ec class would cook for us to make money. We loved these days with sloppy joes, hot dogs, chili soup, and the like.

During the '40s and '50s there were many businesses in Coal City. There were three grocery stores, a hotel, a school, a hardware store, a drug store, a barbershop, two gas stations, two restaurants, a post office, a train depot, four churches, and others. After the high school closed in 1965 many of the businesses also closed. Sadly, now there are only the post office, one restaurant, four churches, and the volunteer fire department remaining.

Growing up in a small town in the 1940s and '50s was very special. Money was at a minimum for many families, as it was with mine. With five kids it was very difficult at times for my parents. We always had enough to eat, but maybe not what we wanted. My mother wore the same winter coat for fifteen-plus years in order to save money. I wouldn't trade my growing-up days now, but back then there were times when I wanted to trade with some of my friends who had more—like an indoor bathroom and a car fit to drive!

I left Coal City in 1958, after graduation from high school, to attend Indiana State Teachers College (now Indiana State University). I became an elementary school teacher and counselor. My siblings also attended college and became teachers. With the role models of some of our teachers (Miss Morris, Mr. Sandburg, Miss Ley, Mr. Fulford, and others) we learned that hard work and passion pay off. The small rural school has left us with wonderful memories of the 1940s and '50s.

Judy Inman Foltz Bullock

Evansville

I hate red.

And yet for fourteen years of my life it was the rule, the color of my school pride—red and black Hornets. Crimson and cream Hoosiers. Even my mother's hometown, Tell City, felt like my own, and I was just as comfortable in its Marksmen's red and white as in my own Bulldogs' scarlet and grey. Washington Middle School, a brick beauty just blocks from the brick beauty that was my high school, offered the only reprieve from red I will likely ever have.

I hate red, but blue makes me sick. In Bloomington—a town like Tell City, carved out of hills and forests and emptied quarries—at least blue is safely guaranteed to stand for pro football. But there is no such safety in my hometown of Evansville. It lies right on the river across from Kentucky; the college merchandise in big-box stores in Evansville is all blue, rather than the red it is supposed to be in a self-respecting Indiana city. No, no—black and yellow are also taboo. (Or at least, the highest and most offensive form of gag gift-giving.)

While Evansville's private university (purple and white) defines the city, IU defines the state. In my first semester there, a paleopathologist told her class that around the time of the school's inception there was a major outbreak of malaria—so IU was moved from its intended home in Evansville inland to Bloomington. Maybe this is why some truckers don't even know there's an Evansville in Indiana, despite its being the third largest city in the state.

As a big city without big city fame, Evansville is somewhat confused in its identity. Its drivers seem to think they are in Chicago, aggressive in their every-man-for-himself mentality. But there are few Chicagoans who wouldn't flinch at street names like Weinbach, Burkhardt, or Boeke. They wouldn't know that Lincoln is north of Washington, while Adams and Madison are south of it. They wouldn't just accept that the expressway has traffic lights.

It's a large enough city than you can pick from its culture as you will. Five public high schools offered little of the community cohesion inherent in single-school towns. As a child I knew the story of the Grey Lady of Willard Library, but always as another person's folklore, not my own urban legend. Few of my peers knew the natural history museum, but it was instrumental in determining my own path; the museum's diorama of a nineteenth-century Midwest homestead and the tiny Chinese silk slippers for bound feet sparked my lifelong affair with history and other cultures. I spent a few summers as a preteen at the YWCA just blocks from the riverfront, and we'd walk to the (red-roofed) Pagoda Visitors Center or to the park across the street from it, or to the old home of Central Library, a spectacularly historic building with odd levels and creaky staircases. Its new location is beautifully modern, but far less charming.

Evansville is the River City, and in my eyes it lived and died by the Ohio. The riverboat casino brought in revenue and visitors, as did the summertime Riverfest (now ShrinersFest) and its flagship events, the hydroplane boat race and air show (now only an air show), culminating in fireworks on the Ohio for Independence Day. Parking downtown is always a nightmare—even more so for this week in midsummer—but the festival is worth it. I remember one evening in particular, sitting under the riverfront in a light rain, as ash and grit crunched between my teeth, a half hour of popular country and patriotic classical themes the sonic backdrop to the bombast of explosions, full of color.

And oh, the Fall Festival, perhaps Evansville's primary claim to fame, widely believed to be nearly the largest street festival in the country, behind only Mardi Gras in New Orleans. Whether or not this is true, it is community spectacle at its best, shutting down huge swaths of local-commercial West Franklin in favor of traditional festival fare and food truck delicacies I would never touch (brain sandwiches and crickets in suckers, for example). Bosse Band's Jamaican jerk chicken, served in a white paper cup with toothpicks for utensils, is an absolute must.

I now consider myself a native of both city and state, with one parent each made of Evansville purple and Indiana red. My father attended the University of Evansville and still did his banking at the Old National bordering campus when I was a child. I loved going in with him to get my cream soda sucker and to stare at the huge, vaguely impressionistic mural across from the tellers' stations. And living in IU's X-shaped Read dorm was like returning to my ancestral home, the home where decades prior my mother placed her hand on the painted lines of the maze-like basement walls, where we followed the right colors back to the right wings.

I never even saw Bloomington until my senior year of high school. But entering Assembly Hall for the first time, I felt déjà vu and nostalgia at once, because like so many of us, I grew up watching Hoosier basketball. As a child I wore little red cheerleading uniforms with little white turtlenecks, and I cheered for white jerseys without names stitched on the back, flashing across an unpainted yellow court, against the backdrop of a red audience—these are the colors of my oldest memories. I was startled to realize, as an adolescent, that the Indiana University trident was actually the letters I and U; since before I could read, before I can remember, it had just been a symbol that meant IU.

Evansville may be confused about its identity, but I know mine. I hate red, but it is the color of Indiana, and as the state that raised me, it defines me nonetheless.

Kristin Emge

* * *

In Evansville, the first full week of every October brings with it the Fall Festival, sponsored by the West Side Nut Club. With the dubious unofficial slogan "If you fry it, they will come," the festival is annually covered by television personality Mr. Food. Some also claim for it the reputation of being the nation's second-largest street festival, surpassed only by New Orleans's Mardi Gras Festival.

For other people, autumn may mean gorgeous leaves, Friday high-school football games, hayrides, bonfires, and the brisk chill undertones that nip at your face in the early evenings. But for natives of Eville, no fall could be complete without the annual festival that brings with it delicacies of the fried variety that become more exotic and quixotic with each passing year.

My husband and I were once vacationing in St. Lucia with friends who were also from Evansville. While on a tour sponsored by our resort, we discovered yet another couple also vacationing from Evansville. During the bus tour, our guide held a contest to find the person who had eaten the most exotic or unusual food item.

When everyone had reiterated their most unusual food, the three people who won were all from Evansville. Their exotic fare had arisen from the fruits of the Fall Festival: alligator, cow brains, and "icky lickys," or bugs encased in candied sugar.

However, this type of curious edible is not the only element that makes the festival so renowned and acclaimed. The rides that fill one large and two small parks should be attempted only prior to any fried food consumption: however, even the most fearless daredevils will find some attraction that will fulfill their desire for adrenaline junkie-ism. In high school, two friends and I ended up on a terror titled the "Zipper." Little did we know that the car in which we were riding would flip a total of thirty-two times over the course of the four-minute ride. Needless to say, not much more fried food was consumed that night.

Equally important to the festival are the family-based events that take place every night, such as the local talent shows (acceptances based on prior week auditions), the Pet Parade, the Lighthouse Parade, and the big parade in the final weekend of the festival. A local king and queen are chosen, based on participants from each of the middle schools located on the West Side. In the final parade, local marching bands, cheering squads, dancing teams, and other types of organizations march or ride on a float down the entirety of Franklin Street.

Then there is the sense of tradition that envelops the entire festival. Booths stay in the same spot for decades, and their food offerings remain largely the same, with only a few variations presented from year to year (and those are primarily devoted to the quest of achieving the most exotic food item that year!). TKE fraternity from the University of Southern Indiana offers their strombolis; the best sausage burgers can be found at the Corpus Christi Catholic Church booth; Resurrection Church boasts the best chicken 'n' dumplings and pizza; the freshest cobbler is made by SWIRCA (Southwestern Indiana Regional Council on Aging), complete with a vanilla ice cream scoop; and the Nutty Bar booth across from the park has the same delectable dessert year after year after year. Although a new Munchie Map is published every successive year, the foods listed for each booth, the majority of which are for nonprofit organizations, seem to be almost exactly replicated from one year to the next. Clever West Siders have even produced a Munchie App, but tried and true Festival-ers know exactly where to find their favorite foods without the benefit of geographical guidance.

Finally, the people-watching at the festival is perhaps as entertaining as consuming the vast varieties of foods—or even more so. One of my friends swears he saw four generations of mullets, all eating corn dogs, one year. Other people wear the most interesting outfits or costumes, including a man dressed as a cow walking down the crowded street as though without a care.

A history of the festival published online reveals that the festival was first conceived of in 1921 by a group of businessmen on the West Side. The festival began as a Halloween night, gradually expanded through the addition of decorations and dances, and began featuring rides about twenty years into its existence. Although its occurrence was suspended for a few years during World War II, it returned even stronger than ever as the more modern attractions of the festival, such as its opportunities to serve as a fundraiser for nonprofit groups, began around the 1950s; the talent shows and other similar attractions were introduced in the years following.

Overall, the taste of apple cider just isn't the same unless you're consuming it in the crowded, noisy streets of the festival. Kind of like how a hot dog tastes different at a basketball game, apple cider has its own distinctive bite when you're drinking it in the midst of the second-biggest street festival in the United States.

Grace Waitman-Reed

* * *

Residents of southern Indiana were excited in the fall of 1991. Outside of basketball season, excitement isn't often the emotion tied to Hoosiers. Yet, just earlier that summer, Columbia Pictures had announced the shooting of a major motion picture in the small city of Evansville and its neighboring rural areas. The filming of *A League of Their Own* included major Hollywood stars like Tom Hanks, Geena Davis, and music superstar Madonna.

Columbia Pictures' decision to bring production of *A League of Their Own* to Evansville prompted multifaceted enthusiasm by Hoosier residents. Some younger kids just wanted to catch a glimpse of their musical Material Girl idol and perhaps reach far enough out for an autograph (the twentieth-century selfie).

The childish dreams of perhaps finding fifteen seconds of fame were not the only source of excitement for Evansville's citizens. Fully aware of the economic benefits of a three-month-long Hollywood production, local leaders and business officials warmly embraced outsiders into their communities. "They've dropped a lot of money here," television station general manager Skipp Simms explained. "They're renting a lot of homes and hotels, spending a lot in restaurants and night clubs and stores and the malls. These are largely California dollars being spent in Evansville, Indiana."

Evansville saw this as a win-win situation. With hardly any investment required from itself, the city reaped big financial rewards, and its citizens got a chance to see their community on the silver screen and possibly run into a few celebrities. After all, Columbia Pictures graciously promised Evansville the movie's premiere, sure to be a huge event in the city's history. Evansville and the surrounding communities worked hard at being on their best behavior in hopes of having Hollywood film crews return for more films. Hoosiers boasted of their unique hospitality that would surely bring about more movie crews.

For all intents and purposes, principal photography went on without a hitch in southern Indiana. Some celebrities found time to talk with the locals. Comedian Rosie O'Donnell explained how her "normal person" persona endeared her to local residents. "You get to be a millionaire and it's hard to identify with things like dry cleaning and what's on sale at The Limited," O'Donnell explained. Later media reports suggested Madonna stayed mostly to herself during her time in Evansville, though she sometimes ventured into the city. Paparazzi swooped in when rapper Vanilla Ice paid Madonna a visit during filming and the two saw a movie at a local theater, undoubtedly a thrilling experience for those same young fans who wanted an autograph. Radio stations invited Madonna on air, suggesting she was bound to get bored in their quiet community. "Hopefully she'll break down after all this boredom and call me on air," said WEHT sportscaster Alan Lee. Radio deejays over the Kentucky border in Owensboro invited the queen of pop and the movie's other stars over so they could show off their local cuisine "to give them a taste of the barbecue capital," 96 STO-FM's Cindy Mercer explained. Local bars held even celebrity look-alike contests. A movie crew in their backyard certainly added something new to regular life for most of these Hoosiers. Granted, some of the attention the outsiders got was downright creepy. Doug Burton, a construction worker from nearby Boonville, Indiana, spent $2,100 on an unwashed baseball uniform that an Evansville auctioneer suggested "still ha[d] the scent of a mega-star." That aside, it seemed the humble Hoosier community served as gracious hosts. Production wrapped up, the studio vans left town, and Evansville returned to normal.

Then, Madonna gave an interview to *TV Guide*. In the beginning of a November 1991 issue, Madonna blasted Evansville as a place "she will not be revisiting in this current lifetime." She felt like she was living in Prague, she said, in reference to former communist rule in isolated Eastern Europe. "For the first time in my life, I felt very disconnected," Madonna explained, especially since she could not get MTV in her hotel room. According to *TV Guide*, "she found herself reduced to watching regular TV . . . 'an oddly disturbing experience.'" Clearly, life in southern Indiana was not something she was accustomed to, which is ironic since the Material Girl was born and raised in northern neighboring Michigan, far from the glitz and glamour of Hollywood or New York.

In the end, Madonna's comments made up nothing more than a few paragraphs of a much larger, somewhat standard and boring celebrity interview. Evansville's residents, however, took her short comments to heart. The local Indiana press declared "Madonna Raps Evansville" and quickly interrogated the local cable companies about whether or not she was really that cut off from the vast wasteland of television. She did indeed have MTV. In fact, she had twenty-three out of the top twenty-five satellite-delivered cable services. After all, United Artists Cable of Evansville was not, in their words "a Podunk cable service," pushing back against Madonna's claims of Evansville isolationism.

Perhaps the most visible sign of this resentment of Madonna's remarks took place on a sunny December day in 1991, when residents converged onto Roberts Stadium in Evansville to participate in a "Human Madonna Billboard." A local radio disk jockey, Brian Jackson, called on residents to come out on a Saturday afternoon and make their anger known, beyond, of course, the vast numbers of irate letters to the editor. To his amazement, over 300 citizens showed up and laid down their bodies on the asphalt to pose for a helicopter photographer, all the while chanting "Get a life Madonna!" and "Madonna, get a real day job." Evansville parents arrived with their children as young as nine years, hoping to communicate that they had enough of child indoctrination. "She may have a big influence on kids," one mom explained while at the protest, "but it's the parents who buy her tapes, and when she gets the parents mad, she's in real trouble."

Some of this criticism seemed a little much, but Evansville's Hoosier distrust of outsiders before its encounter with Hollywood was in many ways confirmed. For example, that much-hyped premiere of *A League of Their Own* was changed to "the midwestern premiere," two days after a much larger premiere in Los Angeles. The Evansville premiere included no stars from the production. In reality, it served as just a large community viewing party, an excuse for the upper-class Evansvillians to pay fifty dollars a ticket, fancily dress up, and walk down a red carpet like superstars, if just once in their lifetimes. Betrayal? Perhaps, but they did not put up another fight. They were content with two worlds—one in Hollywood, and theirs between the cornfields. Hoosiers went about acting like everything was normal; they had their "Hollywood fling." To them, that was enough.

Eric Nolan Gonzaba

Fort Wayne

My grandfather, Charles F. Krudop, was born in Fort Wayne in 1866. As he grew up he was considered one of the "West End Boys."

This was during the time that the Wabash Canal was flourishing. As it went through town, it came to a place where it had to cross the St. Marys River near Swinney Park. To make the crossing, an aqueduct was built over the river. It was a magnificent structure. It was 204 feet long, with a flume 17½ feet wide and 6 feet deep. The floor was 6 feet thick in order to support the 500 tons of water flowing over it. It very much resembled the covered bridges for roads that still can be found in parts of Indiana.

It's noteworthy that the spot where the aqueduct was built was the highest elevation of the canal above Lake Erie; thus Fort Wayne's nickname: the Summit City.

Picture a cool, shaded, protected stream of slowly moving water and then pretend you are a young boy out on a hot summer day. You may be running an errand, or just hanging out. You spot one of your friends and he flashes you a sign: holding up his hand he gives a signal that people today would call a peace sign; but, oh, no, this was an invitation to join him for a quick dip in the aqueduct.

This was a favorite pastime for my grandfather and his brother, George. Of course, it was "illegal," but when would that stop some boys from having a great time? You had to keep a lookout for canal boats, and especially for Constable Kelly, who'd love to catch you, and oh, yeah, other boys who loved to play tricks on you. Their favorite was to take the clothes you had discarded on the banks of the river, soak them with water, and then tie them into almost impenetrable knots. Since getting the knots out entailed trying to pry them apart with your teeth, it reminded them of trying to eat some tough beef; so as the perpetrators took off, they would call, "Hey, Charlie! Chaw beef—chaw beef!"

Around 1912, some of the former West End Boys happened to meet up on a street corner and began discussing the good old days of their youth. They decided they should commemorate their experiences by forming a club. The Old Aqueduct Club was born, and for many years they would meet for an annual "swim." They collected funds and placed a monument at Orff Park, a small tract of land on Main Street near where the aqueduct stood. It features a statue of two young boys with the caption: "Let's Go Swimmin'." Plaques surround the monument with the names of the club members.

As the railroad industry began to flourish, the canal was no longer economically viable. Around 1881, the Pennsylvania Railroad bought the rights to the canal property. They laid the tracks along the old canal right-of-way and, after destroying the aqueduct by blowing it up and dropping it into the river, built a bridge for the trains, using the same foundations that supported the aqueduct. You can follow a pathway under the bridge and see the old foundations.

In the September 12, 1956, edition of the *News Sentinel* over the caption "Three Made It" is a picture of my grandfather, along with the other two of the eleven remaining members of the club who made it to the "swim." That was the last time the club met.

Ellen Krudop Buuck

How many electric light bulbs does it take to light up the Christmas spirit? For some of us it takes just one. Maybe that's the reason 24,717 colorful lights can get the greater Fort Wayne community up and running headlong into the Christmas spirit when the Wolf and Dessauer's Santa and reindeer display is energized on the PNC Bank building wall, casting a glow over old "Transfer Corner."

The story has been told of how some wonderful people, including G. Irving Latz, of the-no-longer-in-business Wolf and Dessauer department store, and Frank Dunigan, of the Brinkman Corporation, first hatched the idea; how Isabel Wilkerson Parker sketched out the concept; how Leslie Pope transferred it to its actual size; and how the employees at Brinkman produced the unique Christmas display. We've heard, too, the story of how the display was stored away and forgotten, gradually falling into a state of disrepair; how the IBEW 305 with the Ironworkers Local 147, combining their time and talents with the resources of Northeast Indiana Electrical Contractors Association and the Chamber of Commerce—along with untold numbers of interested businesses and citizens—refurbished the display, making it the reality we can enjoy in our day.

The intersection of Main and Calhoun Streets, where holiday crowds gather to watch the lighting of the Santa display, is a site that has long attracted people. For many years it was known as "Turntable Corner" and later "Transfer Corner" because a rotating track had been placed in the street to direct departing trolleys onto assigned outbound routes. Between the 1890s and the 1960s, this corner was where all the trolleys, and later buses, converged from a network of routes. As horse-drawn street trolleys rolling on rails gave way to the electrified trolley buses in 1892, it remained an energized place. During the 1890s, Marmaduke Marcellus Slattery, an inventor working for Jenney Electric Company, was experimenting with battery-powered trolleys. Although he was a forward-thinking fellow tinkering with a technology whose time was yet to come, his experience was a little like Noah's last dove, that sent from the ark full of energy, never came back from somewhere in the "out there." When Slattery sent his trial trolley out on a test run full of hope and vim, the battery drained of energy and the car failed to return.

True, many towns and cities have established favorite customs such as parades, festive window displays, church pageants, school plays, orchestral performances, and the like, but Fort Wayne has a long-treasured tradition that extends back to the days of the Wolf and Dessauer Department Store, when window displays drew holiday seekers and shoppers from miles around. Those nostalgic days for the older generation may be gone; however, they have been replaced by a symbol of the season that can light up the legacy of those exciting November and December animated store windows. Another of the remaining artifacts is the gigantic wreath, festooned with lights just like Santa Claus, placed nearby on the north side of Fort Wayne's signature high-rise building in November. But it's Santa Claus that gets the nod with his twinkling, blinking blue eye, officially opening Christmas season in the Three Rivers region and energizing the crowds of thousands in the streets below.

Best of all is watching the eyes of the children of all ages sparkle. Once Santa and his reindeer cast their radiance over the town, it sparks a veritable festival of Christmas trees, gingerbread houses, and model holiday villages, with music in the air all over town.

Tom Castaldi

Greenwood

When I was a little girl in the 1950s small town of Greenwood, the biggest celebration of the year was held right before Halloween. Just after dusk in late October all the children would gather in the parking lot of a downtown building. The street in front of us was closed to vehicles while the children marched north two blocks to the Community House. This building was built by wealthy residents early in the twentieth century. It held everything from the library to a kindergarten to a movie theater.

As the goblins and witches and ghosts reached the Community House they were separated by age. A few kids at a time in each age group walked out on the stage of the theater, blinking as the stage lights blinded them. If you were lucky enough to be chosen in each age group as having the winning costume you were handed a shiny silver dollar. My mother made many adorable homemade costumes over the years, but the closest I ever came to winning was when I was older and I pulled together a hobo costume out of old clothes, the ragbag, and a giant cigar that my uncle had picked up somewhere. I was chosen for the final round, only to lose to another child. No one went home sad, however, as we were all given a small bag of candy and returned home to await October 31.

Greenwood was a perfect place to grow up.

Jo Ellen (Jennings) Villines

Huntington

To this day, whenever I tell anyone my hometown is Huntington, I get the response: "Oh yeah, that's where Dan Quayle is from, right?" Inevitably, that's always said with a big grin and a comment about how former vice president Quayle couldn't spell the word "potato" correctly.

If it's a fellow Hoosier with whom I'm speaking, I always ask, "Have you heard there's a Dan Quayle Museum? It's now the Quayle Vice-Presidential Learning Center, devoted to information about vice presidents in general." I'll then mention that I was present at Quayle's very high-profile visit to Huntington, early in my youth.

If I'm speaking with someone who's not a Hoosier, I make a point of talking about the other things for which Huntington is well known, such as the delicious breaded tenderloin sandwiches at Nick's Kitchen, or the wonderful down-home atmosphere of Johnny's Restaurant at breakfast time. After all, it's not all about Quayle.

Angela Eck

Indianapolis

It was 1905 in Indianapolis. The outset of the twentieth century brought many stories of change and growth to cities around the country. One such tale is about a historic new restaurant that opened just three years earlier. What was to be known as St. Elmo Steak House became an eatery that drew salesmen to it from around the country. This restaurant, located less than 500 yards from the Union Station Depot in the heart of the Warehouse District, provided the perfect meal to salesmen traveling long distances by rail to the capital of Indiana.

Salesmen literally would exit the train station and walk across the street to find the Warren Hotel (today known as Le Méridien—formerly known as the Canterbury). Once registered, the traveler found himself steps away from St. Elmo's. For a weary traveler, the restaurant offered a well-aged steak dinner together with what would be later known as its signature appetizer—shrimp cocktail. The restaurant was then and remains today a highly sought after restaurant in the capital city.

On the local scene at that time was an Indianapolis businessman, J. V. Stout, who began to visit the steakhouse on Friday evenings after his one-of-a-kind family laundry closed for the week. Progress Laundry, as it was known, was located on Market Street near New Jersey and just north of Washington Street. The consumer laundry, unique to the city at the time, provided families a cleaning service that offered an alternative to cleaning it yourself.

It was during a visit in 1905 to the restaurant that Stout, sitting at the end of St. Elmo's bar (that very bar is still in existence today) met a dapper gentleman with whom he would forge a solid, if periodic, friendship. Mr. Stout noticed that his friend wore a neatly pressed three-piece suit and sported tiny round glasses. The two would banter back and forth about current-day topics when Stout's friend was not engaged in writing while at the bar. Little did Stout know that those writings would become known to us all in the gifted poems and other pieces the author would later publish.

The friendship grew, and Mr. Stout frequently took his friend home via his horse and carriage after their meal and spirits at St. Elmo's. He did it so often that the horse that was part of Stout's carriage did not need prodding to find its way to the gentleman's house in Lockerbie Square a little over a mile away.

Now, this story might seem to the reader bland and not very interesting. This is true unless the owner of the Progress Laundry, J. V. Stout, happened to be your grandfather—my grandfather. More important, the well-dressed friend of Mr. Stout's wasn't just anyone. The resident of Lockerbie Square was none other than James Whitcomb Riley, the famous poet. Friendships grow from everywhere, and if you're lucky, you find one with a famous background.

Fast forward to 2013. The writer is in St. Elmo's and is visited by Craig Huse, the current owner, together with his father, Stephen. It was at that time I took Craig over to the bar area to point out the very seats where J. V. Stout and James Whitcomb Riley would reside on those Friday nights during the very early years of the restaurant's existence. For a restaurant steeped in history, tradition, and a rich cast of famous visitors and conventioneers, it was another story that the Huse family can bring to the table about their iconic restaurant.

Robert E. Desautels

✳ ✳ ✳

Broad Ripple High School in Indianapolis, circa 1961–1965, was like most high schools then and now, so an extensive exposition of the social class structure is not necessary. There were the jocks, the nerds, and the overlappers, who seemed to effortlessly glide between the two groups and were usually also the class officers. Then there was, in our minds anyway, the class of dudes and dudettes who seemed to care less about fitting in, and by that very trait established their own counterculture. That culture seemed to be one of rebellion, indifference, and threat, both perceived and expressed, affecting even the most together of the social elite. Finally there was the faceless mass that comprised the rest of us, all just trying to figure out how we fit in and desperately hoping that the right connections would move us up into that rarified air of recognized high school personalities. Fifty years later, I admit we were unknown to most others in a high school of 2,000 insecure teens, but we had a group of friends that made us feel socially superior to other castes, categorized by our own rating system, who themselves felt superior to still others.

My friends' loosely formed car club included my '48 Plymouth, Gary Sims's 1950 Chevy (won for a dollar in a raffle at the high school during lunchtime and worthy of its own story), Steve

Wood's 1955 Chevy, and, the class of the club, Dan Straney's 1956 Chevy. That is, Straney's Chevy was the class of the club until Larry Mills had full access to his dad's 1962 Corvair Monza Spider or 1963 Ford Falcon Futura. We took turns going out in each other's cars. The choice was sometimes based on where we thought we'd cruise or end up and partially on who had gas in their tank. (After all, at twenty-six cents per gallon, no one of us could afford to be "the ride" all the time.)

Generally, our evening was "cruising" through the parking lots of Steak 'n Shake, Dog 'n Suds, Knobby's, Frisch's Big Boy, A&W, Merrill's High Decker, and the Tee Pee, all northeast Indy hot-spot drive-ins. The former four were more or less equal in nightlife and activity. A&W was more or less out of our league except for a brief pass through, just to say we did it. Of the drive-ins, A&W's draw was more for the hardcore car clubbers with seriously sweet rides. Only the finest of rides parked for a root beer at A&W.

On the other hand, Merrill's High Decker was the coolest, mostly because Dick Summers and later Jim Shelton of WIBC Radio broadcast from a glass-booth studio on the roof (thus the "High Decker") each evening. We backed into our parking stalls around the lot where he could see us; we could hear him on our car radios. He'd play the Top 40 record hits, and an audience participation activity each night was "Make it or Break it" (MI or BI). After talking to other guys in other towns later in college and adult life, I think every city had a variation of the show, but Jim Shelton at 1070 AM, WIBC, had it for Indy.

In MI or BI he would play a couple of new 45 hits, and after each song you turned your headlights on as he instructed. All who thought the song would "Make it"—lights on. Then all who thought he should "Break it"—lights on. By popular vote, each song either would go into his playlist or would be smashed with a hammer on air, to the delight of all tuned in that night.

An evening at Merrill's High Decker was magical, whether with a date or just your buds. It was also expensive. You had to order food and drink from the roving car hops to keep your place, and there was a minimum purchase, so Merrill's on 38th Street was a highlight, not a nightly routine.

A cruise of all of the drive-ins would probably connect us with carloads of guys we knew and girls we'd like to, and there was no better place for that than the Tee Pee. Many a car chase through the streets and neighborhoods of the northeast side started after a few loops around the Tee Pee drive-in lot, until a carload of girls pulled out, stopping in front of us and begging to be chased. And off we went—usually up Fall Creek Parkway and north on Keystone, past Glendale Mall, when they would suddenly turn into one of the many subdivisions east of the boulevard. Sad to say, since they knew where they were going and we didn't, they always lost us eventually. Probably a good thing. Not sure we knew what we'd do if we caught them.

Those were good nights, and there were a lot of them. But then there was the night Rodney and Steve Johnson entered our "cruise world"; for a time, they became a greater threat to our peace and security than the Red Menace with the atomic bomb or facial acne with its own explosions.

It was a hot summer night, and a serious ride was in order. I cannot remember why there were only three of us, but Straney showed up with another friend, Steve Burns, driving his mom's 1958 Mercury station wagon. A family car like that was not our first choice for "cruising," and we were certainly not going to be seen at the Tee Pee in it, doubting that any carloads of females would give us a second look for a car chase. But since my Plymouth was running on fumes and Straney's had a flat, we "lowered" ourselves to ride in Burns's. You know, "any port in a storm."

Since Burns didn't have his own wheels and seldom got the family car, he was fine with driving, and loved showing how the 409 cubic-inch Mercury engine had some guts. Since he was driving, with the lone instruction of "no Tee Pee," he could call the rest of the route. Things went fine until we cruised through A&W on Keystone.

As I said, we usually made the A&W drag quickly and without a lot of fanfare. We didn't belong, but if we didn't hang long, we weren't hassled. The night in question was one when we drew attention to ourselves and almost didn't live to tell about it.

Actually it was Burns's fault. I guess, looking back, I can't blame him. He didn't usually drive. He didn't realize the defined pecking order of cruising that put high school geeks with family cars low on the cruise chain. But couldn't even Burns see that his mom's station wagon was obviously beneath the candy apple red 1957 Chevy Impala, tuck and rolled interior, lake pipes and 327 V-8 engine, belonging to Rodney Johnson? You'd think so, but Burns was an idiot. THAT would become abundantly clear on this evening.

It began as we started our loop through A&W, avoiding the Tee Pee for reputation purposes and Merrill's High Decker for financial ones. This made the A&W the farthest south of the drive-ins, and our cruising "map" meant we'd go south to north, A&W, followed by Frisch's, then Dog 'n Suds and a U-turn through Steak 'n Shake and Knobby's, before heading back for a an exaggerated conversation of boasting, probably at my house where it all started.

One last bit of landmark information is necessary to set the stage for what was about to transpire. From the traffic light at Millersville Road, just north of the A&W driveway, to the traffic light at 46th was just about a quarter mile, and thus qualified as the unofficial National Hot Rod Association nonsanctioned location to establish bragging rights. In the early morning hours races became serious. Cross-town, inter- as well as intra-street club drag racing took place, and occasionally pink slips were even exchanged. And we were about to roll onto that track, albeit early.

As we left A&W, we turned right onto Keystone, into the right lane heading toward the traffic light at Millersville Road. As we pulled up to the then red light, Steve put the automatic transmission into neutral and revved the engine, showing us the power of the 409, made famous in the Beach Boys' tune. (I don't think their song was about a station wagon). Anyway, what Steve hadn't noticed was that Rodney Johnson with his brother, Steve, sitting at shot gun, both class hoodlums, had rolled out behind us, more or less oblivious to us as well, maybe planning on the same cruise route, certainly drawing more attention than we ever would in a wagon.

At the exact moment of Burns's demonstration of the Mercury's raw power, Rodney pulled up on our left, and was surprised to think anyone, let alone occupants of a Mom Squad car, would challenge his ride. Anyone in their right mind wouldn't challenge or even cross Rodney. He had been in juvenile hall often, almost to the point of it being his second home. Some thought he had his own reserved cell. He had dropped out of school at sixteen but still hung out, waiting for the close of school daily, to make sure all knew BRHS was still his turf. And he ruled Keystone as a drag strip.

Further, most in the know figured when Rodney went "up the river" for a long stint, brother Steve would assume his position and Johnson rule would remain. Tonight they traveled together.

Burns's ill-advised escalation of his mother's Mercury engine's RPMs took place around 7 PM, not the usual time to drop a flag. But either Rodney couldn't tell time or he just couldn't accept the idea of a high-school lowlife invading the cruise of his kingdom, no matter the time of day. For whatever reason, when Burns tached his engine up, Rodney, at his brother's urging, did the same. (If I hadn't been so scared, I probably would have heard any number of Beach Boys or Jan and Dean car songs running through my head.)

There was still time for us to do a mea culpa and slink away. "Good evening, Mr. Johnson. Didn't mean to do that, Rodney, sir. Have a nice evening." But, have I mentioned? Burns was an idiot. You see, when Rodney responded by flexing his own RPM muscle, Burns pushed his accelerator even farther to the floor.

As poor timing would have it, the traffic light that had been red turned green, and Burns did the only thing you should do at that point. He dropped his gearshift on the column into overdrive. That directed the RPMs of a revving engine automatically to the drive train and rear axle in order to leave the intersection—very quickly—and very loudly.

It was the perfect storm for a vehicle that was never to be driven so hard or aggressively, but that if it had a soul, would have longed to do so. The Mercury leaped forward, squealing its tires but flying off the line. In any other setting it would be Burns's finest automotive moment, but this setting included the Johnson brothers.

You see, Rodney was still in disbelief that any fool would call him out, much less in a "family car." This sense of disbelief meant that when crimson turned to green, he didn't even begin to rise up—immediately. So as Burns left the line, tires screeching, anyone observing the proceedings would have to say, "Burns left Rodney in the dust." It took Rodney only a brief moment to realize the potential embarrassment of astronomic proportion that was about to occur if his Chevy were beaten by a Mercury station wagon! In that brief moment he, too, was off.

He power shifted through the gears, but a quarter mile passes quickly, and we arrived at the light of 46th slightly ahead, before braking to a stop at its red light. (In the early morning contests, stopping at 46th Street, the finish line, wasn't necessary since accomplices idled their cars in the east–west lanes, allowing contestants to fly past without slowing, red or otherwise.)

As the Johnsons pulled up on our left, I urged we all stare straight ahead, suggesting we were merely airing out our car, seemingly unaware that we'd drawn the attention of the occupants of another set of wheels. It didn't work.

"Hey, Punk," Steve Johnson said very evenly and clearly. He said it several times, each time a little louder. "HEY, PUNK!"

"Don't look!" I whispered from the back seat. "Eyes forward." I didn't have to tell Straney more than once. We were both 6'5" on the outside, but on the inside we were Munchkins. We preferred to explain it by saying we were lovers not fighters, but we were actually similarly underskilled in both areas. Without further embarrassment, let's just say, we both knew we didn't like what potentially lay ahead.

Meanwhile, this was the course of the conversation for the full time we both sat at the light, an ever-heightening crescendo of, "Hey, Punk." "HEY, Punk!" "HEY PUNK!!" It seemed to be working. We were seemingly oblivious to Steve's calls and the Johnsons were becoming distracted by other cars cruising, some driven by girls who wanted the Johnsons to chase them. Maybe their short attention spans would work to our advantage. Maybe we'd get away because of their distraction toward a higher calling, a more basic and primal calling.

THEN, as further evidence that Burns was an idiot, he inexplicably looked over, returning Steve Johnson's attention to the lowlifes that had tried to embarrass them on their strip. Shaken back to the task at hand, the younger Johnson uttered those words that have become epic and etched in Primrose Chronicle lore. The zenith of expressions coming from all the stories of my childhood legends.

"FOLLOW US AND WE'LL RUMBLE."

Yep, that's exactly what was said, and it was an invitation that the Johnson brothers would not let us decline. There was no way we could say, "Oh, thanks, Mr. Johnson, but we have plans. Thanks just the same." The light changed and Burns obediently dropped in behind the '57 Chevy, only recently desecrated by its loss to a station wagon. The perceived desecration was about to be avenged by the Johnson brothers, a modern-day example of the basic Darwinian principle—survival of the fittest.

We started to slow down, hoping they'd soon tire of the whole episode: realize the losers behind them were not worth their effort and head on to other drive-in haunts with others they could rightfully intimidate. Instead, when we slowed, they slowed.

We were pretty much on a south-to-north trek. Keystone was a major thoroughfare with a raised center median, narrow but effective in keeping folks from turning wherever in the block they wanted, much to the disappointment of the businesses that could be reached only by customers coming from a particular direction. In other words, any escape routes were few and far between, virtually nothing to the right, only shopping centers, Willowbrook Golf Course, and Lake Maxinhall. On the left was the median, and when there was a break for an intersection, oncoming traffic. No immediate opportunities to flee.

We followed our "captors" all the way up to Kessler Boulevard, driving past each of the drive-ins we expected to cruise that evening. Instead, if we were noticed by anyone, we were observed as being in tow by the Johnsons—the casual observance perhaps accompanied by a grateful exhale of relief and a "better them than me" expression.

Just before Kessler, the Impala made a U-turn, and we were expected to follow. Now we were headed south and beginning to wonder if we'd ever see our families again.

I suddenly realized Rodney had perhaps made a mistake, and, if we were lucky, and a little daring, we might escape "the rumble." We were now on the side of Keystone, as we headed south, that had several street intersections into subdivisions that could eventually connect us with Primrose and home. I became backseat navigator and Straney became the "scout/speed-racer encourager," since Burns was not a regular as either chaser or chasee. We were about to begin a perilous flight to possible freedom, and we had a rookie at the wheel. It was a risk we would have to take.

We crossed through the light at Keystone and 52nd. The next cross street, beside the Dodge dealership, was 51st Street. We began slowing behind the Johnsons as we approached 51st, and so did they. As soon as the nose of the Chevy got beyond the opening onto 51st, at my instruction, Steve again floored it, while turning right onto 51st Street, and we began to make our escape.

Rodney slammed on his brakes, backed up, and proceeded to chase us across 51st. But we were in my neighborhood. The slow expansion of boundaries given in trust to me by Mom, first on foot, then bicycle, and now car, had made these streets as familiar to me as the proverbial back of my hand.

We flew past Hillside, deciding to not be slowed by another turn. School 91 and its playground, full of so many better memories, whizzed by on the right. Burns (you know, the crazy one that got us into this to begin with) proved to be just as crazy when it came to escape-driving maneuvers.

I set us on a course that for the most part had us approaching four-way stops, and Steve figured someone else would be stopping, so it needn't be us. The family car was not made for cornering, and we couldn't quite lose the Chevy, initially. A series of zigzag turns became our escape route—left on Evanston, right on 49th, left on Crittenden, then right on 47th.

It was at that turn that the fickle finger of fate became a friend.

Every summer, the side streets between 42nd and 56th Streets, north to south, and between Primrose and Erie, east to west, were rock-chipped, with a combination of oil base and gravel. Early on, the mix made the streets tacky and noisy. More to the point, many a child's summer wardrobe was ruined by a fall in the tar, while many a new car finish was pocked by the rocks and tar.

It was early August as we made our dash for life, and by that time, the streets were in various stages of dustiness. None was worse than 47th, or in our case, none was better. Immediately the spinning and fishtailing of a nearly out-of-control station wagon put up a smoke screen of dust that forced Rodney to slow significantly. The loose rock base was probably not doing his paint job any favors either.

As a result, three blocks on 47th, a left turn onto Ralston, had us leaving the pursuing duo farther and farther in our rear-view mirrors. If only 46th would be clear of cross traffic . . . it was, and as Straney looked first left and right to see if we'd be T-boned, he looked back and said, "We've lost them."

Fearing they had merely fallen back, or taken a parallel route, we sped down Ralston, past Straney's. His driveway was full of his older twin sisters' friends' cars, so no escape there. So down to 44th, a right turn and around the bend, pulling into our drive, sufficiently up near the house that the car wasn't immediately noticeable from the street.

Burns rammed the gearshift into park, and we all tumbled out and up to the patio, where, as dusk was approaching, Mom and Dad sat with their glasses of iced tea and their third or fourth Winston since supper. We were about to invade their serene space, possibly exposing them to the danger we had for the moment eluded, but grateful we'd made it this far.

It didn't take too much to coax the story out of us. We weren't certain how long before we would be exterminated, and wanted to make sure someone knew who to come after with arrest warrants for murder, or at least assault and battery with intent.

As we told the story of our brush with death, the responses of my folks were markedly different from each other. Mom appeared visibly fearful for our safety. At different points in the narrative, she would shake her head, and perhaps express either a "Martin" or a shocked "Martin Scott." Straney was one of Mom's favorites, so an occasional "Daniel" also was voiced. Burns was a newcomer, and if she'd chosen to verbalize, would have laid the entire evening's events at his feet.

Meanwhile, Dad sat quietly, listening to the tale unwinding by three breathless, scared-spitless teens, one them his eldest and heir to the Young fortunes. He never asked a question or offered a comment, merely taking an occasional sip of tea or a drag of his cigarette.

When it became apparent that the story was starting over with each of us filling in more and more of the basic elements, Dad arose and, without a word, climbed the stoop and went inside.

"Are you okay, hon?" Mom asked.

"Yeah, I'm coming back," Dad responded, tight-lipped as always.

Mom turned her attention back to the youthful trio that were beginning to realize they had, perhaps, dodged a situation of great peril. The story began to turn on tales of my artful navigation and Burns's skillful driving. In truth we each felt we had cheated death.

About then Dad came out the front door. It had become just dark enough that I couldn't see that he was carrying something, but he certainly was. He eased his 6' 4" frame into his lawn chair and, now closer, we saw he carried a tool of his Citizens Gas and Coke Company appliance installation trade—a 14-inch pipe wrench.

After sitting comfortably, having laid the wrench across his lap to take another swig of iced tea, he set down his tea and picked up the tool. Thinking back, I recall a 10-inch wrench would have looked a toy in his right hand, and a 2-foot one would have been unwieldy.

But he handled the 14-inch perfectly, tapping it firmly and intentionally in the palm of his left hand. Then came the statement that for hundreds of chapel kids and a trio of his grandchildren became the battle cry for all really cool dads everywhere. Evenly and deliberately, in time with the tap, tap, tap of the pipe wrench, my dad spoke:

"LET'S GO FIND RODNEY!"

I couldn't believe it. My dad wanted to take the Johnson brothers up on their invitation. He wanted to be the aggressor. He wanted to find them and "rumble" . . . so that's what we did. At Dad's urging, we got back in the car, that family car, that vehicle created for vacations and car pools, and we went looking for the Johnson brothers, Straney and Burns in the front seat, me and my dad in the back. We backtracked. We revisited the drive-ins. We cruised, but with a purpose.

In truth, the rest of the evening was an answer to my silent prayer. I didn't want to find Rodney . . . and we didn't. Steve drove up next to one of his buddies' cars from school, just to talk, and I remember Dad slouching down in the back seat, not wanting to be seen but ready to spring if a rumble initiated. But we never found Rodney.

We headed back home. By then Mom had gone in. It was time for Straney to be home and Burns to get the car back. We said good night in the driveway and Dad and I headed inside, side by side, Dad with the wrench hanging from his right hand.

Mom, sighing a deep sigh of relief and shaking her head as we entered the living room, simply said, "Donald Eugene, what were you thinking?"

Dad didn't answer; he just grinned and took the wrench back to the basement and put it in his toolbox. And I looked back at Mom. She'd already returned to her magazine, but with a proud knowing smile on her face. Her son had seen firsthand the knight in shining armor she'd pledged her own protection to years before, and that was a good thing.

I have to admit I had had my doubts about Dad before that. I had the typical teen idea that he wasn't that cool, had some old-fashioned ideas, and really was kind of boring. A great part of that thinking evaporated that evening. In the days that followed, Dad, *my dad*, had moved into the rarified air of rock stars with my buddies. His words of mission were on the lips of them all. "Let's go find Rodney!" one of them would say, and the rest would hoot their approval. And it couldn't be said by any of them without mimicking the deliberate gesture involving an imaginary pipe wrench and the palm of his hand.

Marty Young

Michigan City

One perfect summer morning I was awakened at my condo overlooking Lake Michigan in Michigan City, Indiana, by a loud male voice over a loudspeaker coming from the beach. "Please clear the beach. There is a mad dog on a jet ski." I could not believe what I was hearing! This statement conjured up all sorts of weird images in my mind, so I decided I had better have a look for myself into what was happening.

As I peered out from my deck on the fourth floor and looked toward the water, I saw people scrambling in all directions to clear the beach. At first I could not find the "mad dog," but finally I did see a jet ski at the water's edge. And as I looked closer, there was a rather large dog sitting on the jet ski all alone. As people would approach him (or her, as the case may have been), the dog would growl, bark, and bare his teeth, managing to look rather ferocious and scary. I thought to myself that it really did look like that a dog on the jet ski was mad. Maybe he had rabies?

Well, it turned out that several people tried to coax the mad dog off of his jet ski perch, mostly with little or no success. But one rather ingenious young woman crawled slowly in the sand toward the dog, spoke to him in a very gentle voice, and actually was able to get close enough to slip a leash over his neck. As soon as he was leashed, the dog quite willingly jumped off the jet ski and went quietly with the young woman.

Just when it seemed that this incident would be concluded, as the woman would likely turn the dog over to the animal control authorities, she took off running at full speed with the dog and headed toward the sand dunes and the parking lot. I had no idea if this was her dog that she was taking to her car, or if she just planned to keep this new dog she had found on the jet ski.

Now things really got interesting. As the girl ran away with the dog at full speed, an animal control vehicle sped after her down the beach in hot pursuit. It wasn't hard to predict who was going to win that chase. The officials used their microphone to tell the young woman, "Stop running. That dog may have rabies and needs to be checkout out by a veterinarian." To her credit, the woman did stop and immediately turned over the now seemingly docile dog to the authorities. Things then returned to normal, people returned to the beach, and that was the last time I ever saw that dog.

But because I had several questions about what I had just observed, I was able to find out the rest of the story. First, the dog had been swimming too far offshore and had to be rescued by a young man on a jet ski. The dog was cold, wet, tired, and scared. He barked rather ferociously at the jet ski driver, scaring him so much that he jumped off when he hit the beach, leaving the "mad dog" alone on the jet ski. After the dog was checked out by a veterinarian and found to be perfectly healthy, he was later reunited with his owners, who had lost track of him while they were engaged in a hotly contested beach volleyball game. Everything turned out fine in the end, but each time I think back on that day, I get this image in my head of that dog riding on a jet ski in Lake Michigan in Northwest Indiana.

James B. Dworkin

Muncie

It was located on Broadway Avenue in Muncie—now Martin Luther King Boulevard—and it smelled bad. At times, it smelled really bad. It was the meat packing company that started as Kuhner and closed many years later as Marhoefer.

Although I can't imagine wanting to see meat packing in action, some of the local schools used to tour the plant. My mother once told me that after going through the plant as a child, she swore off meat, especially hot dogs, until her memory of the tour faded sufficiently.

Gottlieb Kuhner and his sons founded Kuhner and Company which, by 1913, included nine retail butcher shops and Kuhner Packing Company. The packing company produced bacon, sausage, dried beef, ham, lard, and other products. The Kuhner's tag line, developed by advertising manager Robert H. Myers Sr., was "Kuhner Meats Make Keener Appetites." In the 1950s, Kuhner Packing Company became Marhoefer Packing Company. That company closed in the 1970s.

In the early 1960s, Muncie Community Schools built a new junior high school on North Elgin Street and named it for the Kuhner family. According to a fairly knowledgeable source—my husband—the students were allowed to choose the school nickname and colors. Apparently, several of the students, including my husband, wanted to be the Kuhner "Wieners," but the administration nixed that idea. Instead, the Kuhner Junior High nickname was the "Falcons."

Kuhner Junior High School was in existence for only about ten years. The building currently houses the Muncie Area Career Center.

Karen M. Vincent

Peru

Growing up in Indiana left me with a lifelong love of nature, because I was lucky enough to be born in Peru, a small town lined with large trees set along its tidy streets and backyards filled with extravagant displays of flowers.

Rows of towering elms and maples reflected the town's early founders' hopes for a settled future and gave testimony to their faith in that future. A sense of security surrounded us as children, emanating from those grandfather trees, as we played under their sheltering branches.

Mysterious shapes in small patches of the trees' bark nearer to eye level and gnarled roots burrowing under sidewalks, cracking open the cement and pushing it aside to reveal the world under that section, showing a root's progress as it led its own life in a world bumping up against our own, made us believe in the magic of life and our ability to accomplish our dreams just by sharing in the strength of the trees.

Alleys became avenues to more adventure, providing glimpses into backyards all uniquely designed by the many folks who loved to garden, creating rows of color and vitality that seemed to anchor a world bigger than the backyard itself. Large stands of peonies, marigolds, zinnias, and other flowers too numerous to name dotted the landscape and rimmed our hearts with joy.

Giant hollyhocks often lined the alleys just outside the fences or leaned up against the back of a garage. These were our favorites as we took the blooms and, turning them upside down, made hollyhock dolls, the bell-shaped flowers turning into skirts and the stems into faces.

Our favorite alley led to Grandma's house, a block away from home. We gravitated there nearly every day. The gravel lane crunching under our feet marked the boundary between everyday life on the sidewalk and arrival at the fairyland of her backyard. No one else nearby had a yard like hers.

A dense row of 9-foot-tall lilac bushes stood like giants guarding the yard, planted as a natural fence. A break between the bushes formed a narrow entryway.

Inside the yard a child's playhouse waited, surrounded on one side by blackberry brambles, with low bushes under the shade of the trees in the side alley. The playhouse, weathered with time, had been built for our mother years before, when she was a child.

In the fall, a tall apple tree dropped its fruit with distinctive plops onto the roof of the back porch. In muffled thumps more apples thudded to the ground, as if the tree were alive and communicating its secret tree code to us.

In the spring, five dark-limbed cherry trees began to blossom, and soon we would race the birds for the prized cherries that thickened the branches, our metal buckets slung over our arms, ready to start the contest.

Snowball bushes ran alongside the next-door neighbor's fence, their blossoms scoops of white floating on top of mountains of green leaves. They led the way into the front yard, passing the spirea bushes that lined the side of Grandma's house. Their delicate blossoms danced in the spring wind.

Around the corner, forsythia bushes massed along the front of the house, their yellow fingers shooting up higher than the bottom of the windows, their exuberant energy expanding our joy.

Gracing the front yard, a towering spruce tree, so mighty and so silent, captured a moment of our attention. Great-grandmother had brought the young spruce with her from Minnesota when she moved to Indiana, and planted it in the yard. The spruce found its home in Indiana soil and flourished.

We often played in this yard until early evening when lightning bugs blinked in the dusk. We caught them, their wings tickled our hands, and we let them go, watching their lights lead into the distance across the yard. And we felt an endless sense of possibility, for them and for ourselves.

Growing up in Indiana made us strong.

Judy Collins

Petersburg

Hoosiers are renowned for doing their own thing. The courtship of John "Arthur" Bilderback and Flossie Belle Morrison was a true Hoosier one.

While many turn-of-the-century courtships in Petersburg, Pike County, Indiana, took place in front parlors of the Victorian homes standing along Main or Ninth Streets, Arthur and Flossie enjoyed the peace and quiet of Petersburg's Walnut Hills Cemetery.

Arthur, the son of Pike County treasurer Franklin R. Bilderback and Elizabeth (Skinner) Bilderback, enjoyed a comfortable life growing up in the county seat. Flossie, quite differently, the eldest daughter of two orphaned parents, moved from place to place. Meeting in Petersburg in the early 1900s, the two began seeing one another socially and shortly thereafter started the courting ritual.

Why the cemetery? To this day it is not known; however, the importance of the location to Arthur and Flossie is clear. Their October 8, 1908, wedding photo was taken at the spot where young Arthur proposed to Flossie . . . in the Walnut Hills Cemetery.

Upon Arthur's death in 1953, Flossie acquired a plot as close as possible to their one-time meeting location. As a young child in the 1970s I recall accompanying my great-grandmother to place peonies on Arthur's grave each Memorial Day. After placing the flowers in the vases we would stand silently for a moment as she quietly thought to herself. Each year, as my family continues the Memorial Day pilgrimage to the Bilderback plot at Walnut Hills, I reflect upon my great-grandparents and their courtship that was undeniably Indiana.

Lee Bilderback

Richmond

No matter how much a place changes, nothing can erase its footprints. Down dirt paths and concrete walkways now overgrown by forest, some neglected buildings in Indiana's Whitewater Valley Gorge still recall music history made in the east-central city of Richmond after World War I and before FDR's presidency. Before time swallowed up great men and women who came to this once-vibrant city nestled between Dayton and Indianapolis

The Gennett Records building.

to record their songs. Before federal financial follies forced the Starr Piano Company and its recording division, Gennett Records, to close their doors—and thus close a chapter on a progressive and burgeoning music venture.

While the gorge retains remnants of its former tenants—the Starr Piano Company's more-than-100-foot brick smokestack and Gennett's six-story shell still remain stark and imposing against flourishing trees despite their age and neglect—it's the ghosts who speak louder than the rambling, rushing river that flows through the city. A city founded by Quakers and boasting Earlham College, a Quaker institution renowned for its liberal arts education. A city known as the Rose City because of the extensive variety of thorny, coddled flowers once grown here. A city dominated by the Ku Klux Klan in the 1920s and rocked by a devastating natural gas explosion in 1968. A city that now heralds itself as the cradle of recorded jazz—where murals around the city remind visitors and residents about those who built their reputations on songs recorded in Richmond.

These are the rare signs that something amazing once took place in the county seat of Wayne County. And jazz wasn't the only kind of music that performers recorded here.

This is where Gene Autry, the Singing Cowboy, recorded what are now considered early country-and-western songs in the early 1930s. In the 1940s and 1950s, he starred in many films, and he had his own TV show, which featured his signature song, "Back in the Saddle Again." His music continues to delight children and adults alike each holiday season with his renditions of "Frosty the Snowman," "Rudolph the Red-Nosed Reindeer," and "Here Comes Santa Claus," which is a song he wrote.

This is where blues legend Blind Lemon Jefferson made his final recordings, dying a few months after his 1929 recording session. The bands Blind Melon—an anagram of "lemon" and a quintet led by Shannon Hoon, a Hoosier from Lafayette—and Jefferson Airplane paid tribute to Blind Lemon with their names. Jefferson admonished listeners to "See That My Grave Is Kept Clean," and after some years of neglect, his gravesite in Worthham, Texas—in a memorial park now called Blind Lemon Memorial Cemetery—is indeed kept clean by a cemetery committee.

This is where Big Bill Broonzy would record his Chicago blues sound, built upon Robert Johnson's Mississippi blues and Huddie "Lead Belly" Ledbetter's country blues foundations. His tours in Europe in the 1950s would in turn inspire some British youths—Eric Clapton, Ray Davies, Ronnie Wood, George

Harrison, and Steve Howe, among others—to learn how to play guitar. He also influenced fellow blues musicians Muddy Waters and Willie Dixon, whose songs and vocalizations are so infused with Big Bill's prowess that such music overflowed the Mississippi delta and formed new tributaries, inspiring folk music by Pete Seeger as well as rock-and-roll music by Chuck Berry.

This is where Lawrence Welk first recorded his novelty polka music before hitting it big in Chicago and eventually hosting his own variety TV show—one of the longest-running such programs in the United States. One reason why he was able to sustain many cultural changes from 1955 to 1982 was his ability to adapt his champagne music—light and bubbly—to popular recordings of the time, such as those by the Beatles, Burt Bacharach, and Paul Williams, while still appealing to an older audience.

This is where future bandleaders Artie Shaw and Guy Lombardo made their first recordings. The studio masters from Shaw's sessions with Joe Cantor and His Orchestra were destroyed—which happened if someone with the studio didn't like how a master turned out or there was some other critical flaw—but Shaw eventually formed his own orchestra, which featured Billie Holiday, making Shaw the first white bandleader to employ a full-time African American singer. Lombardo later started the tradition of playing "Auld Lang Syne" on New Year's Eve—a custom that continues throughout the world each year on December 31.

This is where William Jennings Bryan recorded his "Cross of Gold" speech in 1921—some twenty-five years after he had delivered it at the Democratic National Convention in Chicago. Although he would lose the 1896 presidential election to William McKinley (and would lose again in 1900 to McKinley and in 1908 to William Howard Taft), he continued to give the speech throughout the years—an oration meant to encourage silver to be considered on equal footing with gold in terms of monetary conversion in order to help boost the American economy. Despite his speech and his best efforts, the United States continued to rely on the gold standard until the early 1970s.

This is where the Ku Klux Klan perhaps unknowingly recorded in the same studio that cut what were then called "race records." Gennett would allow anyone to record at its studios, and the Klan took advantage of this to produce its own propaganda recordings. By the end of the 1920s, when Prohibition—a caused backed by the Klan—began to dry up and economic conditions began to improve (before the stock market crash in 1929), the Klan also became less visible and less influential. In fact, Gennett Records and the Klan in Richmond disappeared around the same time—not long after Congress repealed Prohibition in 1933.

But this is also where some jazz legends made their first recordings.

Bloomington native Hoagy Carmichael first recorded "Stardust" in Richmond in 1927. Although Hoagy had recorded at the Gennett studios in 1925 and would go on to have an amazing career as a songwriter and performer, "Stardust" became an American standard, earning that original recording a place on the National Recording Registry—one of the first fifty songs so chosen by the Library of Congress in 2004.

In 1922, a young cornet player from New Orleans joined King Oliver's Creole Jazz Band, and they recorded in Richmond in 1923—the first time Louis Armstrong put his music, his soul, and his fire onto wax. This was also the first time King Oliver and his band would make recordings, helping to solidify him as a jazz force. As most know, Armstrong would become the most famous trumpet player in the entire world—and he had his start in Richmond, Indiana. He also fell in love with King Oliver's piano player, and he and Lil Hardin would eventually leave the group

The Louis Armstrong plaque.

to marry and to form Louis Armstrong and His Hot Five as well as Louis Armstrong and His Hot Seven—two groups that would lay down some of jazz's most classic tunes, including "West End Blues," "Potato Head Blues," and "Heebie Jeebies."

Bix Beiderbecke, another cornet player, also recorded in Richmond—first with the Wolverine Orchestra in 1924 and later with the Sioux City Six, as well as with his own Bix and His Rhythm Jugglers. Many music historians put Bix in the same influential class as Armstrong, but his early death at age twenty-eight prevented him from making a more lasting impression on future cornet players. His playing on "Riverboat Shuffle," "Davenport Blues," and "Copenhagen" is perhaps a little more crisp than the kind of jazz Satchmo played, but they're recordings that have also stood the test of time.

Jelly Roll Morton, a pianist as remarkable as Scott Joplin, recorded his own solo compositions for Gennett in 1923—tunes that bridged the gap between ragtime and jazz. His recordings with the all-white New Orleans Rhythm Kings achieved another milestone that would thankfully continue to permeate music: integrating bands and celebrating the diverse backgrounds for many different musical genres. Morton's influences would be as far-reaching as those of Duke Ellington and Charles Mingus, who wrote a song called "Jelly Roll" that appears on *Mingus Ah Um*, his masterpiece album.

And then there are the recordings that have been lost to history, including Burl Ives auditioning for Gennett on July 23, 1929, with a song called "Behind the Clouds." Although the studio passed on him and the song master was destroyed, Ives still had an award-winning career as an actor and musician, and he'll forever be known as Sam the Snowman from the *Rudolph the Red-Nosed Reindeer* Christmas special.

Richmond isn't the bustling town it once was, drawing musicians from miles around to record their music and satisfying people's desire for home entertainment, but skeleton edifices still present imposing figures in the gorge, and the Gennett Walk of Fame, with its mosaics shaped like vinyl records, showcases more than thirty enshrined performers and acts. And if you walk down that lonesome valley and listen intently, you can still hear Hoagy tickle the ivories, Welk cascade his fingers across his accordion, and Satchmo blow his horn—blowing you away.

Christopher Stolle

It was 1968 and I was fourteen years old. We went to Richmond every Saturday. My mom and dad needed to buy groceries for the next week, and there were errands to run. We had a routine we always followed.

The first stop was the grocery store to be sure we could get everything we needed before those items sold out. The store held all of our refrigerated and frozen items for us so we could pick them up before we left for our home in Liberty, a 20-mile trip.

Our next stop was Joy Ann Cake Shop. Mom had a standing order for cinnamon buns! On this particular Saturday, April 6, the day before Easter Sunday, the State Theatre right across the streetwas showing an Elvis movie—*Stay Away, Joe*.

By the time we finished our shopping, it was time for lunch. We went to a diner near Main Street. Tammy Wynette was singing "D-I-V-O-R-C-E" on the jukebox, and I was choosing the next song with my quarter.

Out of nowhere, we felt and heard a huge explosion. Everyone ran outside to see what had happened. As soon as we turned onto Main Street, it looked like much of Richmond had been destroyed.

There was debris everywhere, mixed with piles of broken glass. In places, the debris was a foot deep. I remember noticing one building with a huge piece of glass shaped like a sickle hanging out of a window. And all we could see several blocks down was the smoke. We had just been downtown.

The police kept everyone back. No one knew what had happened, but Martin Luther King had been shot just two days before, and many were afraid there had been an act of violence. Then we heard that the explosion may have originated at Marting Arms, a sporting goods store that sold ammunition and gunpowder.

There weren't enough police and firefighters to handle what had happened, so private citizens jumped in to help wherever they could.

We knew our family would be worried, and in 1968 the fastest way to reach them was to drive to their homes. We went to my brother's and my aunt and uncle's to let them know we were OK.

We would hear later that the explosion did indeed originate at Marting Arms. Forty-one people were killed and several injured. Many of them were in beauty salons, in stores shopping for Easter, and on the street.

We saw pictures of the devastation on television and in the newspaper, and they were horrifying, but neighbors were helping neighbors and students from Earlham College assisted with the search for survivors. For the people helping, race didn't matter in Richmond—the people of the town helped each other. The *Richmond Palladium Item* said that "amidst the tragedy, it was Richmond's finest hour."

Joy Fox

Trail Creek

I grew up in the Town of Trail Creek. It is located in LaPorte County just outside of Michigan City. When I was young, our town had only one law enforcement officer, and he was the town marshal. His name was Charlie Congdon. No one ever called him Marshal Congdon; he was always Charlie to everyone, young and old. I remember he would give us neighborhood kids a ride in his squad car to Kienitz Grocery Store to buy penny candy.

Now, Kienitz Grocery Store was one of those great old-time corner grocery stores that did it all. On top of selling groceries, they had a meat market and a gas station. Mr. and Mrs. Kienitz ran the store all by themselves. You could go in and buy a pound of hamburger and a can of soup, then fill your tank, and they would put it on your tab, and you would pay it off on payday. I can remember on trick-or-treat night that they would give out the big Hershey bars instead of the small ones.

I can remember summer evenings catching lightning bugs in old mayonnaise jars. The neighborhood kids would get together and play softball and Red Rover, Simon Says, and Red Light/Green Light. We even made up a silly game called Mighty Mouse to the Rescue.

Where I lived in Trail Creek, the creek ran behind my house. You could not get to it from there because the woods were too thick. My friends and I would walk down to Trail Inn, which is now the Fraternal Order of Police lodge, and get to the creek from the driveway going down the hill. We didn't fish, but we would look for snakes and tadpoles and watch the fish swim by.

It was a great place to grow up.

Jackie Wiencek Weaver

Versailles

James Tyson left a unique legacy at Versailles, Indiana. Cofounder of Walgreens, Tyson left a trust that gives money to his hometown; his gift has totaled millions over the years. A water works, a beautiful church, a school, and a library are totally funded and maintained by his gift to our town. Versailles has around 2,000 grateful people.

Jo Westmeyer

Wakarusa

I arrived in Wakarusa, Indiana, back in 1994, flanked by a fortress of freshly packed moving boxes and feeling as green as the forest, the seafoam, and every shade in between.

And although I might've landed on this little land of the countryside with that same wide-eyed stare made famous by a female sitcom star from the 1960s, my mouth agape, this was by no means a transition to the "big city" for me. In a sense, it could have been considered a step backward, for I was leaving behind my small town for one even smaller still.

It was my great leap from a writing career consisting of working at a weekly paper in my hometown to the hustle and fervor of the daily news circuit. My new "beat" would include coverage in the area collectively known as "Wa-Nee," encompassing the communities of Wakarusa and Nappanee.

I knew no one and nothing about this modest burg to which I was going to be entrusting my family, my residency, and my life's endeavor. My initial introduction to the town consisted of a quick jaunt there in the 1980s, stopping by Truex Auto Sales with a friend who was looking to purchase a car. I had never really known how to find the place on a map, and would not have believed I would one day return to meander through the picturesque southern Elkhart County landscape.

But years after that lone excursion, I was back, this time to stay. As I made my first tentative, patiently executed introductions about the area, one of the comments I consistently heard first was, "Well, if you really want to know what's going on around here, you need to talk to Helen Klein."

Indeed, this was a woman in the know. Diminutive in stature, but hardly so in spirit and moxie, Helen was a lifelong native who was more than happy to show me the sights. All in very good time, I learned abundantly about this quaint and quirky place called Wakarusa, the name of which is reputed to be derived from a Native American expression for "knee deep in mud."

Here the tradition of creating perfect maple syrup is such a beloved part of the communal heritage that there is a festival dedicated to celebrating the trade. Here folks can relish a taste of inarguably some of the best pizza in northern Indiana, the art of which was perfected by a pair of local brothers. Here one can sample what are surely the most generously proportioned jellybeans in America. And here one can develop a profound appreciation for a sprawling museum complex that boasts a collection of some of the finest memorabilia and glimpses from rural life to be found anywhere.

My fondness and affinity for the people and the ways of Wakarusa consumed me sincerely as my familiarity flowered. According to the dictates of my profession, I wrote of civic and governmental affairs, the passages of community leaders, the development of new businesses and events, and the accolades and triumphs achieved in our distinguished schools.

Over time, our family grew to include three children, and it was always our will and our wish to raise them here. We knew full well that this was a town founded securely and steadfastly on faith and that becoming one of Wakarusa's brethren goes far beyond bloodlines and boundaries, for we watch out for and over one another. Some may find it slightly unnerving to fall under that spell of seemingly knowing all that there might be to know about the neighbor's "business," but here it takes on a more comforting meaning, because in that knowing lies the reassurance that people possess an unwavering kindness and give without reservation or hesitation.

Nowhere was that illustrated more eloquently than in 2008, when this region was thrust unceremoniously into the national spotlight. We all became a reluctant symbol and a rebellious symptom of a desperately ailing economy. The jobless rate for this area ascended at a dizzying rate, to the extent that President Obama paid a visit to the community, attempting to rally the weary and downtrodden citizens about the prospect of positivity and change.

Our own family was mired in that abysmal scenario, as my husband was laid off from his job and we subsequently lost our home. When my family of five was forced to shoehorn into a minuscule rental until the tidal wave of uncertainty began to recede, the very essence of my enchantment with this place arose in virtually indescribable ways. People brought food. They gave money. They showered us with gift cards, with notes, and with prayers. Some knew of us in name only, and it mattered not to them. We were still considered graciously, by so many countless people, to be as precious as kin. And eventually, for our family, along with others marred by that selfsame despair, better days came around.

But of course, all along we stayed in Wakarusa. Where else would we have gone?

All these many years have fatefully marched by with poetic precision, now and again marked by memories behind and beyond me. I still marvel at the sense of belonging and of peace that this place has gifted to my soul. And I always smile when I travel about and somehow manage to gravitate toward people with connections, sometimes tenuous and sometimes tenacious, to this community. It's a little bit like the "six degrees" phenomenon, where all roads somehow lead to Wakarusa.

I now serve on the board of directors for the Wakarusa Historical Museum, a site I toured so long ago with Helen Klein, one of the original founders, who has since passed on to her heavenly respite. Whenever I am strolling the hallowed museum grounds, many precious memories fill my mind. I think of the many conversations she and I shared about my volunteer work there and how she never missed a chance to remind me that I should be on the board someday. I think of how I strive to carry my responsibilities dutifully and honorably, to preserve the past for future generations to reflect upon and learn from. I think of the myriad ways in which we instill the importance of "paying it forward" to my children, as it is but one way to tangibly illustrate that as we have been blessed, so we must share likewise to others.

Nowadays, I am still a writer and a chronicler of life's gaffes and panoramic glimpses, and when the occasion strikes, I can and do unabashedly sing the praises of this town. And I still seize every opportunity to offer gratitude for each and every person who has walked with my family and me on this journey that has never been dull, never been complacent, and never been ordinary. But it certainly has been unforgettable.

Within that grand and glorious oasis where hope, happiness, and the heart join together harmoniously, I have at last come home.

Amy Lant Wenger

Winona Lake

The quaint little village of Winona Lake, tucked along the lakeshore adjacent to the Kosciusko County seat of Warsaw, is a treasure trove of historical lore from the three distinct periods of the north-central Indiana town's history.

Winona Lake—then called Eagle Lake—rose quickly to star status as a recreational destination known as Spring Fountain Park in the late 1880s. Three brothers named Beyer purchased approximately 125 acres that now comprise the town, planning to use the many springs, artesian wells, and creeks along the shore to cool the milk and butter from their creamery business.

But they quickly realized that the gently sloping lakeshore property had recreational potential, and they began clearing trees, killing rattlesnakes (twenty-two in one day, according to one workman's diary), and creating recreational venues. They built a towering slide for swimmers to glide into the lake. They created a round cyclorama building containing 15,000 square feet of paintings depicting the Civil War battles of Chickamauga, Missionary Ridge, and Lookout Mountain. Most of the

Kosciusko County Civil War veterans had fought in those battles, so the scenes were familiar to the returned veterans.

A gravity-fed switchback coasting railway, modeled after La-Marcus Thompson's original switchback railway at New York's Coney Island, was installed, giving riders of a bench-like car a 600-foot ride down one track to another tower, where the vehicle was switched to a return track.

A horseracing track was built around the perimeter of a 55-acre peninsula jutting out into the lake. The interior was a military parade grounds, Carnahan Military Park, named for James Carnahan, a well-known Indiana Civil War veteran, lawyer, and judge.

The Beyer brothers also created venues for Chautauqua speakers and performers. Named after a lake in New York, the Chautauqua programs were designed to bring culture out to the countryside. Over time, the list of those performing or appearing on the Spring Fountain Park Chautauqua playbill was astounding—Helen Keller, Admiral Byrd, James Whitcomb Riley, Jane Addams, John Philip Sousa and his band, the New York Symphony Orchestra under Walter Damrosch, Will Rogers, William Jennings Bryan, Colonel Herbert Petrie and his White Hussars, the Russian violinist Efrem Zimbalist Sr., Metropolitan Opera stars, including Schumann-Heink and Galli-Curci, and many more. According to press reports, as many as 250,000 people visited Spring Fountain Park during a summer season, all coming by rail. At the time the town had only about 500 year-round residents!

Although Eagle Lake and Spring Fountain Park had a tremendous pull and reputation as a tourist destination, everything changed when, in 1894, the director of home missions for the Presbyterians in Indiana, Dr. Solomon Dickey, bumped into one of the Beyer brothers on a train and explained that he was looking to buy property to establish a religious retreat and

Bible conference center. "We've got Spring Fountain Park and we're willing to sell," exclaimed the Beyer brother, setting in motion an entirely new set of developments for the picturesque little lakeside town.

Dickey got together with some friends and financial backers, who included John D. Rockefeller of New York (Standard Oil), H. J. Heinz of Pittsburgh (pickles, relish, condiments), John Wanamaker of Philadelphia (department stores), John Studebaker of New Carlisle, Indiana (Studebaker automobiles), Alexander McDonald (president of Standard Oil of Kentucky), William Jennings Bryan (three-time presidential candidate, secretary of state under Woodrow Wilson, and the most popular Chautauqua speaker), and others. These titans of industry and influence immediately purchased the entire town, changed the name of the town and the lake to Winona Lake, and formed a management organization entitled Winona Assembly and Summer School Association.

Thus began the second phase of the town's colorful history, when it would eventually come to be labeled "Home of the World's Largest Bible Conference." Dickey and his associates continued the Chautauqua programs, but programming was increasingly geared toward theology, Bible teaching, and the rising evangelical movement in America.

Billy Sunday, the famed evangelist who rose from being a major league baseball player to become the best-known evangelist of the time, decided to relocate to Winona Lake from Chicago with his wife and four children. In 1911 they built an Arts and Crafts bungalow just a few hundred yards from the main Bible conference auditorium and named it "Mount Hood." Mount Hood today is available for touring as the Billy Sunday home and is in nearly pristine condition, containing a vast number of original Sunday artifacts, including artwork, furniture, dishes and silverware, and personal effects. During his career, which ended with his death in 1935, Billy Sunday preached to more than 100 million people, averaging delivery of about forty-two sermons per month. Most of his crusades were conducted in temporary tabernacles, erected for the purpose, and in 1920 a permanent tabernacle seating 7,500 and featuring the same wooden benches and sawdust floor as his crusade tabernacles was erected in the heart of Winona Lake. It served as one of the largest venues in northern Indiana until maintenance became untenable and it was razed in 1992. Sunday's song leader, Homer Rodeheaver, established a gospel music publishing company in Winona Lake that owned copyrights to a vast number of the day's popular hymns and gospel songs.

During this second period of the town's history, British theologian G. Campbell Morgan founded a summer school of theology that trained thousands of pastors for the churches of America. Grace Theological Seminary, at the invitation of the director of the Bible conference, relocated from Akron, Ohio, to Winona Lake in 1939. Subsequently Grace College was founded in 1948 as a feeder to the seminary, and was then enlarged to become a Christian liberal arts college in 1954. Today Grace College and Seminary have a combined enrollment of about 2,200 students and make a major educational, cultural, and financial impact on Kosciusko County and its surrounds.

An organization entitled Youth For Christ (YFC) was founded in Winona Lake in 1944, as leaders of youth movements across America sought to learn from each other and to fraternize in the conduct of their ministry. YFC's first full-time employee was a lanky young preacher from the Chicago area named Billy Graham, and Graham worked as a YFC evangelist until 1949, when he decided to expand his own evangelistic ministry. So an all-night prayer meeting was held in the summer of 1949, with a number of youth leaders, denominational officials, and para-church leaders gathering around Graham in the Rainbow Room of Winona Lake's Westminster Hotel to pray God's blessing on Graham. He subsequently went to Los Angeles to conduct his tent crusade, where Olympic champion and famed POW Louie Zamperini made his religious conversion commitment, and where William Randolph Hearst gave his famous command to reporters to "puff Graham."

Meanwhile the best of the best in American fundamentalist and evangelical Christianity were on the speaker's roster at Winona Lake, drawing thousands each summer to programming sponsored by Moody Bible Institute, Youth For Christ, and many other organizations.

Eventually the Bible conference movement began to decline, and facilities were suffering from age and disrepair. The Bible conference was facing bankruptcy in the middle 1960s. So the managing board approached the board and administration of Grace College and Seminary, offering the schools to take complete control of all the Bible conference's facilities, and also to assume its indebtedness of about $700,000. Grace's board agreed, and many of the conference facilities now became college dormitories, offices for student organizations, and student unions.

Still suffering physical decline, Winona Lake reached a low point about 1990. In that year a young Grace College student, Brent Wilcoxson, devised a plan which he presented to his business professor to re-envision and revive Winona Lake as an artisans' enclave and tourist community.

Several years later Wilcoxson connected with one of the cofounders of the orthopedic giant Biomet, Dr. Dane Miller, and his wife, Mary Louise. Together they formed an organization called Winona Restoration Partners and set about rehabilitating old buildings, tearing down those no longer viable, and creating venues along the canal and lakeshore for painters, glassblowers, woodworkers, weavers, potters, and other artisans. The concept was that the artisans would live upstairs, have their studios and galleries downstairs, and the remainder of the town would be developed into restaurants, recreational trails, confectioners, and coffee and specialty shops.

Thus, in the third phase of the town's history, the Village at Winona was born, which today contains those artisan and specialty shops, has two world-class restaurants, and includes nearly 200 acres of recreational facilities, including scenic mountain-biking trails and a greenway winding through the forest dotted with sculptures and artwork created on commission.

The Winona History Center is open in the west wing of Westminster Hall at 105 Ninth and contains a treasure trove of artifacts and materials from the town's history. Tours of the Billy Sunday Home are also arranged through the guides on duty at the History Center.

Winona has once again become a tourist destination, not only with its shops and historical features, but with many weekend festivals throughout the year, including a Fat & Skinny Tire Fest (bicycle festival), a juried art fair, Canal Days, holiday events, and many weekend specialty exhibits of antique automobiles, Porsches, British cars, and more.

Terry White

Zoar

Undeniably, Hoosiers love summer festivals! From Indianapolis to Zoar, gatherings of people enjoying good food, entertainment, and the outdoors make summer in Indiana fun.

This is true the first full August weekend when the folks of Zoar, Indiana, host the Zoar Mosquito Fest. Held at the Dubois-Pike county line in tiny Zoar, the fest, since 1972, celebrates the Hoosier summer. From thirteen flavors of homemade ice cream (over 160 gallons of it, including pumpkin), to a twenty-four-team Wiffle ball championship and baked goods sold in a 118-year-old one-room school, the festival is undeniably Indiana.

Even the annual parade tends to be a unique one. Zoar is so small, basically two blocks—one in Dubois County and one in Pike County—that the parade entries remain stationary while the visitors walk around them! Sack races, an egg toss, and a water balloon toss remain favorites of all ages, but perhaps it is the socializing of locals and guests from throughout Indiana that gives the fest its unique flavor. While many summer celebrations have creative themes, the Zoar Mosquito Fest is definitely Hoosier folk!

Lee Bilderback

Just Wait till It Changes

A Meteorologist's Life with Indiana Weather

Some people mark their life events by keeping newspaper clippings, taking photographs, or collecting memorabilia. As a meteorologist, I mark my life events by the weather that occurred that day.

My mother told me that on the day I was born in 1954, a severe thunderstorm occurred right at the moment I was being born. I'm told that just as the storm broke, I rushed out of the womb after my mother had been in labor for twenty-four hours. I consider this My First Storm Chase.

My first real memory of weather comes from back in 1961 when my father, who was a petroleum geologist, took my sister and me on a field trip (read: got us out of our mother's hair) for an afternoon. We went down to southwestern Indiana, where he was checking gas well readings when a thunderstorm blew in and dropped a tornado, which was heading for us. My father ran to get my sister and me into the car. My sister was petrified, and I'm sure I was too, except that I remember seeing the ghostly gray funnel heading for us and thinking, "Cool!" I was hooked.

My parents quickly learned not to bother me when Bill Crawford's weather broadcast on Indianapolis channel 6 came on every evening at 6:15. I would dutifully copy his weather map (in one minute!) and compare it to the newspaper weather map and his previous day's map. I didn't know this, but I was getting a grounding in synoptic forecasting, and I started making my own forecasts.

My teachers and my parents' friends thought this was awfully cute until I was in fifth grade and announced on a Friday in February 1965 that we were going to have a big cold wave. No one took me seriously until that weekend, when the temperature dropped to –13 degrees on Sunday morning. The next Monday, I walked into class and announced we were going to have a blizzard. Sure enough, it began to snow on Wednesday, and by Thursday night winds howled at over 65 miles per hour. The next morning schools were closed, and we were all digging ourselves out. I now had credibility: whenever I made a forecast, people listened.

I remember Palm Sunday of 1965 being wonderfully warm when my sister and I went to church that morning. We were playing with friends that afternoon (with the temperature hanging around 80 degrees) when I noticed the sky turning a beautiful golden-tan color. We were watching TV when the first weather warnings came on: a tornado had been sighted in northern Indiana. Then another tornado was sighted. And another—and another. Finally, Bill Crawford himself came on the air and announced that so many tornadoes were on the ground that they couldn't keep track of warnings. He said if we could hear his broadcast we should consider ourselves under a tornado warning and take cover immediately.

The golden-tan sky was caused by dust and dirt sucked up by tornadoes to the west and northwest of us in Illinois and thrown into the atmosphere. I sneaked out of the house, walked up to the intersection of Cottage Grove and Walnut Street in Bloomington, which was situated on a high hill, and looked to the northwest.

That's where I saw it: it looked like a thunderstorm, but with what appeared to be an atomic bomb shooting up through the middle of it. I was looking at my first supercell thunderstorm, which was producing a tornado that Dr. Theodore Fujita would later rate F4 on his Fujita scale.

Two weeks later, we went to Frankfort to visit my aunt and uncle, who took us on a tour of the tornado damage. Here and there we ran into houses that had been demolished, but as we approached Russiaville the trees—big trees—became shorter and shorter, and the road disappeared as though someone had pulled it up. We could see where homes had been because of debris in the basements or concrete foundations, but the homes were gone. This was my experience of the Palm Sunday tornado outbreak—the worst tornado outbreak to hit Indiana since the Tri-State Tornado of March 18, 1925.

Indiana weather during the Christmas holiday season is notoriously variable: balmy one year, icy the next—sometimes balmy one day, icy the next. I remember the Thanksgiving Day of November 1966 when we ate dinner outdoors in sunny, balmy weather with temperatures in the high 60s at the Skyline Restaurant outside Spencer. The next day, storms bristling with F3 tornadoes struck the state just after sunset, and we ate pumpkin pie while sitting in the basement. The next day was one of those archetypally cold, raw Indiana days with highs right at freezing.

One of the most terrifying winter storms I ever experienced was in January 1978. I was a student at Indiana University, majoring in an area completely unrelated to weather, when I noticed an area of low pressure deepening rapidly in Georgia. I also knew a strong Alberta clipper was approaching. When I went outside to go to afternoon classes, I observed a very peculiar steely-slate color to the south—exactly the same color of sky I remembered from before the big blizzard in 1965—and promptly went to the store for groceries, which I brought home before going to class.

I took the bus to school—something I did commonly; but after class was over my father and sister were waiting for me in the four-wheel-drive used by his office for field work. I looked at them oddly, and my father said, "Hurry, there's a severe blizzard warning!" We rushed home (it was already snowing heavily), and my father rushed to the store to buy groceries, quite unaware that I had already done so.

Actually, it was probably a good thing he did this, because it would be two weeks before we could make it to the store again.

It snowed heavily during the evening, but nothing really alarming until just after midnight when I heard a hard WHOMP. I was in our garage, which was heated, and noticed that the garage door was bowing in and snow was coming in through the crevasses in the door. I went into our house and saw snow being driven through the space between the windows and the tracks they rolled on into the house. I had an anemometer, so I checked the wind speed and saw the winds were already gusting to 70 miles per hour.

My father had a large gardenia plant that he'd grown for several years, which he had brought in to winter in the garage. Gardenias are *extremely* sensitive to freezing temperatures, and the temperature in the garage was dropping as snow was being driven in.

I looked around and found a large sheet of Visqueen plastic, which I stretched and tacked over the garage door to keep the snow from blowing in; then found a very large blanket and put that over the door to try to keep at least some of the cold out; then rolled the cars (which we had put in the garage) back against the door to try to keep the door from blowing in.

I went in to make some coffee, and noticed the house was getting cooler. I looked at the thermostat: 66 degrees. "That's odd," I thought, "The furnace should be on." That's when I realized that our oil furnace WASN'T on and putting the thermostat at 72 only caused the furnace to turn on for a minute and then shut off.

I very tentatively and gingerly went in and woke up my father to ask him what I should do. He turned over and grumbled that the furnace had a reset button, and I should punch that button and the furnace would come on. Dutifully, I went to the garage and punched the button—and the furnace came on for exactly one minute.

I emptied the pot of coffee into a thermos, took the thermos outside with me, and for the next six hours dutifully punched that button, waited a minute, and punched the button again. The temperature continued to drop in the garage: through 45 degrees, then 40 degrees, then 37 degrees, then 34—closer and closer to the deadly 32 degrees which would doom my father's prized gardenia.

About 6:30, I went in to use the bathroom and to check my weather instruments. Wind gusts were exceeding 70 miles per hour and my barometer was registering 28.40 inches. I had always wanted to see a barometric reading below 29 inches, but was hardly expecting to see a reading below 28.5 inches. Then I noticed the furnace was on, and it was staying on.

I checked the thermometer in the garage, which had climbed from 33 to 35 degrees, then went in and made a pot of coffee for my parents. They came out and noted how cold the house was, and I explained what had happened: the blizzard had hit, the oil furnace wouldn't fire up, and I had been punching that damned button all night!

My father went in to build a fire in the fireplace and was greeted with several inches of snow that had fallen down through the chimney during the night. Our little dog went outside for his morning constitutional, sensed what a 0-degree temperature and 70-mile-per-hour wind gusts felt like, did his duty (which immediately froze!) right on the porch, and raced back inside. Frankly, I couldn't blame him for not wanting to go out into the yard!

All those groceries held us through the next two weeks, when roads statewide were closed (and when they did open, were open only in one lane), and actually, we ate rather well. I dug a large tunnel from our front porch out to the road. Once the blizzard finally ended on Saturday evening, we went out and found my sister's car, which to nobody's surprise wouldn't start. When we popped open the hood, we found out why: snow had blown up into the engine and was packed solid.

About that furnace: The suction in the chimney caused by the wind, plus the low pressure in the blizzard, combined with the extreme cold, made it very difficult for the furnace motor to pump up enough oil from the oil tank to keep the furnace lit. Once the winds were below 60 miles per hour and the barometric pressure had begun to rise, there was enough pressure for the pump to work.

High school graduation is a happy occasion, made perhaps somewhat less happy by the inclusion of tornadoes during the baccalaureate service just before the formal graduation exercises. This happened on my sister's graduation day on May 27, 1973, when twin tornadoes struck Bloomington during her baccalaureate service.

The sky darkened to the southwest of Bloomington at about 4:30 in the afternoon. My uncle, who was watching this, urged us to come out and see what was about to happen. Sure enough, a tornado dipped down, then back up; then another, then another, and another, and finally two tornadoes established themselves and started growing and moving northeast. I could tell this whole thing was heading toward my sister's church.

I called over to the church—interrupting the service, but someone finally answered the call—and I explained that I truly hated to interrupt the service, but *there were two tornadoes heading directly for the church!*

There was a pause (I presume whoever I was talking to was looking out the window), followed by an expletive—and the guy came back, thanked me, and said he had to go. The tornadoes passed near my sister's church, but fortunately did not strike the church, and continued right up SR37.

That was not the worst I was to see. Anyone who has grown up in the Midwest knows that there are days when the atmosphere just doesn't feel "right." The best word I've heard to describe this feeling is by someone who experienced the May 3, 1999, Moore/Oklahoma City tornado: the word he used is "hinky." April 3, 1974, was one of those days when I felt "hinky."

What appears on a weather map prior to a tornado outbreak is remarkably subtle. In this case, there was an obvious warm front, which had bowed sharply north because of strong jet stream winds from the south: a cold front undercutting the warm air from the west and a strong, upper-level jet stream coming in from the northwest. Low pressure was established at the surface and at the upper level of the atmosphere. All that was needed was a trigger.

April 3 started out cloudy, but the sun finally broke through at midday and temperatures warmed rapidly in the sun. THAT was the trigger: warming by the sun caused the air at the surface to rise and reach the "cap," which is an area of somewhat warmer air above the surface that prevents the warming air from the surface from rising further. The air continued to warm, and eventually the warm surface air punched through the cap—erupting into monster lines of thunderstorms all the way from Michigan and Ontario down through Indiana and Kentucky, into Alabama and Mississippi.

Normally, the air stabilizes behind a thunderstorm. This didn't happen on April 3: three separate lines of incredibly intense thunderstorms moved through, one after the other. Because the low-level and upper-level jet streams were moving in somewhat different directions, and the upper-level jet was moving faster than the low-level jet, the thunderstorms actually tilted forward. This allowed the warm updraft feeding the thunderstorms to avoid coming in contact with the cold downdraft—essentially a perfect tornado-producing machine.

I was walking to class at IU when I looked up and saw the sky was pink. I've seen many colors and gradients of sky—blue, indigo, green, icy blue (beware this one if you see it in conjunction with thunderstorms: you're about to get hit by giant hail)—but outside of sunsets, I had never seen a pink sky.

Then it began to hail—and hail, and hail. I'd just made it to the building where my class was and saw people scurrying to get inside from this downpour of ice that was cascading from the sky. My professor watched this, and then wisely announced that she thought we all ought to get away from the windows.

And then it was over. There was enough hail outside so that it looked like we'd had a snowfall, but no wind, no roar, and everything seemed fine. Later we would find out we were on the north side of a system of tornado-producing thunderstorms that killed four people near Columbus.

By the time we went home for the evening, we were all seriously spooked as we received news that tornadoes had flattened Monticello, Indiana; Xenia, Ohio; and Brandenburg, Kentucky; once again we were told that there were so many tornadoes on the ground that the National Weather Service could not keep up with warnings and those hearing the broadcast should consider themselves under a tornado warning. I decided to chance it and drove home. I had just reached the intersection of SR37

and SR45 west of the city when I felt the car literally bounce—
and the traffic light was also bouncing. I rolled my car window
down to ask the driver next to me if he'd felt that, and he responded affirmatively.

On top of EVERYTHING that had gone on that day, we'd just
had an earthquake!

Mark Carpenter

Restoring the Place We Love

Adam and maybe even Eve had been knocked down. Traffic
stopped because of 100-year-old trees lying across the main
roads surrounding campus. Enormous limbs had fallen across
brick paths and broken out third-floor windows.

I stepped out the front door of my office building on Third
Street to survey the destruction to the Indiana University
Bloomington grounds from the storm the night before and was
amazed that there was not a single car in the usually busy road.
I walked down the empty street as if in a postapocalyptic movie:
taking pictures, assessing the damage, stopping to talk with
other people, also stunned at the wreckage of tree limbs and
glass and stone fences.

And I felt it. I felt the damage to the beautiful scenic paths
and monuments. I felt the holes in the thick forest greenery. I
ached over fallen trees and contorted iron gates and the sad, sad
figure of Adam twisted and bent off his pedestal, bowing low
to Eve, who was buried deep in tree limbs that surrounded her
at her bronze neck.

Anyone who works or goes to school here believes in the IU
mission, reveres their time spent here, and loves to recite the
values of a liberal arts education. We believe; we really do. But
beyond the admiration for faculty, the learning, the classroom

experience, there is a deeply felt connection to the physical place. I have been on dozens of college campuses throughout the years, walked the paths of many quads, and gazed at many ivy-covered walls, and absolutely none compares to this campus at IU in Bloomington.

The magnificence of the campus is not accidental. People work hard at making the place stunning and picturesque. Campus Division employees plant and grow armies of flower-filled baskets and planters: in the peak of summer hundreds of huge pink and red angel wing begonias cascade from pots hung from lampposts and tall, purple flowering grasses and red geraniums burst out of containers; in the spring multicolored pansies and tall, red and white tulips form perfect rows in planters; in the fall full, lush, orange and purple chrysanthemums hold on to the last pieces of summer beauty. A local storm-water drain turns into a river as soon as it bubbles up on campus and wends its way around trees and over rocks and around ancient buildings. Wooden bridges traverse this storm-water ditch, a.k.a. the Jordan River, over and over until it leaves campus as a drainage pipe again. It charms us as if the river that runs through campus is the Seine flowing through Paris.

I frequently walk to meetings and feel lucky that I get to work on this stunning, historic, and utterly enchanting campus. I have a friend who swore that when the famed president of IU—Herman B Wells—died, the campus would no longer be so well cared for and tended because it was Wells's vision that kept the place so gorgeous. That has proven not to be true. In the sixteen years since Wells passed away, the campus has gotten even lovelier. Clearly, Wells was not the only person who appreciated the traditional splendor of well-kept university grounds.

They've meticulously paved walkways in red brick, kept up with repairs on sidewalks and retaining walls, valued the century-old limestone buildings with gargoyles and steep slate roofs by polishing and restoring them. The Old Crescent at IU Bloomington is a fine example of historic restoration at its best. Strolling these sidewalks one can imagine IU's founders ambling from building to building teaching Latin and Greek to well-heeled young Hoosiers.

But here we were, roaming the quiet campus, noting that those 100-year-old trees had been felled in a single storm and precious artwork lay in pieces. Dunn's Woods, once a dense forest, was now see-through and rather spare.

Then the sound of chainsaws began. After many hours of people climbing over tree trunks, figuring out where the most damage had occurred, and choosing new paths to get from one building to another because regular routes had been cut off, the sound of gas-powered tools filled the quiet summer air. If silence was the aftermath of the devastating storm that tore up the picture-perfect campus, then the shrill grinding of chainsaws was the return to normalcy, a signal that we were mopping up and moving on.

It was weeks, the rest of the summer even, before all the tree limbs and green detritus was hauled away. Campus art curators removed Eve along with the remains of Adam because you can't have one there and not the other. We watched as the cultivators of IU carefully worked their plan and returned the campus to the place we love.

There were changes to be sure. Dunn's Woods was sunnier, and more wildflowers began to grow. The landscape looked a bit sparser. Windows and felled walls were replaced with shiny new ones. Money was raised for a fund to restore the hallowed grounds should something like this happen again. A plaque in the president's garden attests to the damage of the storm of 2011 and the vow that we would always maintain this place of beauty. And finally, in the summer of 2014, Adam and Eve made a quiet return to their familiar spot at the edge of the woods as if there had never been a moment when they weren't there to greet each other.

Amy L. Cornell

If You Don't Like the Weather . . .

Every Hoosier has heard, if you don't like the weather in Indiana, wait a while, it'll change. My two youngest sons and oldest granddaughter learned very young how true this saying is.

My husband, Craig, had a marvelous plan for a canoe trip down a quiet local river. We would begin at Morsches Park in Columbia City, follow the Blue River to Eel River, and as we passed behind Eberly's mobile home park, where our oldest son, Nathan, lived, Craig would blow the air horn to announce our arrival into South Whitley. Nathan would then meet us at the city park to help us bring the canoe and three little ones safely to shore.

The sun shone bright and warm, perfect spring weather for a relaxing Saturday. A picnic lunch and cooler of water was packed into the canoe along with three preschoolers and two seemingly competent adults. We launched into Blue River about 8 AM. Excited chatter bounced between the banks of the otherwise serene waterway.

We paddled from the northeast side of town to the southwest before running aground on rocks. Craig had to get out and push us off. Shoes and pant legs soaked below the knee, he got back in, and we continued on our way.

The banks, far above our heads, kept any breeze that might be blowing above away from us, making us all quite comfortable. Suddenly a loud bang followed by a poof of dust at the top of the bank sent panic rushing through my brain.

"Somebody's shooting at us!" I cried.

Craig remained calm. "We're too far below the bank, they can't hit us."

Another shot. Another poof of dust, proving that a bullet flew over our heads. My fear blossomed into anger. Who would shoot at a family canoeing down the river? A farmer miffed that trespassers disregarded signs posted along the road and sent his livestock into a mad dash across the field? At any second I expected to see an angry man in jeans and a seed cap hovering over us with a shotgun.

Craig called out, "Hey, we're down here!"

I pulled myself together. It was more likely that a deer hunter was practicing his aim at a target mounted on a bale of straw. At any rate, I paddled faster. There was no sense in taking the chance that the kids or I or my calm husband would be shot. I paddled feverishly for several feet before feeling safe again.

The sun, and I'm sure our recent fright, warmed us to the point of shedding our sweatshirts, and still perspiration beaded on our foreheads. The only sounds were the gentle splash and swish of the paddles moving the water and our own low voices We were surprised to see a kingfisher perched along the bank. He must have thought we were an odd sight, too, because he was more curious than frightened.

Ahead a sandbar stretched nearly from one bank to the other and was several feet long—a good place to stretch our legs and eat our lunch of sandwiches and cookies. The kids played, doing well to keep their feet out of the water, which was unusual, especially for our youngest son, whom I had dubbed a water magnet.

Back in the canoe, Craig once again pushed us off, making sure the rest of us stayed dry. By now, he was waterlogged from the knees down.

We rowed lazily, soon meeting the Eel River, only slightly wider than the Blue. We chatted about this and that, enjoying each other's company. We came upon a Canada goose standing midway down the bank. Craig and I instructed the kids to whisper so we wouldn't frighten it. As we drew closer, the goose paced but didn't fly. Almost upon it we spied his mate, mostly hidden behind weeds and grass, sitting on a nest. They both stayed their ground. The five of us watched in silence. One family nervously waiting, the other in awe, as we floated by.

Not long after, clouds moved over us, and we put our sweatshirts on again. Sure we were past the halfway mark of our journey, Craig and I decided it would be wise to paddle harder in case rain was on the way. The wind began to blow cold, even though we were sandwiched between two high banks. I was getting tired. The wind slowed our progress. The kids were complaining of being cold. I assured them it wouldn't be much longer until we reached South Whitley. No one said anything that wasn't necessary.

The sky turned a threatening gray. The wind pushed against us, slowing us even more and forcing our tired muscles to work even harder. The kids were almost crying now from the cold.

"Get down on the floor," I told them. "Make yourselves as small as you can. Stay close together." I hoped this would protect them from the freezing wind that now penetrated to the bone.

My arms were numb. I didn't dare stop to rest. The paddling motion could only be done by my muscles' memory. Cold had shut off my control. I wasn't sure the canoe was moving forward anymore. White caps rushed toward us, now and again splashing into the canoe. White caps on this little river barely wider than our canoe was long! How could that be?

Craig, because of his height, had been sitting cross-legged the entire trip. His pant legs were frozen, and he couldn't feel his legs. One of the kids wanted to get up and take their life-jacket off.

"No," I said. "It will help keep you warm. Stay down."

We approached a bend in the river. Relief swept over me. Nathan's mobile home was just around that bend. But it wasn't. Nor was it around the next. How much farther did we need to go? My arms couldn't keep going. I didn't want to frighten the kids any more than they were so I kept my thoughts to myself. My frozen lips couldn't have formed the words anyway. My arms moved mechanically. The cold pounded deep inside my ears. Snowflakes stung our faces. Craig tried the air horn. It was too cold to blow. How would we signal Nathan? Could we get to the docking ramp ourselves against this wind? Craig stuck the air horn under his shirt hoping it would be warm enough by the time we really needed it.

Finally we rounded the bend heading toward South Whitley City Park. We fought against the waves to steer the canoe to the ramp. Nathan was there, thankfully, to grab the bow and pull us up out of the water. He helped each of us onto land, struggling to help Craig, so frozen and numb he couldn't move on his own.

"How did you know we were coming?" Craig asked. "The air horn didn't work."

"I've been watching," Nathan said. "It's 28 degrees and 6:00, we've been worried. And we knew you'd all be frozen."

I took the kids to the truck while the two men loaded the canoe. Our ordeal over, we headed home for a hot supper.

Of course this happened before cell phones were as common as today, and weather apps were unheard of. I don't know who "invented" the weather app, but I'm fairly certain it had to be a Hoosier.

Ginger Crosson

The World Enriching
Our Home

Francis Vigo

Francis Vigo, after whom Vigo County is named, is a forgotten hero in the annals of American history. Originally from northern Italy, Vigo arrived in the New World at age sixteen on a Spanish ship. Vigo had been serving in colonial Cuba with a band of Carignans (who were like Navy SEALs) from the Alpine regions of Western Europe. Having mustered out of military duty, Vigo left his ship in New Orleans, hollowed out a massive tree, and paddled it north against the Mississippi's current, with his only map being an etching on a piece of leather depicting the river and its tributaries. He wanted to enter the fur trade, and having an ear for spoken languages—Spanish from the west side of the Mississippi and French from the east side, his native Italian, and native tongues and sign language—he did very well making contacts with all sorts of people. Although he was illiterate in the written form of any language, his word was gold, so he was always welcomed and trusted. Eventually he became the silent partner of the Spanish don serving in St. Louis, Don Fernando de Leyba, and became known as the "Spanish Merchant."

Most Hoosier fourth graders learn how Vigo spied for and financed General George Rogers Clark in the taking of the British-held fort at Vincennes, which helped to secure the Midwest as part of our new nation. Later, Vigo housed General Clark's youngest brother, William, helping the young man recruit tough local frontiersmen for the Lewis and Clark Expedition of 1803.

When he was in his fifties, Vigo married and settled in an artistic, self-designed home in Vincennes and hosted an array of individuals. These included Vincennes's first resident priest and territorial governor William Henry Harrison, whose mansion was under construction, as well as various tribal chiefs. Vigo toyed with electrical experiments and anatomy and came up with culinary innovations such as introducing tomato juice to the wilderness settlers. He also started the first circulating library in what became the Midwest. His admiration of science and print, art, adventure, and people of all walks of life helped him earn the nickname of the "Ben Franklin of the West."

Then, after years of representing native interests of leaders such as Little Turtle and Tecumseh at the annual tribal/government councils at Carlisle, Pennsylvania, Francis Vigo seems to have fallen out of history. As I see it, Vigo realistically saw that the cause of the local natives, with whom he had always dealt so fairly and appreciatively, was a lost one, but he simply could not advise them to sacrifice their lands and lifestyles for new unfamiliar ones west of the Mississippi. This is perhaps why the government lost interest in him.

As we all know, history forgets more than it remembers. Yet as time passes and perspectives evolve, the things forgotten often become the things most worth remembering. I think this is the case with Vigo. He died a pauper—the new American government never repaid in his lifetime the monetary debt owed him for financing General Clark's efforts during the Revolutionary War. But I'll bet Vigo never cared too much. He was humbly proud to be a man of the people, eagerly doing his part in rampantly changing times.

Chris Vogel Haley

"Gypsy" Royalty of Evansville

The final resting place for several members of Romany (commonly known as "Gypsy") royalty and their descendants is, improbably, Evansville's Oak Hill Cemetery. In April 1896, Elizabeth Harrison, born in England in approximately 1835 and known in her day as the "Gypsy Queen," was interred at Oak Hill. Mrs. Harrison died of malarial fever in Corinth, Mississippi, in September 1895, and her body was transported to Evansville and held in the cemetery vault for five months so that her children, relatives, friends, and acquaintances could travel from various parts of the country to attend her funeral. The Harrison family, along with the Stanley family (Mrs. Harrison purportedly was a Stanley before her marriage), owned several large pieces of property in Evansville and considered the city their headquarters, in warmer months living there and hosting an annual convention on the grounds of their large Victorian-style home.

Local newspapers estimated funeral attendance to have been between 6,000 and 10,000, consisting of mostly curious onlookers and approximately 50 Romanies. The record-breaking throng—reportedly the largest ever seen at any Evansville funeral—necessitated a special train to carry people to the cemetery. Harry Harrison, a son of Elizabeth Harrison, debunked the misconception that his mother was of royal blood, saying, "There is no such thing as a queen among our people. We are American citizens." While Mrs. Harrison may have been no monarch, newspaper accounts of her funeral describe her as a "very able and accomplished woman."

While visiting Evansville for Mrs. Harrison's funeral, Romanies camped at Lake Park (most likely located on Evansville's west side), lodging in tents, carts, buggies, and wagons, their horses kept nearby. Dr. E. G. McLean of the First Cumberland

Presbyterian Church officiated at the funeral, and a double quartet performed. Though rumors had swept the city that the deceased's possessions and wagon would be burned, the last rites were quiet and simple and involved no fire. Mrs. Harrison was buried in a family plot that the Harrisons had purchased in 1895.

In 1900, the widower of Elizabeth Harrison, Isaac Harrison, was accidentally shot to death when he intervened between his sons Harry and Richard during a fight. Mr. Harrison, dubbed at least by the newspapers as "King of the Gypsies," was born in England in approximately 1836 and died in Selma, Alabama. His body was transported to Evansville and held in the Oak Hill Cemetery vault until his funeral, some twenty days after his death. Though Mr. Harrison was, like his wife, well respected in his community, his funeral drew only several hundred people, perhaps because it took place on Christmas Eve and, due to the tragic circumstances leading to Mr. Harrison's death, the family kept the news of the services quieter than they had for Mrs. Harrison's. Harry Harrison was the only immediate family member not in attendance; he disappeared after the bullet he fired at his brother accidentally struck and killed his father. Harry Harrison was thought to have fled to South America with his wife. The Reverend Dr. John Davis of St. Paul's Episcopal Church conducted the services, with music provided by a quartet. Isaac Harrison was buried next to his wife, Elizabeth. After Isaac Harrison's death, the Harrison family would begin spending more of their time in the South, selling their Evansville properties and establishing residences in Arkansas, Tennessee, Louisiana, and Texas. For decades, though, the Harrisons would return to Evansville to bury their dead.

In 1961, the last of Isaac Harrison's grandsons, William Harrison of Walnut Ridge, Arkansas, was buried in Oak Hill in a grave near his grandparents'. Relatives traveled from all over the lower Midwest and South for the Masonic ceremony.

According to some local historians, there may have been a Harrison family member buried in the family plot as recently as 1967. The Harrison family plot is marked by a tall granite monument that remains well preserved.

Laura Pinhey

Holland, Indiana, Is All German

The small town of Holland in southwest Dubois County received its name in a typically Hoosier way. Henry Kunz, founder of the town, established his community and christened it "Holland" to say "Thank you." You see, in the 1830s–1850s the vast majority of settlers in the area immigrated from northern German communities in Tecklenburg and Osnabruck.

In the early 1800s poor farmers from this area, bordering the Netherlands—commonly referred to as Holland—needed to supplement their income. Each summer, after their fields had been planted, many of the young Germans left their homes to work in the Netherlands peat bogs. Once there they found a very labor-intensive job, but the Germans were desperate. Over time this yearly ritual became known as "Holland Going." Following a summer of backbreaking work, they returned home to their families in Germany.

During this era letters began arriving from the United States telling of the available farmland in Indiana (in what was then referred to as part of the American West). Using funds saved from their ventures of Holland Going, large numbers of Germans from the neighboring areas of Ladbergen, Lengerich, and Lienen in Tecklenburg and Venne and Holte in Osnabruck made the long ocean voyage to the United States. In time they settled in southern Dubois County in what was referred to by historian George R. Wilson as a "colony."

In 1859, Kunz, a storeowner and businessman, realized the potential of platting a town (with his store occupying a lucrative location in his new community). The area already was referred to as Holland by locals in nearby Huntingburg—due to the fact of so many "Holland Goers" homesteading in the area—and on May 20, 1859, Kunz officially platted his town and named it Holland as a way of thanking the Netherlands for financially aiding (perhaps inadvertently) the early German settlers' quest to come to the United States and Indiana. What an example of early Hoosier hospitality!

Lee Bilderback

Joe Wants a Wife

Just to show what lengths a fellow would go to back in 1877 to find a great Indiana girl to marry, we can look at the story of some young German fellows who had moved out west to Ione, Nevada.

The *North Vernon Plain Dealer* on February 15, 1877, tells about Joseph Merten having traveled all the way from his home in Nevada to find a wife. Joseph's father, Joseph Sr., had immigrated to Jennings County, Indiana, from Germany in 1862 with his five children. The younger Mertens, along with some of their friends and their families, moved to Nevada because of large plats of land being available. They were all Catholics and had been members of the St. Anne's Catholic Church in Jennings County. By 1877 they were doing well and, as the paper tells it, young Joseph said there were only two girls in the area and neither was his choice, so he decided to pay the $80 (now about $1,800) for a train ticket to travel the 2,100 miles back here to try his fortune.

The newspaper article reads like a posting on Match.com, with the paper telling about the 320 acres of land Joseph owns, his twenty-seven horses and thirty-six head of cattle. He has a good brick dwelling house and outbuildings. He sure sounds like quite a catch for a local girl. It says they are only 50 miles from the nearest church, which is a five-hour drive, but the drive is a pleasant one.

It didn't take long for Joseph to find a local girl, Miss Rosa Decker, and by March 7 they were married and headed back to his Nevada home. His friends there were very impressed with his new bride, and on January 2, 1879, his brother Mathias was back in Jennings County on the same mission as Joseph. On February 25, 1879, he married Miss Elizabeth Renie, and they headed back to Nevada to help populate the west. Most of the families who went from Jennings County during this time eventually ended up in Oregon, Washington, and California, but we know those Jennings County girls made a real contribution the settling of the area.

Sheila Kell, Local History and Genealogy Associate,
Jennings County Public Library

Growing up Dutch in Indiana

Of course I wore wooden shoes growing up in Indiana, didn't everyone? Apparently not, but I did not know that growing up in the Dutch-centric town of DeMotte, Indiana.

The story I heard as a child was that the Dutch were brought over to the marshes of the Kankakee River to reclaim the land. They pushed back the soggy, marshy land and claimed the area for their Dutch traditions of faith, family, and farming. Churches were built where services were offered only in Dutch, even as the next generation was born American. The town, named after a French civil war hero, clung to its ethnic roots, celebrating its Dutchness in a summer festival, Touch of Dutch;

many, many Dutch churches; and a real windmill greeting you on the north side of town.

I am fourth-generation Dutch on both sides of my family, and that ethnic heritage was part of every day of my childhood. Wooden shoes for myself and my dolls, Dutch pastries called banket and oliebollen, pies from scratch, and Dutch words were all I ever knew. I went to a Dutch church camp and a Dutch parochial school.

I did not understand how unique this was until I moved away to Evansville for school. I rarely discussed it until I took a multicultural class in graduate school. My classmates asked, "What did it mean to grow up Dutch in Indiana?" It took a while to form an answer because it was my whole life. It was my family, my culture, my faith, my food, my heritage.

I now live in Jeffersonville, in the southeast part of the state. My daughters have their own wooden shoes. I am proud to be a Dutch American and will always be proud to be a Hoosier.

Valerie Fase Milholland

The Memory Work of Gustav Potthoff

While preparing for an NBC documentary on the anniversary of D-Day, television journalist Tom Brokaw began to understand and appreciate the contributions veterans have made to our country and the world. The experience led to his writing *The Greatest Generation*, a book that features dozens of stories about everyday Americans who came of age during the Great Depression and World War II.

Living in Columbus, Indiana, is a remarkable gentleman who credits members of this group with saving his life during the war. A naturalized American citizen, Gustav Potthoff, known to most as Gus, was imprisoned nearly four years by the Japanese.

Gustav Potthoff.

He managed to survive torture, injuries, disease, and horrible living conditions during his captivity.

While thousands of others endured the same conditions, Gus's story is significant because of the unusual way he uses art to deal with painful memories. Most critics would consider this self-taught artist's paintings raw and naive, but it's the story behind his work that makes it impressive. To understand what motivates Gus to create, it's helpful to first know something about his background.

Born on the island of Maluku near New Guinea, Gus enlisted in the Dutch Colonial Army, and he was taken prisoner on his eighteenth birthday, March 11, 1942. After being taken captive, he spent several months on a prison ship before he was sent to a camp near the town of Thanbyuzayat, Burma. There, he worked with other POWs to build Japan's new Thai-Burma railway, which was known to the prisoners as the Railway of Death.

The first year Gus was held captive, he and his fellow prisoners became very ill from eating spoiled meat, and they suffered with cholera and dysentery. As he lay dying one night, Gus heard a Spirit Voice tell him he would recover if he ate hot peppers. Gus gathered all the strength he could muster and crawled to the kitchen, where he begged the cook for the food, which he reluctantly gave him. When Gus awoke the next morning, he found that he was the only one to survive the ordeal. He believes the peppers saved his life, and he promised the Spirit Voice that if he "made it out of that hell," he'd do something good with the rest of his life.

For nearly four years, Gus was a prisoner of war, working alongside his countrymen and soldiers from Australia, New Zealand, Canada, England, and the United States. The prisoners built railroad bridges, including the one over the Kwai River, and they cut roadbeds through the mountains and jungles of Southeast Asia using common hand tools. In August of 1945, Gus and the other prisoners were freed when members of the United States Air Force bombed his camp in Thailand. On being liberated, Gus said, "Oh, we are so glad we are free. Some people are so glad, they pass away."

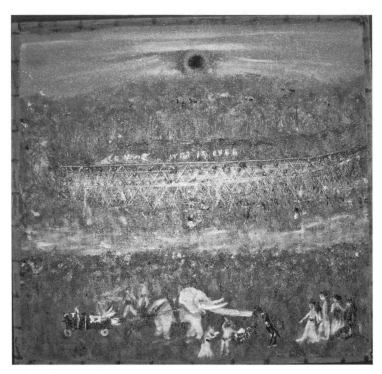

Potthoff painting.

About ten years after the war, Gus immigrated to Holland, where he met his future wife, Adele. In 1959, they were married, and they started a family. Three years later, Gus, Adele, and their daughter came to the United States, and he became a United States citizen. Soon after, a son was born in Indianapolis, and in 1965 they moved to Columbus, where he found work at Cummins Engine Company.

Twenty-five years later, Gus retired from Cummins, and he began to paint in order to do his Memory Work about his experiences as a prisoner of war. While many artists create with hopes of selling their work, Gus instead paints because he feels compelled to do so. Creating the art and painting about his imprisonment has a cathartic effect, and it helps heal his tormented soul.

Gus always paints at night. Working into the wee hours of the morning, he creates haunting scenes to honor his fallen comrades. His subject matter consists entirely of landscapes from the areas where he was held captive, as well as scenes of his life and those of the other prisoners of war. Gus's colors are pure and bright, and his work often includes an elephant, guards, and ghosts of fallen soldiers that he calls "spookies." Sometimes Gus embellishes his paintings with stickers or short sentences such as "War is over. Go home!"

Although Gus creates to do his Memory Work, he insists that he's not an artist. In speaking about being creative, Gus says, "Ya, I am painting, but I am not a painter. The Spirit lets me do it." He truly believes that the Spirit Voice that saved his life during the war also guides his hand in making the paintings. Creating helps to fulfill his wartime promise of doing something good with his life, and it's his way of repaying God for saving him.

This kind and gentle man rarely sells his art, as he prefers to donate it. To accept money for his work seems irreverent, and it would dishonor the memories of his fellow soldiers and the supernatural power that saved him. Gus's work is on display at the Atterbury-Bakalar Air Museum in Columbus, and many times he's traveled overseas to reunite with former POWs and to present his art to museums. In December 2001, he went to Thailand to take part in the dedication of the Thailand-Burma Railway Centre, a museum that honors prisoners who were forced to build the railroad through Southeast Asia.

Since the dedication, he's been busy creating new work to hang in the air museum, and Indianapolis Public Television station WFYI made a documentary entitled *Lest We Forget* about his war experiences as a POW. In the fall of 2006, the film was shown on more than 100 public television stations across the country, and the documentary won an Emmy for Best Special Program.

The former POW demonstrated great courage and caring for others during his captivity in Burma and Thailand, and while more than 100,000 of his comrades died in captivity, Gus learned to have a positive attitude in order to survive. In speaking of his imprisonment, Gus says, "Your medicine is your will . . . your brain . . . not thinking of bad things."

Gus Potthoff is a survivor, and he's proud to be an American citizen. He's grateful to members of the Greatest Generation who served during the war and rescued him and his comrades. However, Gus is most thankful for the Spirit Voice that saved him during one of his darkest days as a prisoner, and for the supernatural power that now uses him as a messenger to do his Memory Work.

Marilyn Hanna Brackney

India . . . ana

For inhabitants of India like me, coming to Indiana has a special meaning. Indiana registered in our mind as "India . . . ana," meaning in Hindi "India . . . Come." It's a warm welcome sign visible everywhere: books, magazines, billboards, license plates, websites, and documents of all types, and at first sight it hits the senses with a warm, fuzzy feeling. Indians entering Indiana must be experiencing its impact like petals of a flower bud opening up when encountering the warmth of sunrise.

Coming to Indiana changed my life dramatically, but for the better. After completing graduate studies on the East Coast in the mid '70s, I moved to Ohio and then to Indiana. On September 7, 1979, I joined Inland Steel (now ArcelorMittal) in East

Chicago. My first commute to work started from Griffith with a cup of coffee in the car cup holder. There I was driving on Ridge Road, re-creating in my mind the 10,000–12,000 year history of the ice lobe of Lake Michigan melting away. Geologically the Ridge Road represents reworked sediments of Lake Michigan deposited as sand bars along its shore. Driving on the top of an actual sand bar of the geologic past was a dream come true for a former student of geology. All I was imagining was the last vestiges of the ice age, when the glacier was melting and giving birth to Lake Michigan. The only distraction was cars passing by and overtaking me due to my leisurely drive. But with each passing car, I started paying attention to car license plates anchored above the back bumpers. They seemed to be waving at me with a sign "India . . . ana" registering in my mind a red carpet engraved with the sign "India . . . Come," implying a warm welcome. During my twenty-two years of working here, the journey has been made easier and more enjoyable, and the sign "Indiana" had contributed a lot to that.

During my college days in the United States, my father, Santokh Singh, sent me an audiocassette tape entitled "The Shortest Day—4:00 AM–10:00 PM." He taped everything that happened in an entire day in the home where I grew up. He ended the tape by saying, "This tape is dedicated to the memory of forgotten ones." It was a tape that reminded me of my roots in Chhindwara and Nagpur, India. The tape was made around the early '70s. His fondest memory was his visit to America in the early '80s. Both of my parents were overwhelmed by the generosity of America and its people. By the end of his US visit, I gifted him with a VHS tape that he played time and time again to everyone who visited our family home in Meerut, India. While he was here, we went to the Indiana Dunes, Lake Michigan, Inland Steel, Ridge Road, Wicker Park, and countless other places where I had spent the latter part of my life. The man who walked on the hard granite gneiss rocks of Satpura Range in Chhindwara was able to garner sweet memories walking on the soft sediments of Indiana! The biggest smile on his face came at the sight of car license plates with the sign "India . . . ana" assuring him that his son and the family belonged here.

Last but not least, I want to say how Sikhs like myself have flourished in Indiana. Sikhism is the fifth largest religion in the world, with about 27 million followers. When I first arrived here, to my knowledge, there were five Sikh families in the close vicinity of Highland, Griffith, Munster, and Valparaiso. Today this area of Northwest Indiana is dotted with a beautiful Sikh Gurdwara (temple) located in Crown Point where about 300 Sikh families worship, and at the end of the services a free lunch is served to everyone. This is a practice started by the founder of Sikhism around 500 years ago so as to bring equality to all regardless of caste, religion, or social status. A Sikh is easily identified because he wears a turban (pagri) and adopts five articles of faith (5 Ks) namely, kesh (long uncut hair), kanga (comb), kada (bracelet), kacha (short), and kirpan (sword). These articles of faith bring in him dignity, courage, and spirituality.

Indiana made it easy for all Sikhs to assemble in its melting pot. The community thrived and benefited from its riches. Now it asks Hoosiers that when you see a Sikh, greet him, visit his Gurdwara (temple), enjoy the langar (free lunch), and allow him to express his thanks and gratitude. This time, his car license plate will be conveying to you "Indi . . . ana," that is, "Hoosier Come."

Hardarshan Singh Valia

The Infamous

The Newburgh Raid

During the days of the American Civil War, the town of Newburgh, Indiana, in Warrick County was captured . . . by roughly thirty Confederate volunteers and two fake cannons.

The Confederates crossed the Ohio River on July 18, 1862. It all began when Adam Johnson recruited a group of men from the nearby town of Henderson, Kentucky, to conduct a raid. The men made their way to the riverfront across from Newburgh. There, before they left the shores of Kentucky, the raiding party improvised two cannons, which consisted of stovepipes, wood, and old wagon parts. The majestic crossing was completed by rowboat and flatboat. The men met little resistance on the Newburgh riverside, as most people were taking lunch.

The raiding party headed straight to a nearby tobacco warehouse, which served as a local armory, found it unarmed, and preceded to collect all the sabers and guns they wanted. Now that the group was fully armed, they headed off to the makeshift Union hospital. At first, the Union soldiers resisted, but the confederates pointed out their two "cannons" on the other side of the river and threatened to fire upon the town. The medical officer in charge surrendered.

At the hospital, the Confederates gathered medical supplies, food, and more weapons. They also declared all the convalescing Union soldiers to be their prisoners. At that time, it may have dawned on them that they had to somehow move eighty prisoners, on one rowboat and one flatboat, across the Ohio River. So they decided to let all the prisoners go as long as they promised not to fight against the Confederates anymore.

On their way back to the riverfront, the group looted a few houses and stores to add to their booty. They crossed the Mason-Dixon line and made it safely to Kentucky. Not one shot had been fired. As luck would have it for the Confederates, the telegraph between Newburgh and the city of Evansville was not working. It took hours for the Union military to find out about the raid.

In Newburgh's defense, the town had few men left to defend it, as many had volunteered for the war. Maybe the town should have stationed someone at the armory; maybe they should have taken lunch in shifts; maybe they should have fixed the telegraph when it first broke. Hindsight is 20/20. However, if they had, the capture of Newburgh might not have been bloodless. Well, it wasn't completely bloodless; two residents of Newburgh, who townspeople thought aided the rebels, were killed by an angry mob.

Johnson's raid of Newburgh gave the Confederacy some much-needed supplies and earned Adam Johnson a nice promotion to colonel and a cool nickname. Colonel Adam Johnson was called "Stovepipe" as a tip of the hat to his use of stovepipes in his fake cannons. And so Newburgh, Indiana, in Warrick County, has the distinction of being the first town in a Northern state to be captured by the Confederacy.

September Lant

The Hanging

There was only one hanging in Pike County according to the early records. It took place on December 23, 1883, in Petersburg.

Charlie Harvey was arrested for the murder of Henry B. Custin, a popular young man of society, during a robbery attempt. A mob of local citizens stormed the jail, dragged him a couple of blocks away, and hung him from a tree across the street from the Presbyterian Church parsonage and the Blythewood Academy. Girls staying at the school during the term woke the next morning to see his body hanging from the tree, covered with icicles. Townspeople refused to allow Harvey's burial in their cemetery. His father had to take down the body, dig the grave, and bury his son outside the fence of the cemetery. Today, due to expansion, the small stone that marks Charlie Harvey's grave is located in the center of Walnut Hill Cemetery.

Sandy McBeth

The Friendly Stranger

In 1933 my Uncle John and Aunt Daisy Evans lived on a farm just outside of Greencastle, Indiana. Uncle John would often gather his eggs and walk into town to sell them to some of the Greencastle residents.

On October 23, 1933, as Uncle John was walking into town, a car stopped beside him. The driver leaned out of the window and asked, "Would you like a lift?" Uncle John gladly accepted the offer. The driver was very friendly and chatted as they drove. He asked Uncle John a lot of questions.

The next day Uncle John picked up the Greencastle newspaper and saw a photograph of his benefactor. He turned to Aunt Daisy and said, "Ma'am, this is the man who gave me a ride yesterday!"

The driver was John Dillinger! He had just robbed the Central National Bank in Greencastle!

Sandy Boswell

Dillinger's Last Bank Robbery

On June 30, 1934, a tan 1930s Hudson automobile pulled up in front of the Merchants National Bank on Michigan Street in downtown South Bend. Several men got out of the car and strolled into the bank holding what looked like handkerchiefs. Once inside the bank, the men revealed that they were actually holding tommy guns and proceeded to rob the bank. At the same time, South Bend patrolman Howard Wagner was on traffic duty around the corner from the bank. Another storeowner close to the Merchants Bank saw what was happening in front of the bank, grabbed a shotgun from underneath his counter, and went outside to confront the gang.

The ensuing gun battle alerted Patrolman Wagner, who proceeded to head around the corner to the bank. As he was coming across the sidewalk, one of the gang who was stationed at the front door of the bank told Wagner to stop. Wagner did not stop, and the robber shot him with a .44 caliber Thompson submachine gun in the left side of his body, instantly killing the officer. The criminals escaped from downtown South Bend with $29,890 of stolen cash.

It was learned later that among the group of criminals in the 1930s Hudson was fellow Hoosier John Dillinger. It was also possible that "Pretty Boy" Floyd was with Dillinger that day.

Dillinger would live only one more month, as government agents killed him outside the Biograph Theater in Chicago on July 22, 1934. South Bend Patrolman Howard Wagner was buried with full honors. He was twenty-nine years old and had been with the South Bend Police Department for only five years.

As Dillinger had always said, "You can't trust a woman or an automatic weapon."

Travis Childs

Sheriff Watson and the Brady Gang

Everyone knows about John Dillinger, but far fewer people have heard of the Brady Gang. Al Brady once bragged that he would "make Dillinger look like a piker." And perhaps he did. Brady and his gang not only committed numerous robberies but were responsible for the murder of a grocery store clerk and two police officers and suspected in the murder of a third officer.

Our family was lucky that one of those officers wasn't my great-grandfather Clarence E. Watson (1888–1942), described by the *Indianapolis Star* in 1936 as the "45-year-old rugged, 200-pound sheriff" of Hancock County.

In 1936, Brady, Clarence Lee Shaffer, and James Dalhover were awaiting trial in the murder of Indianapolis police sergeant Richard Rivers when they were granted a change of venue and transferred to the Hancock County Jail. According to news reports and the recollections of my grandfather, Melville E. Watson —a student at Indiana University at the time—Sheriff Watson was emptying wastepaper baskets in the jail cells that Sunday morning, October 11, when Brady threw himself into the door opening.

"Then began a struggle as terrific as any one man ever waged against three other men," the weekly *Greenfield Democrat* reported on October 15, 1936. "Sheriff Watson fought and grappled with the trio from the time they emerged through the jail door, through the corridor of the jail residence, down the jail steps, and into the street."

Brady had broken off a 15-pound metal bar from the jail and was repeatedly hitting my great-grandfather over the head with it. Sheriff Watson's sister, Edna Tinney, tried to retrieve his revolver, but Dalhover shoved her and took the gun.

Thankfully my great-grandfather did have some help as he fought the three outlaws in the street outside the jail (which still stands but is now the Hancock County prosecutor's office). A local barber, Edgar Ridlen, and his wife were leaving for a day trip when they saw the fight. According to the *Greenfield Democrat*, Mr. Ridlen knocked Dalhover to the ground and hit Shaffer. But Dalhover had the revolver and fired at Mr. Ridlen; the bullet put a hole in his coat but miraculously hit no one.

The *Greenfield Democrat* reported, "The fact that Dalhover carried the gun and not Brady probably saved the lives of both Sheriff Watson and Mr. Ridlen. Brady is said to be a crack shot and is a known killer."

There was one other hero in this story: my great-uncle, Phillip Watson, was twelve years old at the time, and his dog, Trixie, nipped and bit at the heels of the fleeing gangsters as they took off in Mr. Ridlen's car.

While the Brady Gang did escape, it wasn't for long. A year and a day after the escape from Hancock County, the FBI gunned down its public enemy number 1, Al Brady, in the streets of Bangor, Maine. Shaffer was also killed, and Dalhover was captured, only to be returned to Indiana, tried, and executed.

Michelle Watson

The Dark Side of a Town

The county seat of Cass County, Indiana, is the town of Logansport. Incorporated in 1838, the area grew to epitomize the meaning of the word "city." First the Wabash and Erie Canal was routed through, and then the railroad system grew, making Logansport a railroad hub.

The bright side of the arrival of the railroad was the construction of retail shops, restaurants, and hotels that located themselves near the depots. City transit such as trolley cars and city buses planned their routes between the Pennsylvania Railroad and the Vandalia Railroad depots.

But a dark side followed—prostitution. City court records, newspaper stories, and even the 1880 US census—in which many young women listed "prostitute" as their occupation—reveal that there were many houses of ill repute scattered about the community. Arrests would be made and fines would be given, but authorities just could not seem to rid the city of the "oldest profession."

What did happen over many years was that the owners of the bordellos gravitated to one specific area in Logansport. Whether this just happened or whether city authorities made an effort to corral the business is anyone's guess. But the operations seemed contained to one street, which was, believe it or not, behind the railroad tracks. East Wabash Avenue is a short, dead-end street, located over the tracks, just east of the back side of the Pennsylvania Depot, which stood at the south end of 4th Street.

The "Line" as it was called, a row of houses on that short street, became so popular that many out-of-town fellows would ask for the location when stepping down from the train, and it became so well known that fellows traveling from Logansport to other cities were sometimes met with knowing looks and comments such as "Oh yes, Logansport, Indiana—the place with the Line." The unwanted attention for the profession was worsened by the fact that Logansport was identified by the American Social Hygiene Association as a hot spot for the "open toleration of sin" in its nationwide survey of 221 cities. This survey was featured in an article in *Look* magazine on February 26, 1952. Action was taken to close up the area at that time, and things quieted down for a while, but the business was not completely finished. That didn't happen until 1980.

That is when the brothels were closed down completely as local, state, and federal authorities worked together and executed a raid. The success of finally eradicating organized prostitution on East Wabash Avenue, ridding the city of this most unwanted menace, was attributed to the city's first female mayor, Jone Wilson.

The Pennsylvania Depot was razed in the 1960s. All but one of the houses either were razed or burned down over time. The one house that remains was purchased for its historical value. Sometime after the restoration was completed the house was featured in a segment of the TV show *If These Walls Could Talk* on HGTV television network.

Thelma Conrad

The Extraordinary
Ordinary

Betty Frazier

Long ago, in the area that would later be called Fayette County, there lived a couple by the names of George and Betty Frazier. George is described as "a cripple," but information on both the nature and cause of his disability has been lost to time. The story of Betty, however, has been preserved and deserves to be told.

The Frazier family, like some others, came before the land was opened for purchase. They built a cabin on the east side of the Whitewater River, just north of the tiny settlement that would soon be platted as Connersville. Their intention was to purchase their farm at a land auction in Cincinnati in the spring of 1813. Betty planned to sell a number of hogs to finance the deal.

Sometime during 1812, the family received a visit from General Hanna, a government agent who had come to seize the family's property as a penalty for their "squatting" on government land. Betty met him at the door and offered him the family's only horse as payment, telling him he was welcome to go into the barn and retrieve it. As soon as Hanna had begun to untie the horse, Betty secured the barn door, leaving the general confined overnight.

When morning came, she agreed to release him—on the condition that he report that the family had no property to be taken.

Upon his departure, Hanna inquired as to the best place to ford the river. Betty pointed to a spot she undoubtedly knew would result in the soldier and his horse disappearing beneath the water. Having done just that, both horse and rider were able to swim to the safety of the opposite bank, but the general's hat continued its own journey down river.

Having saved her family from this crisis, Betty continued to fatten her hogs for market, feeding them a crop of corn she had wisely raised for that very purpose.

A cold, wet spring arrived, and Betty began the 70-mile trek to drive her hogs to Cincinnati. She estimated the trip would take a week. Accompanied by the couple's two young sons, she set off through the snow.

The family stopped for shelter from a snowstorm at the home of Squire Rockafellow in New Trenton. A deep snow wasn't all that arrived during the cold, dark night. Betty mounted her pony at dawn, now accompanied by her two sons and their newborn sibling!

The family arrived in Cincinnati the day before the land sale, and Betty sold the hogs. The next day, infant in arms and cash in hand, she bought 135 acres at auction.

Land records show this purchase as having taken place on April 5, 1813—a memorable example of the tenacity and resourcefulness of the pioneer women of Indiana.

Donna Schroeder

Adrian Marks

Quiet and unassuming, Adrian Marks was a beloved member of his Frankfort community when he died in 1998 at the age of eighty-one. Like most men of his generation, he proudly served

Adrian Marks. COURTESY OF CLINTON COUNTY
HISTORICAL SOCIETY & MUSEUM

his country during World War II. And like many of the veterans who had seen action, he had a story that he rarely told. Marks's story, however, was a spellbinding, first-person account of one of the war's most harrowing incidents, and it had to be told. It also explained why more than 300 men, who had benefited from his quick thinking, sound judgment, and courage, called Adrian Marks an American hero for the rest of their lives.

The story began the afternoon of Thursday, August 2, 1945, when twenty-eight-year-old US Navy pilot Lieutenant Adrian Marks, a native of Ladoga, Indiana, was dispatched to an area in the Pacific, midway between the Philippines and Guam, where several hours earlier another pilot on an antisubmarine patrol had spotted scores of men thrashing about in the sea. The Navy was unaware that the men were all who remained of the 1,200-man crew of the USS *Indianapolis* that had delivered atomic bombs intended for Hiroshima and Nagasaki. Neither did the Navy know that four days before, on Monday, July 30, 1945, the ship had been torpedoed and sunk by a Japanese submarine. The drowning *Indianapolis* had taken some 400 of its crew down with it, while the other 800, most of them equipped with little more than life jackets and rafts, leaped into the water.

Because of bureaucratic slip-ups, the Navy recorded no distress signals; nor did it realize the ship was missing. By Thursday, August 2, after enduring four days in the shark-infested water, all but about 300 of the crewmen had perished. Those who managed to stay alive suffered terribly from hallucinations, injuries, sunburn, dehydration, and shark attacks. That was the day the pilot noticed men bobbing in the water and, although uncertain whether they were friend or foe, radioed his base to report the finding.

Marks heard the badly garbled call and took off for the site with his eight-man crew in a PBY-5a Catalina seaplane ahead of the destroyer escort, the USS *Cecil J. Doyle*, that had been dispatched. Upon spotting hundreds of men in the sea, Marks cruised over them at a low altitude and immediately realized the "heartbreaking decisions" he faced.

"We couldn't rescue everyone," he recalled at a 1994 reunion of survivors. "There were men in life rafts and swimming with life preservers scattered throughout an area of about 50 square miles. They were in really bad shape. They had been through a lot."

After assessing the situation, Marks disregarded Navy regulations and made a daring landing on the rough sea, maneuvering through 12-foot swells. He radioed back to the base for immediate emergency help, but the message never got to the commanding officer.

"Some moron who took the message sat on it and didn't give it to the commander," he told a crowd at the '94 reunion. "It still burns me up."

Marks and his crew started pulling men onboard, concentrating on the single swimmers who had become separated from the main body of survivors. He believed, as he would later explain, that men clustered together stood a better chance of surviving in the water because they could look after one another. When the plane's fuselage was full, they carried men onto the wings and tied them in place with parachute cord. Responding to shouts for help, two of Marks's men volunteered to go out in a rubber boat. They saved two more. In all, Marks and his crew rescued fifty-six survivors.

Marks maintained a relative calm and instilled optimism through the night awaiting the USS *Cecil J. Doyle*, which arrived a few hours later and loaded everyone onboard. In all, 316 members of the USS *Indianapolis*'s crew lived through the ordeal, thanks largely to Marks's courageous leadership.

Twelve days after the rescue, on August 15, 1945, Japan surrendered, thus ending World War II.

Marks had graduated from Northwestern University and Indiana University Law School before the war. After the war, he joined his wife, Elta, in Frankfort, where he opened a law practice, specializing in real estate titles and deeds.

Admiral Chester W. Nimitz, the Pacific Fleet's commander-in-chief, presented Marks with the Air Medal for his actions. Through the succeeding years, Marks attended many of the USS *Indianapolis* survivor reunions and often was the featured guest speaker. He said he never forgot the tragedy at sea, nor the men who perished, nor the men he saved.

In return, the survivors and their families never forgot Lieutenant Adrian Marks, the man who had given them their lives.

Upon learning of Marks's passing on March 7, 1998, Paul J. Murphy, chairman of the survivors group, was quoted by the Associated Press.

"Thank God for him," Murphy said of Marks. "He was loved by all the survivors."

Janis Thornton

Kurt Vonnegut

Kurt Vonnegut's legacy includes his reputation as one of the nation's greatest writers of the second half of the twentieth century. This unique man hailed from Indianapolis and attended Shortridge High School on the city's near north side. His family and personal life took many twists and turns that gave him a wide variety of experiences to shape his life and writings. As with many other notable writers and public figures, New York City came to serve as home to Vonnegut for many years, until his death in 2007.

His story and that of the city of Indianapolis's notable growth from the late '70s to today came together in 1986 when, on behalf of the Indianapolis Convention and Visitors Association (ICVA), now Visit Indy, I wrote Vonnegut in hopes of dispelling what was then thought to be the prevailing idea that Vonnegut did not have a warm spot in his heart for the city of his birth. The widespread feeling among the citizens of Indy was that Vonnegut's love of Indy was limited to the famous Indianapolis 500 held annually on Memorial Day weekend. That myth took a notable turn when I wrote to request an interview to discuss his native home. Vonnegut kindly agreed, personally wrote me a letter, and later sat down with a representative of the ICVA in 1987 to discuss his feelings for Indianapolis.

The letter that Vonnegut sent to me on August 31, 1987, was brief but to the point. It started by saying he "would welcome the opportunity to kill the canard that I scorn my home town, which gave so much to me." He went on to say, "I remain aggressively and sometimes abrasively [an] Indianapolis person, and will remain such until I die."

Robert E. Desautels

Jill Bolte Taylor

A celebratory story of Indiana must begin with my close friend Jill Bolte Taylor, one of Indiana's best-kept secrets! Perhaps you have heard of Dr. Jill Bolte Taylor—author of *My Stroke of Insight: A Brain Scientist's Personal Journey* (2006), published in thirty languages, and one of *Time* magazine's 100 Most Influential People in the World (2008). Dr. Taylor delivered the very first TED talk that ever went viral on the Internet, and she delivered a second TEDx talk about the teenage brain in Indianapolis. She has been a guest on *The Oprah Winfrey Show* and is working on a feature film adaption of her book. But, most importantly, Jill is an authentic Hoosier!

Jill Bolte Taylor. PHOTO BY KIP MAY

Growing up in Terre Haute, Jill was the girl next door, with wholesome values and a kind heart. From chanting songs in Mrs. Webster's Girl Scout troop, to eating cupcakes at slumber parties, to trudging through snow to Mr. Fischer's math class, to cheering enthusiastically at ball games, Jill was that genuine, fun-loving, and dependable friend. Jill was inquisitive and extremely bright, and none of us were surprised when she went on to become a neuroanatomist and research scientist at Harvard Medical School. Jill began to pursue research about the brain, specifically schizophrenia, to learn more about her own brother's illness. She was elected to the board of directors of the National Alliance on Mental Illness (NAMI) and focused her energies toward advocating for social justice for the mentally ill. While at Harvard, she was featured in numerous journals and began making keynote presentations around the country about the brain and the shortage of brain tissue donated for research.

When she was thirty-seven, however, Jill's life took an unexpected turn. She woke up one cold morning in Boston and realized that she herself was experiencing something highly unusual: she was having a massive stroke in the left hemisphere of her brain. In the next four hours, she watched curiously as the incoming stimulation to her own brain was no longer research to be documented in a Harvard laboratory but actual traumatic changes taking over her own body. In her book, Jill describes the banter taking place within her brain as she worries about the disruption of her work schedule, along with the acknowledgment of impending danger that she is having a stroke. As she stood in the shower and felt the water around her, she began to think of herself as a part of a living world, made up of trillions of cells. She was alone in the moment, studying her own brain and recognizing the preciousness of the human body.

Jill was experiencing a life-threatening hemorrhagic stroke that happens when blood breaks free from the arteries and flows out into the brain. In the early moments of Jill's stroke, when her right arm became paralyzed and she was overcome with exhaustion, she recognized the seriousness of the changes taking place within her nervous system, and this knowledge of what was happening helped her to stay focused so she could eventually seek help. Two and a half weeks after the stroke, Jill underwent major surgery to remove a large blood clot that prevented her brain from transmitting information.

Jill largely credits the success of her recovery to the care and love from her mother, G.G., who, after Jill's surgery, helped her restimulate her neurons to make multiple connections and keep her brain challenged. Also, Jill attributes her full recovery to her advantage as a neuroscientist in believing in the plasticity of her brain, with its ability to repair and retrain its circuitry. Her rehabilitation took place in the same order as a young child goes through normal development. In her book, Jill describes herself on the morning of the stroke as "an infant in a woman's body" who basically had to spend eight years making new connections and recovering all of her mental and physical functions.

Jill's trauma gave her an unparalleled opportunity to experience the ability of the brain to recover. It is astonishing to hear Jill explain the intricate steps of having a stroke through the lens of a scientist who can also recount the anatomy and biology behind the traumatic event! Because of her strong academic background, she understood what was taking place within her brain and could better comprehend its beauty and resiliency. This belief in her brain's ability to grow, learn, and recover extended to her caregivers, as Jill's mother G.G. focused on Jill's abilities instead of her disabilities. Jill adds that one of her greatest lessons was that of choosing to feel joy, and she reflects that although she may not be in total control of her life, she certainly is in charge of how she chooses to perceive each of her own experiences.

As a survivor who is willing to share her personal experience, Jill provides a transformational account of how your reaction to a stroke can save your own life. As is her candid nature, Jill is willing to recall even the personal details of her tragedy for those who are anxious that this may one day happen to them. Likewise, Jill narrates her story for those who have had a stroke or another kind of brain trauma, with the optimistic ending that a full recovery is possible.

Now, years later, although she was just featured on *60 Minutes* and will soon star in a Hollywood movie, Jill is still Jill. We continue to meet for coffee, eat pie in the local café, and walk the dogs on the Terre Haute sidewalks. Jill has never allowed fame to define her; instead she radiates warmth and energy with the same hometown character of long ago. Hoosiers should be honored to call her their own!

Dr. Karen A. Goeller

Billy "Stix" Nicks

Billy "Stix" Nicks is a sharecropper's son turned Motown drummer. He's seen it all and experienced it all, and, at eighty-one, this South Bend music legend is still performing with his band, Billy "Stix" Nicks & the Motown Machine.

He played alongside many legendary Motown greats such as the Temptations, Stevie Wonder, and Marvin Gaye. He performed at the famed Apollo Theater in Harlem and is an accomplished instructor who teaches drumming at the University of Notre Dame.

"The drummer is the cement or the glue that holds everything together," Nicks says of his chosen profession. "I just love relaxing and playing. I feel at peace."

His family got on a train in Greenwood, Mississippi, headed to Chicago in the middle of the night in 1944 after his father suffered at the hands of a plant manager. "He walked on dirt behind the plow and it just destroyed his legs," Nicks says of his father. "The plant manager threatened to whip him because he couldn't work. I was an adult with a child of my own before I knew the story. He wasn't going to let anyone whip him." Nicks picked cotton as a young child before heading north.

The family settled in South Bend, and eventually he ended up at Central High School, where he borrowed drumsticks from his friend Jackie Ivory. He taught himself, practicing on chairs and books and in study hall until Ivory gave him the name "Stix" because the drumsticks were always found in his back pocket.

It was at Central that he became friends with Junior Walker, with whom he later toured and made recordings such as "Road Runner" and "Pucker up Buttercup." While the two had their fallings out over the years and were in and out of each other's lives, they thought of themselves as brothers and kept in contact until Walker's death in 1995.

Nicks uses the word "blessed" repeatedly to describe his life. Despite the discrimination he has faced, he just loves entertaining and says he feels at peace when he is on stage performing. His wife of fifty-two years, Pattie, and his children and grandchildren also enrich his life.

"I've always believed in entertaining," he says, calling himself the "side man," not the star.

Kathy Jonas

Bob Farmer

Indianapolis is a long way from Stuttgart, Germany.

The distance is so great, in fact, that the story of how a kid from east central Indiana would grow to be so attached to the small sports car manufacturer located there is as anticlimactic as it is unlikely. Even more improbable is the fact that it all started in Muncie.

Yes, Muncie. The ancestral home of the legendary "Muncie 4 Speed" transmission, the critical component of many a fire-breathing domestic V8 monster. If Indianapolis is a long way from Stuttgart, then Muncie is in another galaxy entirely.

I still remember the moment I spotted a Porsche for the first time. It was a little white 4-cylinder 944, parked by itself on the outer reaches of Muncie Mall's parking lot in the early 1990s. The concept that someone would care enough about a vehicle to park it a distance that seemed, to a ten-year-old, practically

2 miles from the mall entrance struck a chord with me. Then, of course, there was the concept of how it even came to be there in the first place. This car, peerless in handling performance, had been shipped around the world, across an ocean, and deposited right here. In my home. By the L. S. Ayres.

It was a magical revelation. And that was that.

When my teenage years came around, reality set in. Porsches were expensive, apparently fickle things that provided world-class performance in exchange for high-end purchase prices and hard-to-find parts. When the time came for me to start looking for a car on a typical teenager budget, it quickly appeared that any Porsche from any year was entirely out of the question.

Imagine, then, my shock when I found, less than a mile from my house, a Porsche 944 just like the one that haunted my preteen automotive dreams. Even more amazing was the price—$3,200 for this incredible piece of German engineering! How could I lose? After completing my very first loan application from the local credit union, and having my dad's begrudging approval on the signature loan, I was able to pick up my pride and joy, a gold 1983 944. I was in heaven.

For years, the 944 and I ran wild over the entire state. The car and I charged through the end of high school, then to Bloomington for college. There were single-vehicle accidents, multivehicle accidents, deer struck in the middle of the day, make-out sessions, speeding tickets, expensive repairs, more speeding tickets, and midnight runs to twenty-four-hour diners. I once crammed in six Indiana University Air Force ROTC cadets (including two in the hatch) and drove across campus to a football game. Rumor had it that it would do 140 miles-per-hour flat-footed on a deserted stretch of Highway 3. The car and I were inseparable. There was only one thing that could be better.

Having two.

My budget was slightly larger as a twenty-year-old, and when I spotted a Burgundy 1985 944 for sale in the local classifieds on summer break, I knew I had to act. Soon, 70 percent of my living expenses were tied up in storing and maintaining a couple of "poor man's" Porsches. For a college student working two jobs, it was not my best financial decision.

And then the 1985 944 broke down.

A local shop in Bloomington assessed the situation and, after wiping out my already meager remaining credit card balance, they returned the car to me. It was worse than before, vibrating at speed, shaking when it was turned off, and refusing to accelerate. My dream was rapidly becoming a nightmare. On a test drive trying to make sense of the symptoms being exhibited by my formerly perfect machine, I happened to stumble upon a middle-aged man getting out of a similar vintage Porsche 911 in a parking lot in Bloomington.

Being well aware of the Porsche model hierarchy, a social dynamic roughly similar in scope and complexity to that found in feudal Japan, I waited for this elder to speak. Imagine my surprise when he paused at my parking spot, smiled, and said "Nice car!" I opened up to him immediately.

"I just had it repaired and I don't know what's wrong. Now I don't think I can afford to have it fixed again and I'm worried I'm going to have to sell it." My words spilled out like a fountain. Why I was being so honest with this complete stranger, a man I would never see again, I still have no idea.

The man stood there for a moment and said, as if no problem existed whatsoever, "Just take it to Bob Farmer."

Bob Farmer. My mind raced. Where had I heard that name? Suddenly, it dawned on me. For years I had seen the words in classified advertisements for Porsches:

"Farmer-maintained."

As a teenager, I remember thinking "How arrogant! Besides, most of the farmers I know are cheap as hell! Farmer-maintained just means lots of complaining!" Now, I was suddenly confronted with the fact that this "Farmer" individual actually existed out there somewhere. Even more startling, according to the owner of a superior Porsche, he was the answer to my prayers!

I thanked the man, complimented him on his car, and sped back to my apartment in my wheezing sports car. A quick search on the nascent web revealed Bob Farmer's address—on the far outskirts of Indianapolis. It was time for a drive.

When I arrived at Mr. Farmer's, it was dusk and I was nearly lost. It was fall, with a chill in the air, and the combines were already in the fields. By the time I left Post Road behind me and began venturing into the cornfields that surround Indianapolis like a rustling cocoon, I was becoming more frantic. Surely he would be closing soon and I was getting farther and farther away from civilization. Finally, when I turned down the last county road, I spotted a modest but lovely home with a well-kept barn in the side yard. And then Porsches. Porsches everywhere. At least ten of every year, type, and color. In my young life, I had never seen so many in one place and yet here they were, in the middle of a harvested cornfield on a gravel driveway in front of a barn less than a mile from I-70. Flabbergasted, I pulled in.

A shorter man in his fifties with a square jaw, purposeful gait, and one hand in the pocket of his jeans met me by the manual garage door affixed to the front of the barn. He didn't introduce himself, didn't smile, and didn't appear particularly unsettled by the whirring racket emanating from my engine compartment. I leaned out the open window. "Hi, Mr. Farmer, my name is . . ."

I was cut off by a grunt.

"Pop the hood," the man directed, gesturing with one hand while keeping the other firmly in one pocket of his jeans. In the barn behind him, my gaze fell on a 911 Turbo, the ultimate Porsche, worth more than ten times my meager 4-cylinder 944. I gulped. Its wheels were more valuable than my car. It was on a floor jack with engine components that appeared to belong to an Atlas rocket lying around it. I knew I was out of my league. With hardware like this, I knew that Mr. Farmer was some sort of Porsche shaman, and for a kid with a couple of hundred dollars to his name, I also knew this didn't bode well for my chances of keeping my dream car. But I had come this far. I did as ordered and popped the hood.

The man immediately disappeared behind it. Ready to meet my fate, I left the safe confines of my shuddering vehicle and approached the front of the car, walking up next to this apparition who was now leaning over my engine compartment. I stood for a moment on his right. He didn't acknowledge my presence.

"They put the balance shafts on backwards." Mr. Farmer couldn't see the balance shafts. They were hidden under a plastic cover. He hadn't driven the car. I hadn't revved it. He heard me pull in his gravel drive in idle and had seen and heard the motor for less than thirty seconds. He hadn't touched a thing.

Flabbergasted and immediately reverting back to my penniless college mindset, I blurted out, "How much will it cost?"

"Sixty bucks. I'll have it ready tomorrow evening."

I nearly fainted. Bob headed back inside. Feeling as though I owed this man my life, I cautiously went after him. My girlfriend, having followed me there in an Oldsmobile, joined us. I had questions. Burning questions. How did he wind up in Indianapolis? Who did all of these cars belong to? How long had he been doing this? For the next two hours, I hung on his every word.

My girlfriend was a patient woman.

Bob Farmer was a Porsche-trained mechanic who had quit working for the dealership in Indianapolis nearly two decades before I met him.

"Got tired of 'em," he said.

He started working on Porsches privately and turned it into his profession. His engine modifications had made him a nationally known racing name, and Porsche race cars fielding his engines could be spotted all over the country. Yet, here he was talking to a pair of twenty-year-old kids in his barn at eight in the evening.

The plethora of cars belonged to all sorts of Indiana people. Doctors. Lawyers. And now wannabe Air Force pilots. Bob was reserved at first, but gradually opened up. He worked only on Porsches. He repeated it.

"Only Porsche."

He was married, and he and his wife had one child, a daughter our age whom he clearly adored. He worked alone and he had his own Porsche 911 with plenty of custom modifications.

By this time it was getting late and my girlfriend had class in the morning. I had class as well, but was probably going to skip it as was my heathen custom. There were obviously much more pressing matters concerning this world-class, Stuttgart-focused mechanic who had somehow made a living fixing the greatest sports cars ever made . . . right here in Indianapolis.

After bidding Bob farewell, we retreated into the crisp evening and marveled at the day's events at the Steak 'n Shake on Post Road. Eventually, we made our way back down SR37 to Bloomington in the Oldsmobile.

The next day, I paid Mr. Farmer, the most skilled Porsche mechanic I had ever met, the smallest amount I had ever paid for an automobile repair. Then I fired up the car. It was as if I was starting a new Porsche in 1985. I looked at him, stunned.

"Retensioned all the belts while I was in there."

Still beside myself, I watched him return to his little barn. Through the door, I noticed the 911 Turbo from the evening before was put back together and off the jack. I imagined that the owner, some race-car driver, would be here soon to pick up his daily driver. Bob briskly waved and disappeared into the shop.

I drove my little 944 away as if I had stolen it. We tore across I-465, and down the entrance ramp to 37 like it was Laguna Seca. Then on through Martinsville and into the hills of Monroe County. All was right in the world.

Over the remainder of our time at IU, Mr. Farmer was always there for us. My girlfriend became my fiancée, and she remained behind in Bloomington to finish her degree while I completed pilot training in Mississippi. Once, the car overheated. Once, it needed a new clutch. Then an exhaust fix.

My fiancée was a patient woman.

She would always bring Mr. Farmer cookies when she dropped the car off unannounced for another repair. He would always smile—and have her pull it straight up to the barn. Once, she watched him stop working on a stunning race car when the 944 arrived. She immediately apologized for dropping off our cheap little car and interrupting him while he had such incredible, expensive hardware to maintain as well.

"You don't worry a moment about that," he replied sternly. He paused, then gestured toward the vehicles behind him. "Your car is just as important as theirs."

There was no caste system or model hierarchy with Mr. Farmer. They were all Porsches.

After pilot training, my wife and I moved all over the country with different assignments. Both of our 944s were sold, with tears, over time, and replaced by more and more 911s.

My wife is a patient woman.

I haven't seen Bob for over a decade. To this day, I often see "Farmer-maintained" on Craigslist ads for Porsches for sale in

Indiana. Knowing he is there, working in a barn in the middle of a cornfield, just outside the glow of the lights of Indianapolis, always gives me a reason to smile.

Indiana is a car state. From our motto, to the 500, to the manufacturing base that once called the state home, the love of vehicles runs deep through our veins. Cars need mechanics, and thousands of men and women call that job their own in Indianapolis alone.

Bob Farmer is one of them, but he is also much more. He is a professional. And he fixes Porsches.

Even if he is a long way from Stuttgart.

Micah Jones

John Mellencamp

What would any volume of Indiana stories be without paying homage to the legendary John Mellencamp?

But that's the thing. Despite his legendary status, he lives in a small town. He was born in a small town. And like his own lyrics say, he can be himself in a small town, where people let him be just what (and who) he himself wants to be. And what could be more "Hoosier" than that?

Growing up Hoosier, as soon as I heard the opening riffs to Mellencamp's "Small Town," I'd be able to picture exactly the type of scene he transmitted through those lyrics, the kind of scene that might have stood at the heart of his own daydreams. Acres upon acres upon acres of mile-high corn, waving lightly in a soft summer breeze. Basketball hoops on every house as far as the eye could see, the rhythmic thunking of basketballs hitting concrete courts on every driveway. Banners alternately sporting the striking cream and crimson of IU or the stately gold and black of Purdue.

John Mellencamp made Bloomington his adopted home and Indiana University his chosen palace. With his huge donation to an athletic pavilion named for him and his constant presence in the good seats at the Hoosiers' home basketball games, he is as much of an institution at Indiana University Bloomington as the Sample Gates or the fountain statue of Venus in front of the IU Auditorium. In the commencement speech he delivered at IU's class of 2000 graduation ceremony, he emphasized the importance of being able to "reinvent yourself" at every stage of life. Certainly, his own life and musical career is a testament to his ability to follow and model his own advice.

Every time Mellencamp takes the stage at his concerts, you can feel the way he exudes Indiana, whether it's his distinctive Southern-ish twang or his comments and mannerisms that have something decidedly "Hoosier" about them.

He's made Indiana into a kind of musical trademark, one that implicitly embodies the pride of the state, its strong sense of hospitality (Hoosier-style, of course), and simultaneously also speaks to the toughness and tenacity of anyone who self-iden-tifies as being a "Hoosier."

His lyrics paint pictures of daydreams unfolded, pursued, and lived out. His songs depict the goodness that is life in In-diana, whether it's about "two American kids growin' up in the Heartland" like Jack and Diane, or about being "young and im-provin'" when "dancin' meant everything." The scraps of pic-tures and experiences that he paints with his music exemplify what it means to grow up and to live and to learn in the Hoosier heartland.

And the way he conveys these images is so understated and unexpected, like the way he occasionally presents himself at a bar venue in Bloomington, to serve a crowd of the college stu-dents among whom he has made his home. It conveys itself in the slightly overgrown yet understated beauty of his mailbox near the shores of Lake Monroe; everyone knows where he lives, yet they admire him and his celebrity from afar, similar to how spotting his location at every IU basketball game is tantamount to an in-person game of *Where's Waldo?* with our very own unpretentious celebrity.

Grace Waitman-Reed

Russell Eugene Rogers

Russell Eugene Rogers was born in 1927, in the only place in the world that he could have been born: Scottsburg, Indiana. Or at least that's the way it seems now, but most certainly the way it should have been. Some people it seems were born just to do certain things, and Gene Rogers is one of those people.

Gene's parents, Russ and Myrtle Rogers, owned a Dodge and Plymouth agency in Scottsburg, and growing up Gene spent a lot of time at the business and a lot of time learning about the town. Gene had a tough competiveness about him, and even though he was only 5' 6" tall he developed a deep love for basketball, which placed him on the Scottsburg Warriors high school basketball team. In 1944, Gene's junior year, the Warriors won the Madison sectional, and seventy-one years later Gene takes pride in remembering the final score of the championship game: 30–24 over Dupont. Gene's coach that year was Ralph "Whiskey" Feeler, a legendary coach at Scottsburg. Gene says he heard the reason Feeler was called Whiskey had to do with when the coach was a kid. "I heard he collected empty whiskey bottles and then sold them, but I suppose he may have indulged a little too," he adds with a grin.

Gene loved Scottsburg High School, and it loved him, as he was voted the most promising boy of the future. In 1945, after he graduated, Gene enlisted in the United States Navy and served thirteen months active duty. He then returned to Scottsburg and enrolled at Hanover College, just 20 miles from Scottsburg, of course. After Gene graduated from Hanover in 1950, he married the girl he'd had his eyes on for a few years, Vada Kenney. "The first time I saw her was at the tennis court," he says, "I liked her legs."

After graduating from Hanover, he first worked at his dad's business, and then in 1952 he got a job at the Scottsburg School District, where he stayed until 1993, and where he loved every single day. Fifteen of those years he spent as the Scottsburg Junior High principal; another ten were spent as an assistant varsity basketball coach under Charley Meyer, during some of the greatest years of the storied program in the 1950s.

In the 1960s, twenty-plus years after he played for Scottsburg, a dozen years after he helped coach Scottsburg, he did something at a Scottsburg game that no adult had ever done before, an act that would eventually lead him to the Indiana Basketball Hall of Fame.

During a Scottsburg home game, Gene felt the crowd needed to be roused up, so he left his seat and went out on the floor and urged the crowd to get fired up. The student cheering section cheered wildly, the adults stood and cheered like never before, and Scottsburg won the game. At the next game when the Warriors struggled on the court, some adults looked to Gene again to get things turned around. And, of course, Gene went back out on the floor, and after that, at least once a game, Gene started going out on the floor and leading the Scottsburg fans in cheers for the Warriors. The opposing team's fans didn't know what to think; sometimes they booed Gene, who never seemed to hear them.

Once the act started, and the Scottsburg faithful expected it, Gene decided he needed his own uniform. So Gene asked Doris Prewitt, who sewed a lot for her family, to make him an outfit.

Mrs. Prewitt then made Gene an outfit he wore for over twenty years to Scottsburg basketball games. One pants leg was gold, the other purple, one side of his shirt was purple and the other gold, and Gene loved it.

By now Gene's act had come full circle, as the Scottsburg masses began to chant his name "ROGERS, ROGERS" before he would leave his seat to go on the floor. Gene developed his own cheer and stunt while on the floor, which always occurred at the end of the third quarter and drove Scottsburg fans to a frenzy. Gene would stand facing the crowd and yell "Give me One Big Fight," the crowd would yell "FIGHT." He would then yell, "Give me Two Big Fight," and the crowd would yell FIGHT-FIGHT. Gene would respond with "Give me Three Big Fight," and the crowd would scream "FIGHT-FIGHT-FIGHT!" And then Gene would take off, running in a big circle with the entire gym watching him. At the end of the circle Gene would jump in midair splits and touch his toes, as the Scottsburg fans would go delirious. Gene would then run off the floor back into the bleachers, as fans high-fived him and encouragingly patted his back.

Even at away games fans found his act entertaining. In the 1980s, when the Scottsburg girls' basketball team rose to state-wide prominence before a state championship in 1989, Gene Rogers, now in his sixties, was also becoming a statewide figure. During the final four in Indianapolis others started taking notice of the impact Gene's cheer had on the crowd. With three trips to the girls' basketball final four from 1986 to 1989, Gene started to become the talk of Indianapolis every February. When the director of the Indiana Basketball Hall of Fame asked Gene if he could have his uniform, Gene thought he was joking. "I didn't know what to think, but eventually he persuaded me he wanted to display the outfit at the Hall of Fame. So I gave it to him and it's still on display there; a lot of people have told me they've seen it and that's really something."

Gene quickly replaced the uniform and kept his place on the court for the next twenty years, performing his act up until his early eighties, and every time he did it the Scottsburg crowd would go wild. Gene's pride in being a Scottsburg Warrior has gotten stronger each year of his life and even more meaningful to the community. At a Scottsburg home game last season Gene was sitting on the first row of bleachers under the goal closest to the Scottsburg pep band. When the band started playing the Scottsburg school song, Gene stood and started clapping his hands to the beat of the school song, and then he started walking toward the band while he continued to clap his hands. When he reached the band he stopped, shook his fist in the air encouragingly, proudly, and then he pointed at the band members, thanking anyone that made eye contact with him. He then marched a few feet over to the student cheer block, where the students waved at him and many shouted, ROGERS! He waved back and shook his fist in the air again as the students screamed wildly, and then he strolled on past them. It was the perfect Scottsburg moment, with Mr. Scottsburg thanking everyone he could see for being a Scottsburg fan.

Mike Barrett

Theodore Dreiser

I was born and raised in Sullivan County, graduated from Union High School (Dugger), and went on to earn a PhD in literature (out of state). Imagine my surprise when, during my studies, I discovered that one of America's most important novelists, Theodore Dreiser, not only was a fellow Hoosier, but also was raised for a few years in Sullivan, just a few miles from where I was reared.

In school I had learned that Indiana's state song, "On the Banks of the Wabash," was penned by Paul Dresser, but no one mentioned that Paul's younger brother was Theodore Dreiser, the great novelist whose *Sister Carrie* is considered one of the most important books in American literary history. Paul changed his too-German-sounding name to Dresser to better fit in to show business. He had lived and worked in Sullivan as a youth, but being the elder sibling, he left the family before Theodore and the rest moved back to Sullivan from Terre Haute in 1878. Theodore writes that he spent his best childhood years, from ages seven to ten, in Sullivan.

In his 1916 book, *A Hoosier Holiday*, Dreiser takes a road trip to revisit all his old homes in Indiana, and he notes the changes that have taken place over the years. He begins in Warsaw, stops to visit his companion's family in Carmel, then descends to Terre Haute, Sullivan, and Evansville before heading back to Carmel through West Baden and Bloomington. It's a fascinating book for any Hoosier as it documents places and events in the Hoosier state that don't often get recognized. It may also be the very first "road trip" book ever written—to be followed by many more throughout the twentieth century.

Most interesting to me was Dreiser's peroration on his time in Sullivan County in the introductory chapter of *A Hoosier Holiday*—it fits so well with my own fond memories of the area:

> This lower Wabash valley is an Egyptian realm—not very cold in winter, and drowsy with heat in summer. Corn and wheat and hay and melons grow here in heavy, plethoric fashion. Rains come infrequently, then only in deluging storms. The spring comes early, the autumn lingers until quite New Year's time. In the beech and ash and hickory groves are many turtle doves. Great hawks and buzzards and eagles soar high in the air. House and barn martins circle in covies. The bluejay and scarlet tanager flash and cry. In the eaves of our cottage were bluebirds and wrens, and to our trumpet vines and purple clematis came wondrous humming birds to poise and glitter, tropic in their radiance. In old Kirkwood's orchard, a quarter

of a mile away over the clover field, I can still hear the guinea fowls and the peacocks "calling for rain."

Dreiser writes much more about Sullivan and its environs later in the book, but I'm grateful that the words of such a great writer describe the same fields and forests where I went barefoot as a child.

Still, though, few in Sullivan County seem to know about Dreiser, and there is no historical marker to designate where he lived. My father and I did some searching, and we believe we've found the spot where Dreiser's old home once stood. Dreiser provides many details about the place where he lived in Sullivan, and from what we've found, his old house once stood in what is now the southwest corner of the Sullivan County Park and Lake. If you take Leech Street from the railroad tracks east toward the Park and Lake, and look to the left, you will notice, along the fence that demarcates the Lake property, old gateposts and an old stone walkway that obviously led up to someone's front door long ago. Given all that Dreiser describes in *A Hoosier Holiday*, this location seems most likely.

Maybe one day a historical marker can be placed there, or somewhere in Sullivan, to celebrate the fact that one of America's greatest writers spent some of his formative years here. Maybe schoolchildren will take pride in knowing that someone great lived in the same place they do; and maybe someday they can be great too.

N. S. Boone

Uncle Snuffy

This undeniably Indiana story of my Uncle Snuffy's Christmas Eve starts out in East Chicago, Indiana, in Lake County, during the mid- to late 1970s, on the day before Christmas, and ends happily about midnight, a few miles north of Columbia City, Indiana, in Whitley County, on State Highway 109 at my Aunt Betty and Uncle Lee's home. It is a true Christmas Eve story about our favorite uncle, Paul Pence (a.k.a. Uncle Snuffy), who was good-humored, kind, and generous to all he encountered. Uncle Snuffy was the younger brother of Lilyan Pence Meyers and Betty Pence Dowell of Columbia City. Betty and her husband, Lee, had two sons: my cousins Phil and Keith. The three of us cousins were about the same age and grew up together like brothers. Later, as adults, we remained close and always looked forward to our annual Christmas Eve gathering when Uncle Snuffy came from his home in East Chicago and dressed as Santa Claus for the enjoyment of our younger children.

On the Christmas Eve night of this story, it was getting late and Uncle Snuffy still hadn't shown up at our party. We all speculated about what might be keeping him. Finally about 10 PM my wife, Mary, and I decided to put our three children in the car and head back home. My cousin Keith and his wife, Deany, along with their two children, Stan and Theresa, stayed a bit longer. They were still at Aunt Betty and Uncle Lee's when, about midnight, the front door was thrown open and Uncle Snuffy called out, "Merry Christmas!"

The story he recounted is one that illustrates old-time Hoosier holiday spirit in more ways than one. Back in the mid-'70s attitudes toward drinking and driving were much more lenient than they are today. That day, before he set off for our party, Uncle Snuffy's landlord invited him in for a little Christmas cheer, and they enjoyed some whiskey together. Then Uncle Snuffy went on to Emil's Tavern and had a steak sandwich before getting back on the road. It wasn't too long before he stopped at another tavern and had a couple of drinks before he started out again for Columbia City.

When Uncle Snuffy got back on Highway 30 going east toward Columbia City, the road had become snow-covered and slippery. Near the town of Hanna in LaPorte County, his car slid off the road and came to a rest down a gully in some trees. A trooper noticed the car and stopped up on the road, calling down to Uncle Snuffy to "Come on up here!" But Uncle Snuffy had a bottle of whiskey with him and had been consoling himself with that libation, and he called back, "You come down here!" So the police officer climbed down into the gully and approached Snuffy's car, asking him, "How did you avoid hitting any of these trees?" Snuffy said he didn't rightly know and offered the policeman a drink out of his bottle (which the officer declined). Then the trooper asked Uncle Snuffy where he was going, and Snuffy told him he was headed to his sister's in Columbia City. Snuffy then asked the policeman if he knew Gene Dowell. (Our uncle Lee's brother Ellis happened to live in Hanna, and his son was named Gene.) The officer readily replied, "I went to school with him, and we played on the high school basketball team together!"

With that connection made, the policeman took our Uncle Snuffy home with him, fixed him a steak dinner, and arranged to have his car pulled back up onto the roadway. After Snuffy had dinner and several cups of coffee, the policeman asked him if he thought he was okay to drive. Being satisfied with Uncle Snuffy's sobriety, he said, "I'll be checking on you," and allowed him to continue on toward Columbia City.

That's when the real fun began. Snuffy was stopped by a trooper in Plymouth, Indiana, but allowed to continue. When he got to Warsaw, he was stopped by another officer.

Snuffy asked the Warsaw officer what was going on and why he was being stopped so often. The officer replied, "We got orders over the radio to watch over a friendly little guy in a beat-up Pontiac!" Uncle Snuffy laughed, wished him a "Merry

Christmas," and made him a present of what was left in the fifth of whiskey. Then he drove on and arrived late but safe and sound at Uncle Lee and Aunty Betty's in Columbia City—all because his relative had once played basketball in Hanna with a boy who grew up to become a state trooper!

William L. Meyers and Keith Dowell

Sunshine

In July of 1967, my husband, Larry, became the senior pastor of West Middleton Friends—a little Quaker church in West Middleton, Indiana. West Middleton is a small town about 7 miles west of Kokomo. The gracious people welcomed the new pastor, his wife, and their three-year-old daughter. They welcomed us so warmly that we pastored there for twenty-seven years. They became like our own family.

One of our members was Sunshine—an elderly lady in her eighties. Her mother had named her Sunshine because the sun was shining on the bed as she was born. Sunshine had her own unique vantage point on life. She always kept us amused.

Sunshine's driving was especially entertaining. She was a very slow driver. She would tootle along at about 25 mph in a 45 mph speed zone. She also liked to drive in the middle of the road for safety.

One day one of my friends at work asked where I lived. "West Middleton," I told her.

She replied, "Really? I was driving through there the other day. There was a little old lady in a white car driving down the middle of the road!" Yes, that would be Sunshine!

One Sunday Sunshine told Larry, "I drove into Kokomo a few days ago. Everybody was honking and waving at me." She had been driving the wrong way on the bypass!

Our church was on Alto Road—a road that was fairly busy. Each Sunday morning after church, Sunshine would climb into her car, then back out into the road without checking traffic. Another member, Arthur Allen Horn, became very concerned for her safety. One morning he decided he needed to make her aware of the danger. He cautioned, "Sunshine, you need to check for traffic before you back out."

Sunshine replied huffily, "I look before I get in the car!"

Quakers often have a time of open sharing of their blessings during the week. One Sunday morning during our worship service, Sunshine stood up and spoke. "I'm so glad for how the Lord helps me drive." The next week the police set up a speed trap at the edge of town. Sunshine drove through and knocked it out. We were truly grateful the Lord was helping her drive. I don't know what might have happened if he hadn't been.

Sunshine lived alone and developed her own method of dealing with annoying people. One Sunday she told us that a salesman had called on her. "I wasn't interested in what he had to sell, but he wouldn't leave. He kept talking and came into my house. I just turned on the TV and began listening to it. He kept talking, so I turned the TV up louder. He still refused to leave, so I punched him in the nose."

Yes, that would be Sunshine.

Sandy Boswell

Nelson Price is a journalist, historian, and host of the weekly radio show *Hoosier History Live*. He is author of *Indiana Legends: Famous Hoosiers from Johnny Appleseed to David Letterman*; *The Quiet Hero: A Life of Ryan White*; *Indianapolis Then and Now*; *Legendary Hoosiers*; and *Indianapolis Leading the Way*. Price has won more than 45 national, state, local, and civic awards for his journalism.

Editor: Laura Baich

Director: Gary Dunham

Book and Cover Designer: Jennifer L. Witzke

Project Manager/Editor: Nancy Lightfoot

Marketing and Sales Director: Dave Hulsey

Editorial and Production Director: Bernadette Zoss

Printer: Thomson-Shore Inc.